Passionate Piano Moments

Emotional Piano Music

Tito Abeleda

Music Editor: Michael Roth
Book Editor: Karen Abeleda

Book Cover photo - Ludwig Kwan
Photo, page 78 - Daria Sannikova
Photo, page 16 - Alain Frechette
Photo, page 21 - Felipe Cespedes
Photo, page 27 - Suzy Hazelwood
Photo, page 33 - Jeswin Thomas
Photo, page 39 - Cottonbro
Photo, page 46 - Alex Smith
Photo, page 115 - Jeremy Bishop
Photo, page 154 - Dalila Dalprat

Passionate Piano Moments

Emotional Piano Music

By

Tito Abeleda

ISBN: 978-0-578-24170-8

Published by Visionary Quest Records

Contents

Introduction

Deep heartfelt emotions fuel my creativity. **Passionate Piano Moments** is a collection of piano pieces reflecting emotions I felt at the time I was writing each piece. Included are 10 piano solos, 1 two piano duet (score plus parts), and 1 four piano quartet (score plus parts). Depending on the piece, the music in this piano book is geared for early intermediate to intermediate advanced playing levels. I hope that you will enjoy learning and performing these emotional dramatic pieces. You can listen to each song on its respective album on your favorite music platform or the following playlist:

Visionary Quest Records — http://bit.ly/PassionatePianoMoments_VQR

- **Drifting** (piano solo) - *L' Heure de la Mort* album

- **Dying Breath** (piano solo) - *L' Heure de la Mort* album

- **Missing You** (piano solo) - *Pathos* album

- **Beautiful Memories** (piano solo) - *L' Heure de la Mort* album

- **Silent Night, Holy Night** (piano solo) - *O Holy Night* album

- **Forever Touched by Your Love** (piano solo) - *I Feel* album

- **Running, Searching** (piano solo) - *Pathos* album

- **Phoenix Rising** (piano solo) - *L' Heure de la Mort* album

- **Tempus Fugit** (piano solo) - *Pathos* album

- **O Holy Night** (piano solo) - *O Holy Night* album

- **Descensus ad Infero** (two piano duet) - *L'Heure de la Mort* album

- **Procession in D Minor** (four piano quartet) - *Pathos* album

Enjoy!

Tito Abeleda

Composer/Producer
Visionary Quest Records
https://www.visionaryquestrecords.com

Acknowledgments

I want to thank my friend and professional colleague, award winning Film/TV composer Rob Pottorf for writing the foreword to my book. I am truly honored. This year Rob won Best Score from the Los Angeles Motion Picture Film Festival for the film **"Magic Max."** Some of his other scores can be heard on films that include **"I Am Patrick"** starring John Rhys-Davies; **"When We Last Spoke"** starring Cloris Leachman, Melissa Gilbert, and Corbin Bernsen; the Hallmark Channel's **"The Ultimate Legacy"** starring Doug Jones, Raquel Welch, Brian Dennehy, Lee Meriwether, Bill Cobbs and Ali Hillis; 20th Century Fox's **"The Trial"** starring Matthew Modine and Lions Gate's **"Mountain Top"** starring Barry Corbin, Lin Shay and Coby Ryan McLaughlin and many others. Rob was the Music Director and Sr. Music Composer at Paramount for their theme park division for 11 years. In 1999 he left Paramount to pursue film and television and never looked back. Rob's compositions can be heard on projects for Disney, CBS, Paramount, Lions Gate, 20th Century Fox, The Hallmark Channel, INSP Network, Turner Network, HGTV, CourtTV, Nickelodeon, Dollywood and others.

I also want to thank my dear friend Michael Roth who shared his musical expertise as my music editor. Michael attended my alma mater, Butler University, graduating with a B.A. in Music Theory and Composition. Michael is the music director of the Piper Theatre in New York.

Special thanks also go to the following photographers whose artistic photos captured the essence of this piano book and the emotions of each piece they introduce:

- Book Cover photo- Ludwig Kwan
- Drifting photo, page 8 - Daria Sannikova
- Dying Breath photo, page 16 - Alain Frechette
- Missing You photo, page 21 - Felipe Cespedes
- Beautiful Memories photo, page 27 - Suzy Hazelwood
- Silent Night, Holy Night photo, page 33 - Jeswin Thomas
- Forever Touched by Your Love photo, page 39 - Cottonbro
- Running, Searching photo, page 46 - Alex Smith
- Procession in D Minor photo, page 115 - Jeremy Bishop
- Closing Piano photo, page 154 - Dalila Dalprat

A special shout out also goes to my sister-in-law, Karen Abeleda, my book editor. With her watchful analytical eye, this piano book project became a life-long dream come true. Finally, I thank my father and mother who nurtured and cultivated my aspirations for playing piano by making it possible for me to take piano lessons starting at the age 6 with a life filled with support and love for all the performing arts to this day. None of this would have been possible without them.

Foreword

When you can pick up right where you left off, no matter how many years or how much time has passed; that is a true friend. Tito is a true friend.

Tito has always been one of the gifted few. A natural-born performer, we met in the 80's at a theme park where we both performed. He was an incredible dancer, and his stage presence added that extra spark to any production he was a part of. Years later, we would work together for the same production company; I was a music director. He, a choreographer. Everyone loved working with Tito. His talent always shone through his impeccable work as choreographer and director, but more than that, his kindness and patience with the cast was widely appreciated in a business that can be harsh at times.

Years later, I discovered there was even more to Tito's natural talent. His musicianship included his ability to play piano and compose a wide range of musical styles; from the intimate to a full cinematic and orchestral creation.

It's easy to find people in this business who say they possess a wide range of disciplines, but it's rare to find those who walk the talk. Tito is the rare.

This book is truly one of a kind. It will inspire, as he takes you not only through his collection of music, but into his own journey of creating.

Mozart was the guy who said, "Neither a lofty degree of intelligence nor imagination nor both together go to the making of genius. Love, love, love that is the soul of genius." And so my friend Tito has made with love, this collection of music.

Congratulations my friend. Keep creating with love.

Rob Pottorf

(Award winning Film/TV Composer)

Dedicated to my piano teachers Lola Wolfe and Richard Gray

Drifting

Tito Abeleda

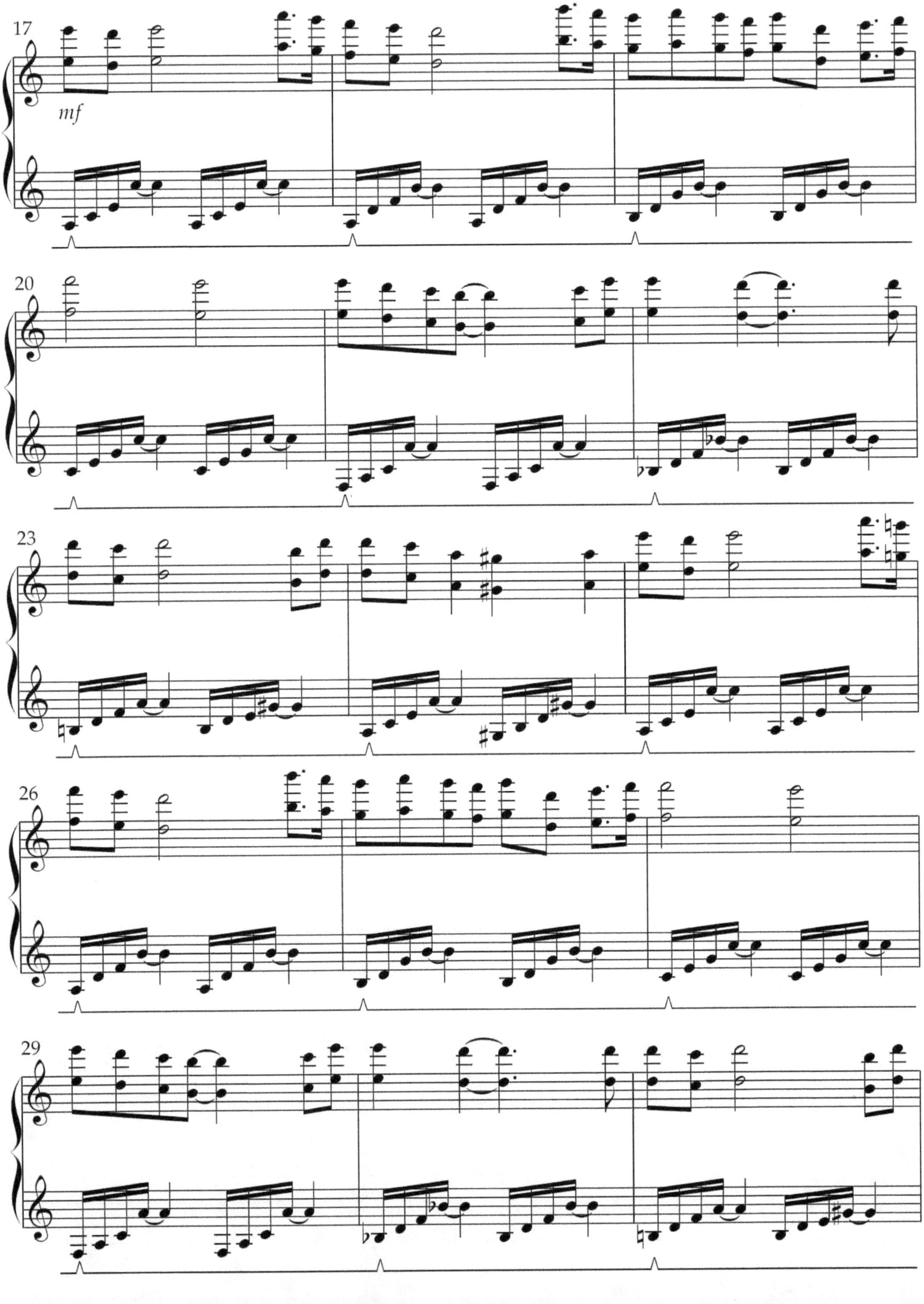
17
mf
20
23
26
29

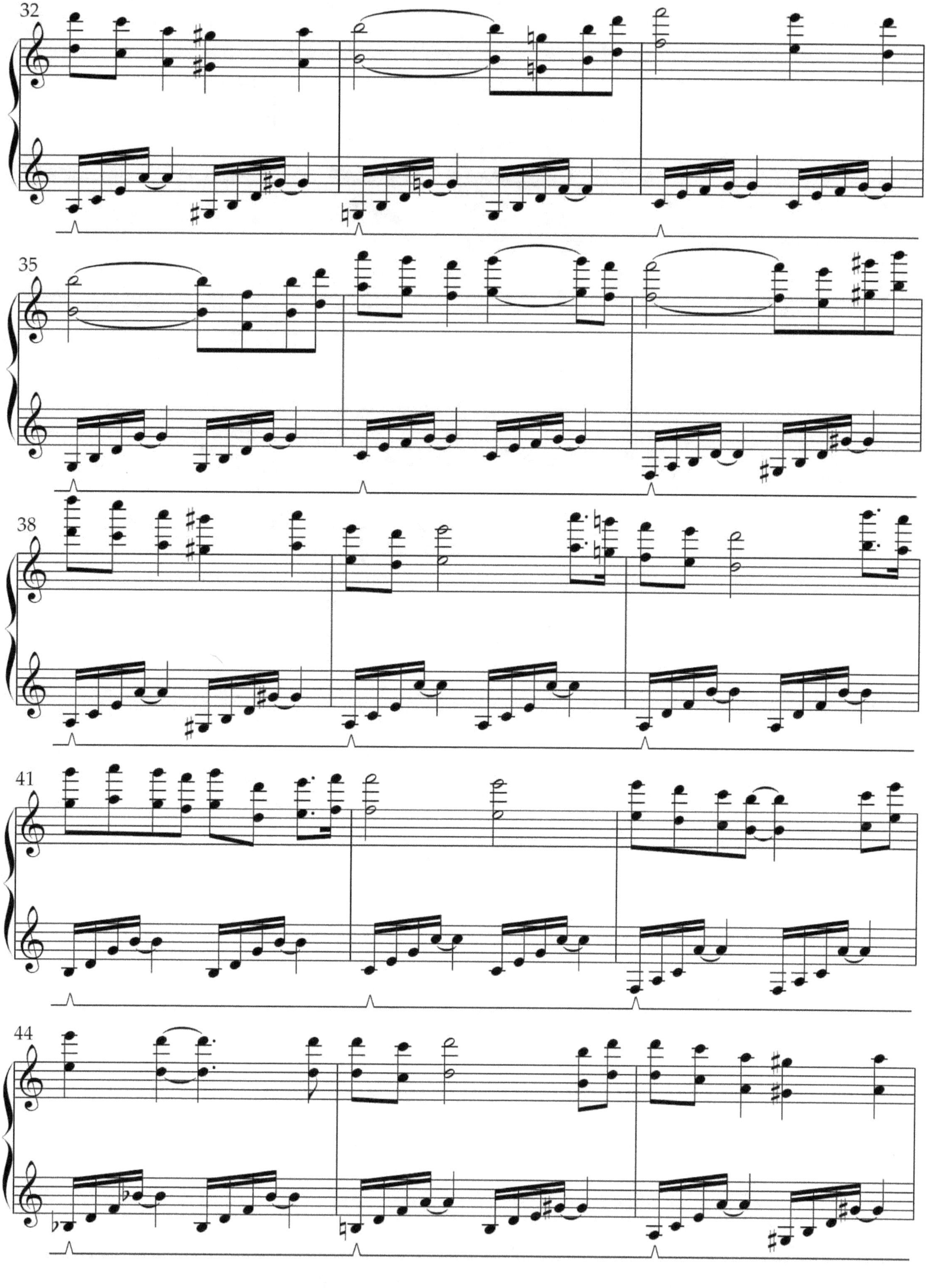
32
35
38
41
44

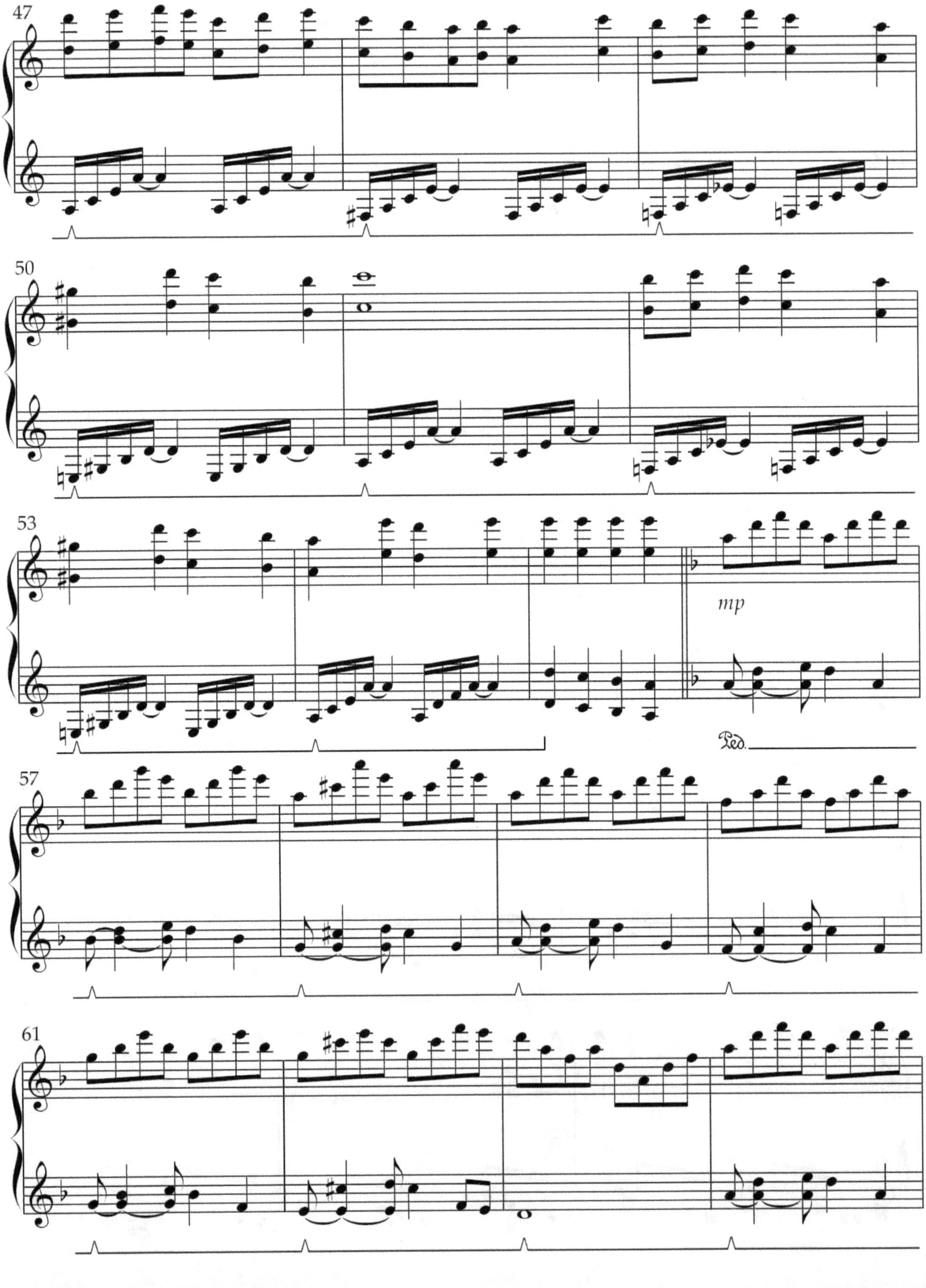
47
50
53
mp
Ped.
57
61

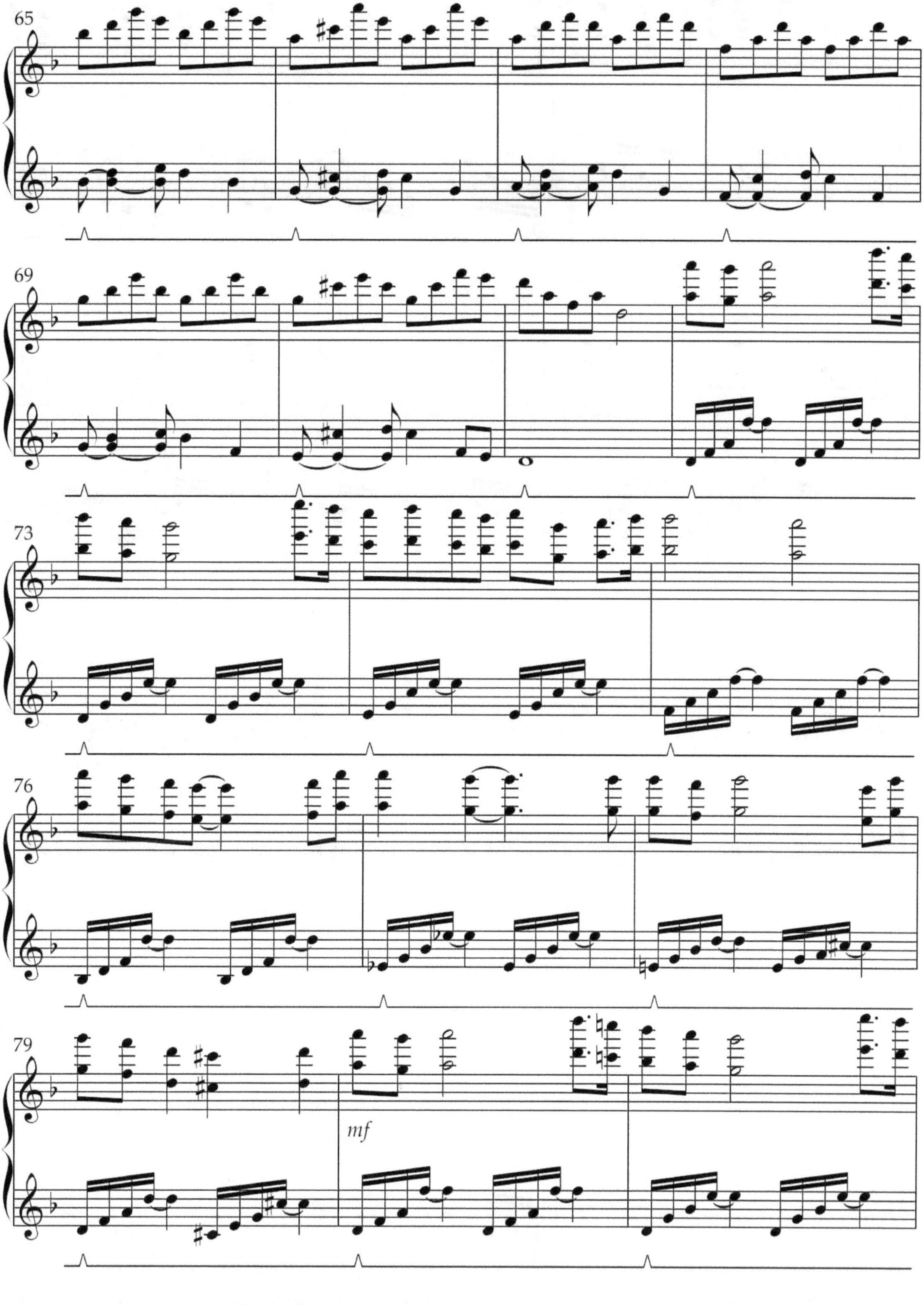
65
69
73
76
79
mf

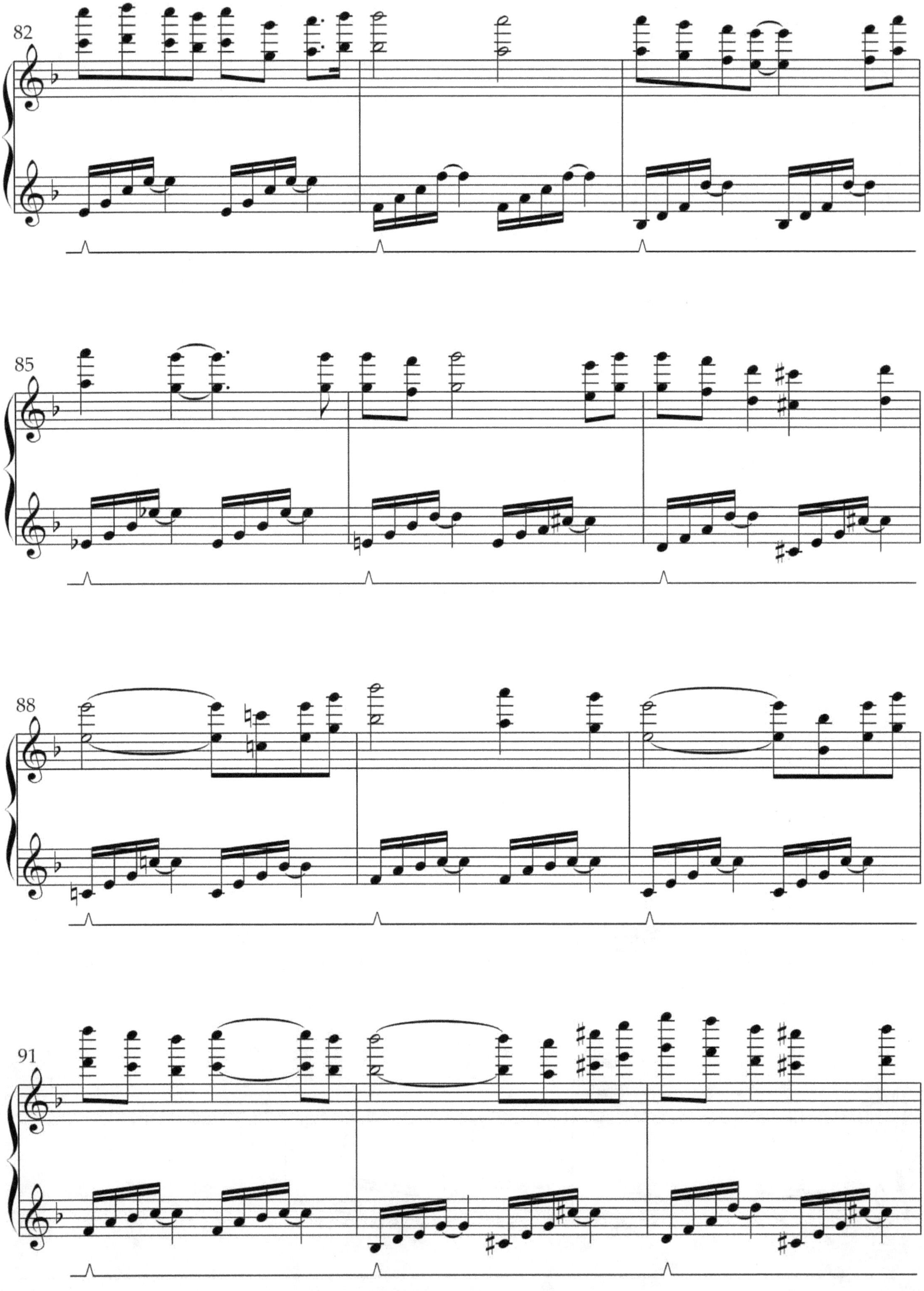
82
85
88
91

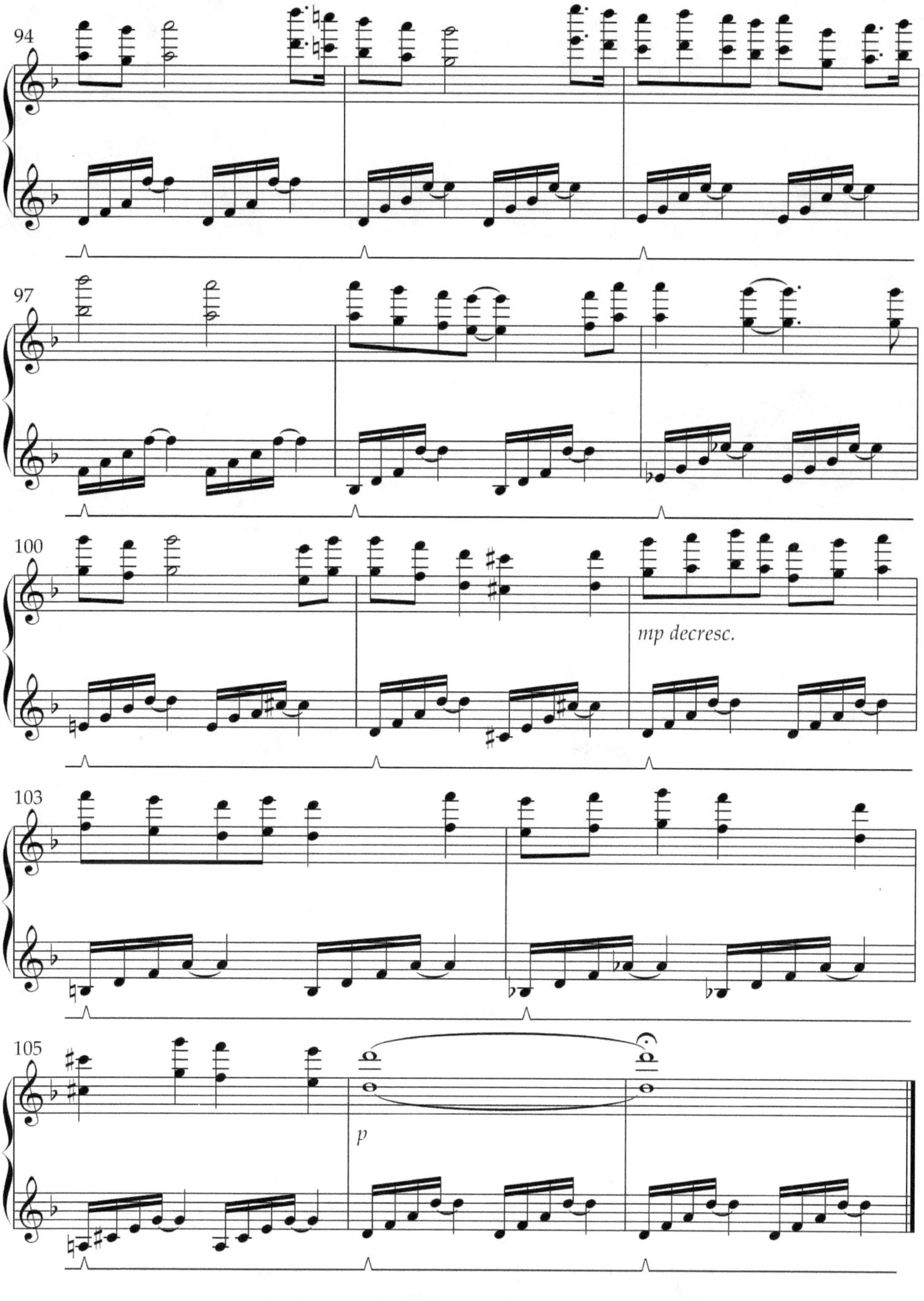
94
97
100
mp decresc.
103
105
p

Dying Breath

Tito Abeleda

Andante ♩=70

A

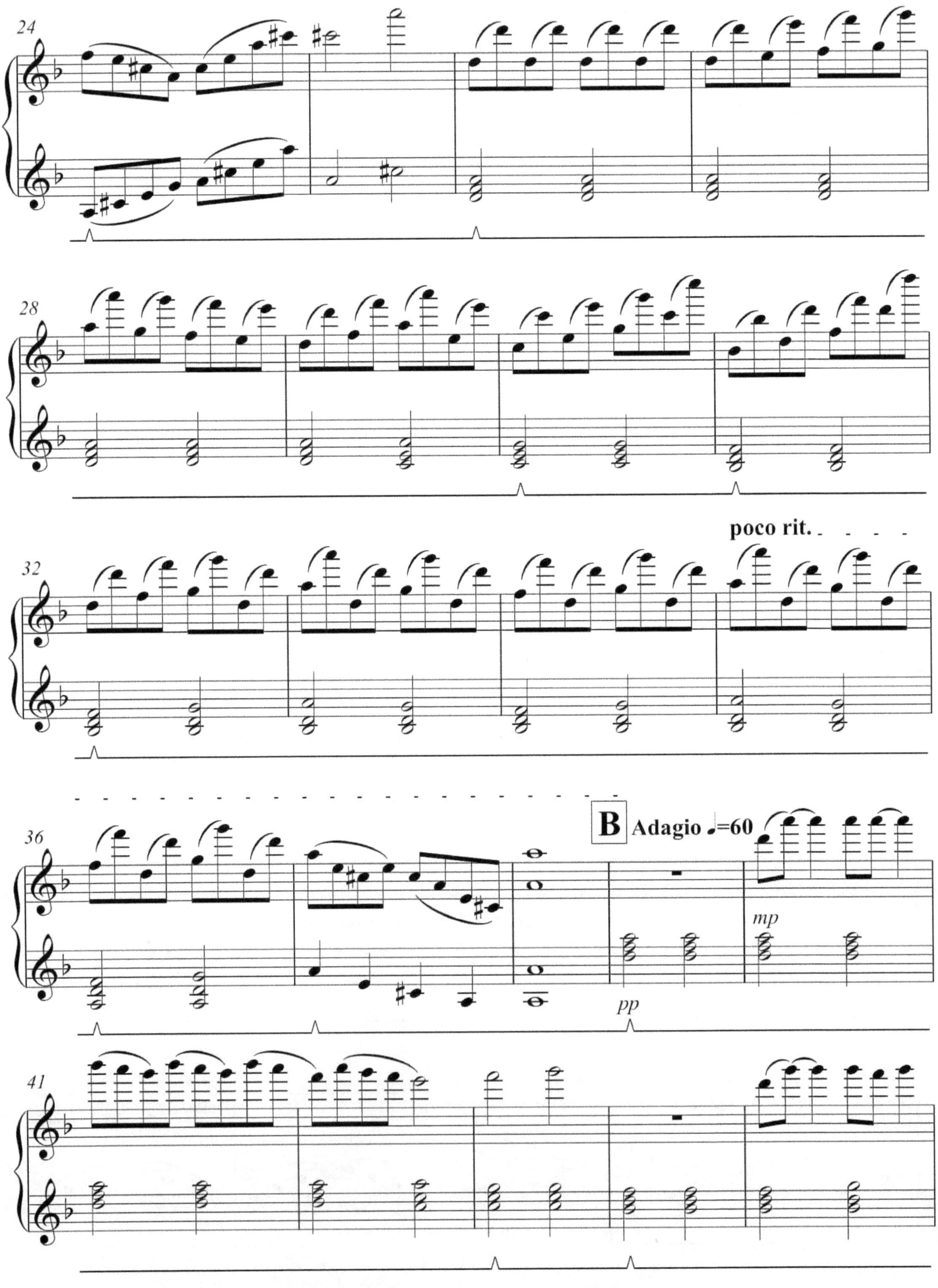
24
28
32
poco rit.
36
B
Adagio =60
mp
pp
41

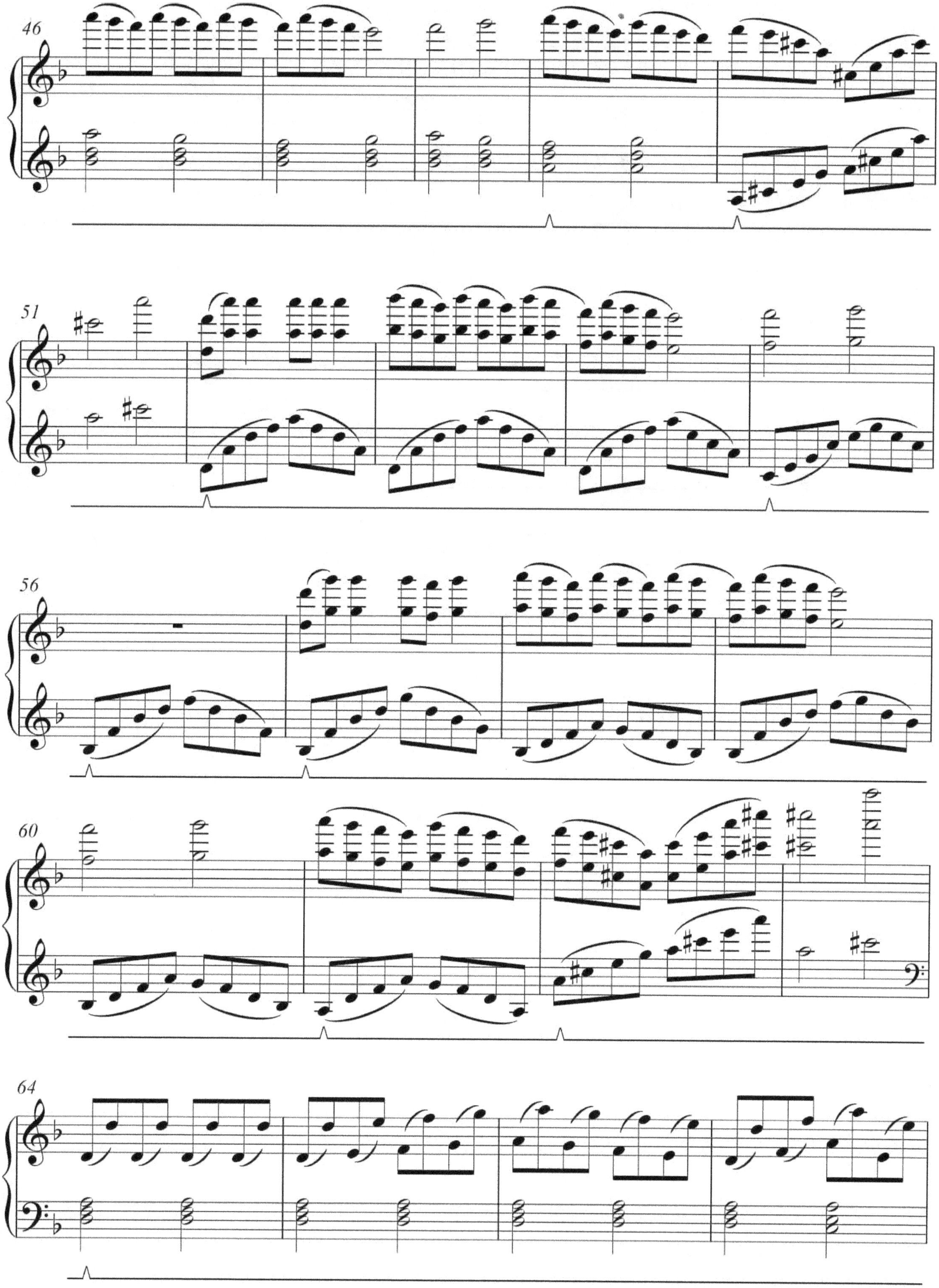
46
51
56
60
64

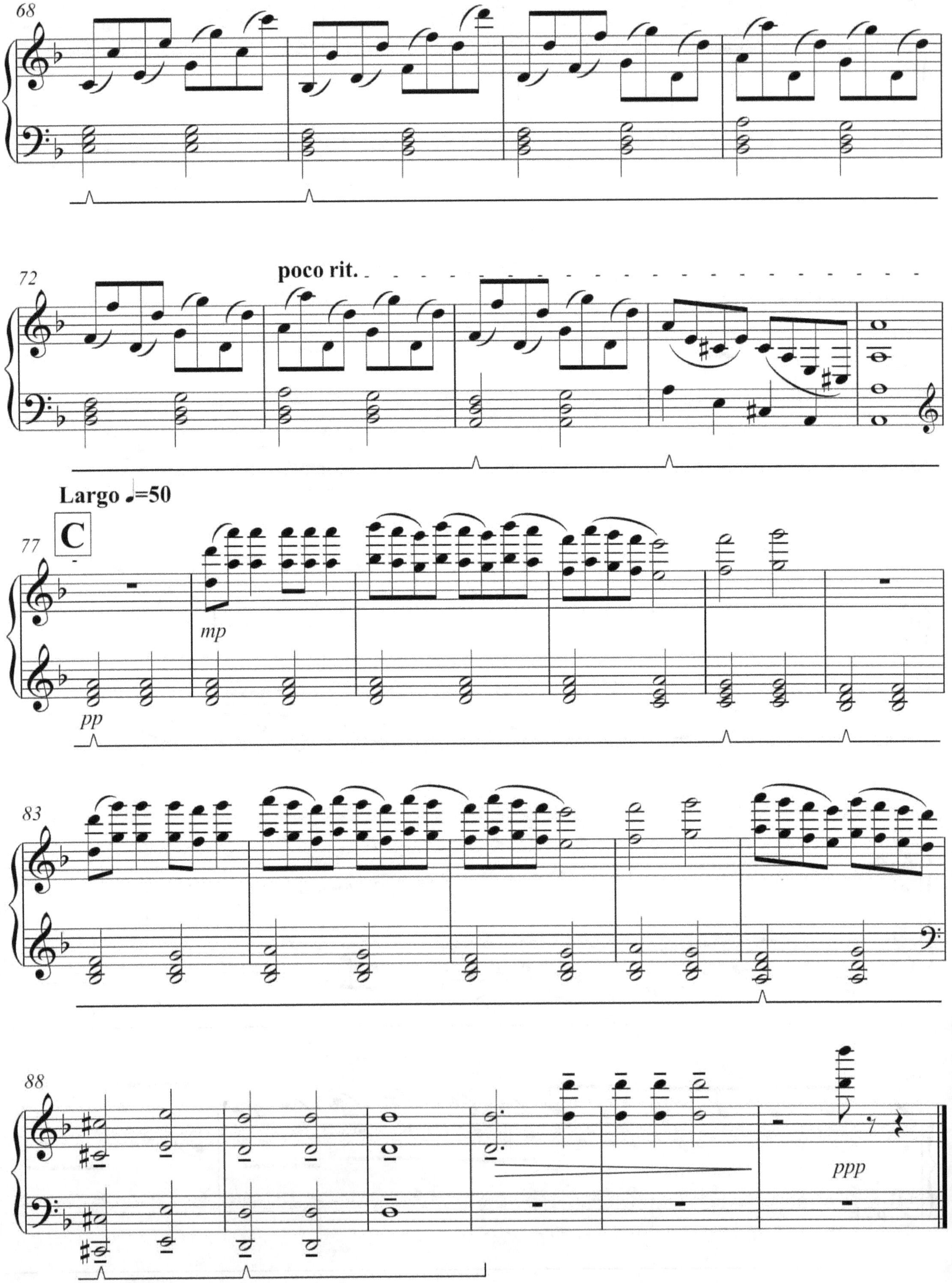
68
72
poco rit.
Largo 𝅗𝅥=50
C
77
mp
pp
83
88
ppp

Missing You

Tito Abeleda

Lento ♩=50

A

mp Legato con moto

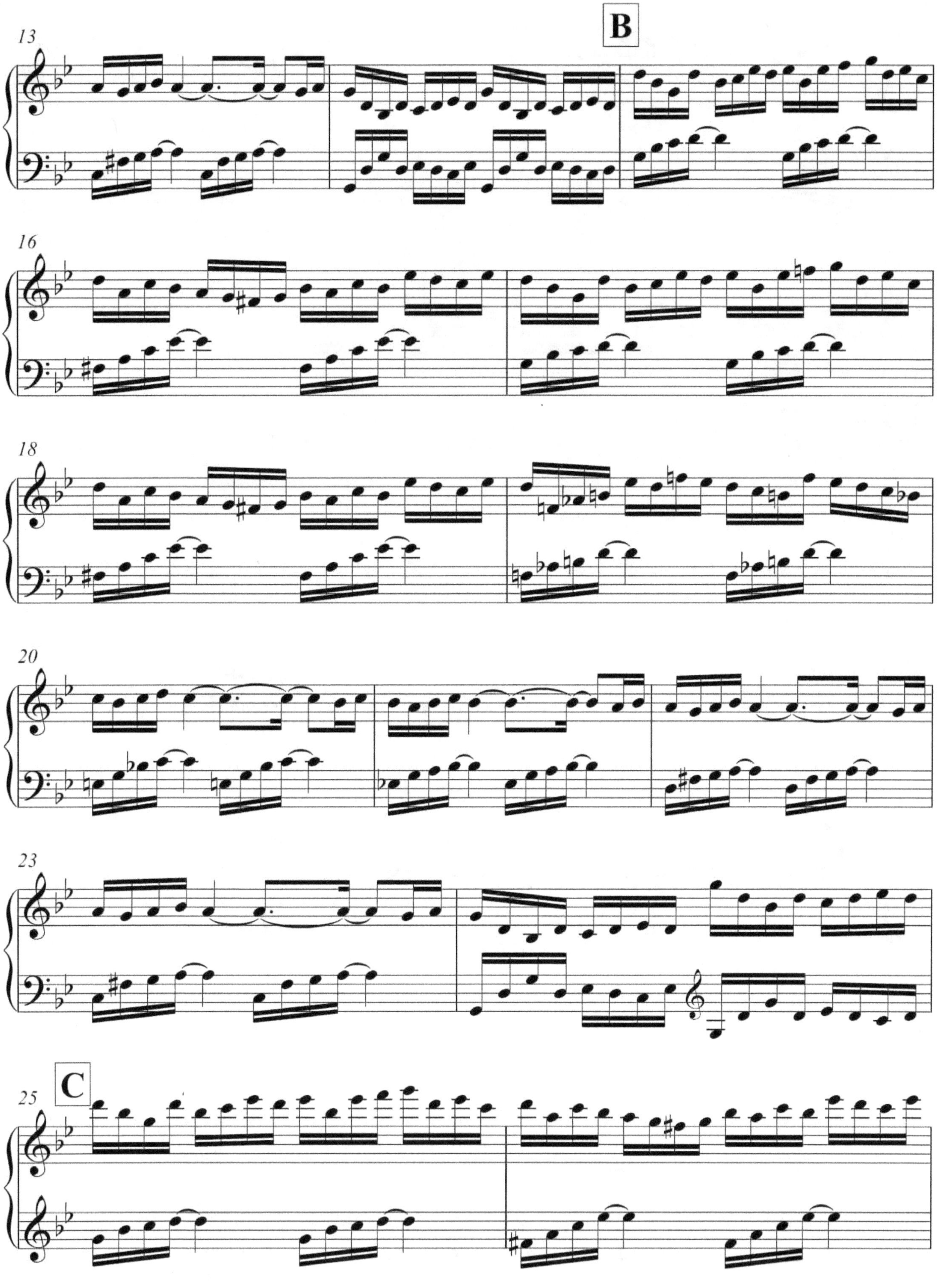
13
B
16
18
20
23
25
C

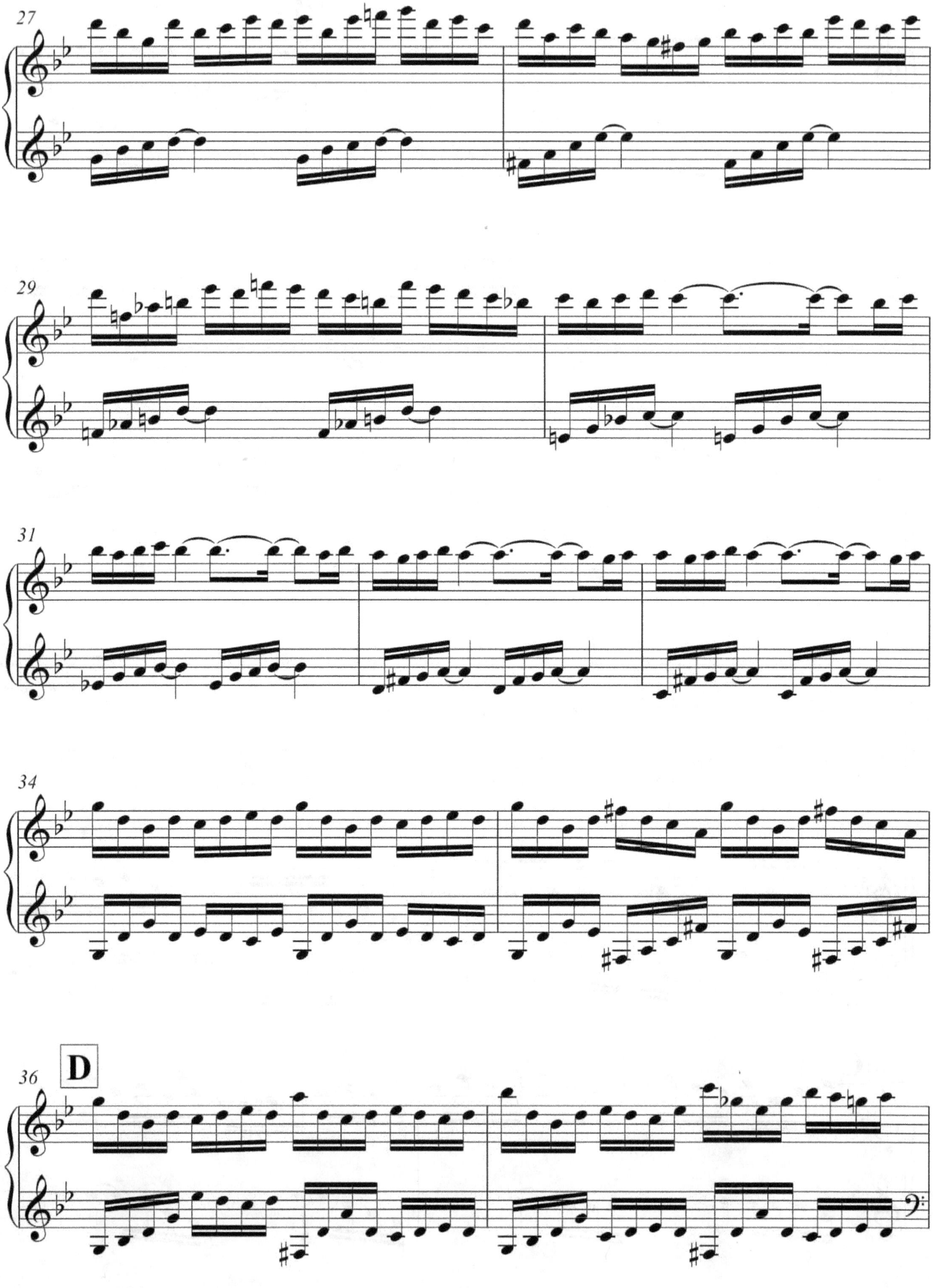
27
29
31
34
36
D

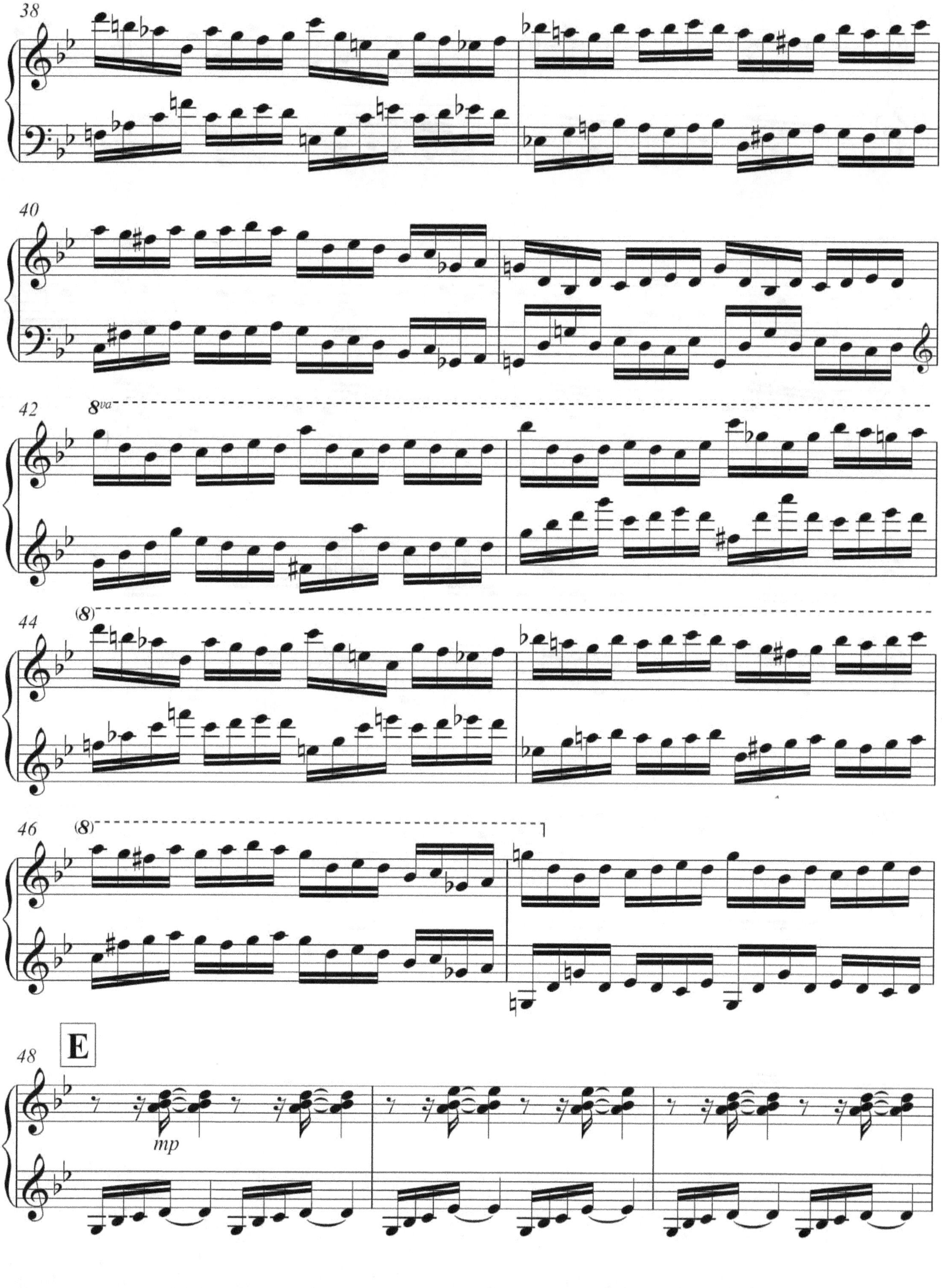
38
40
42
8va
44
(8)
46
(8)
E
48
mp

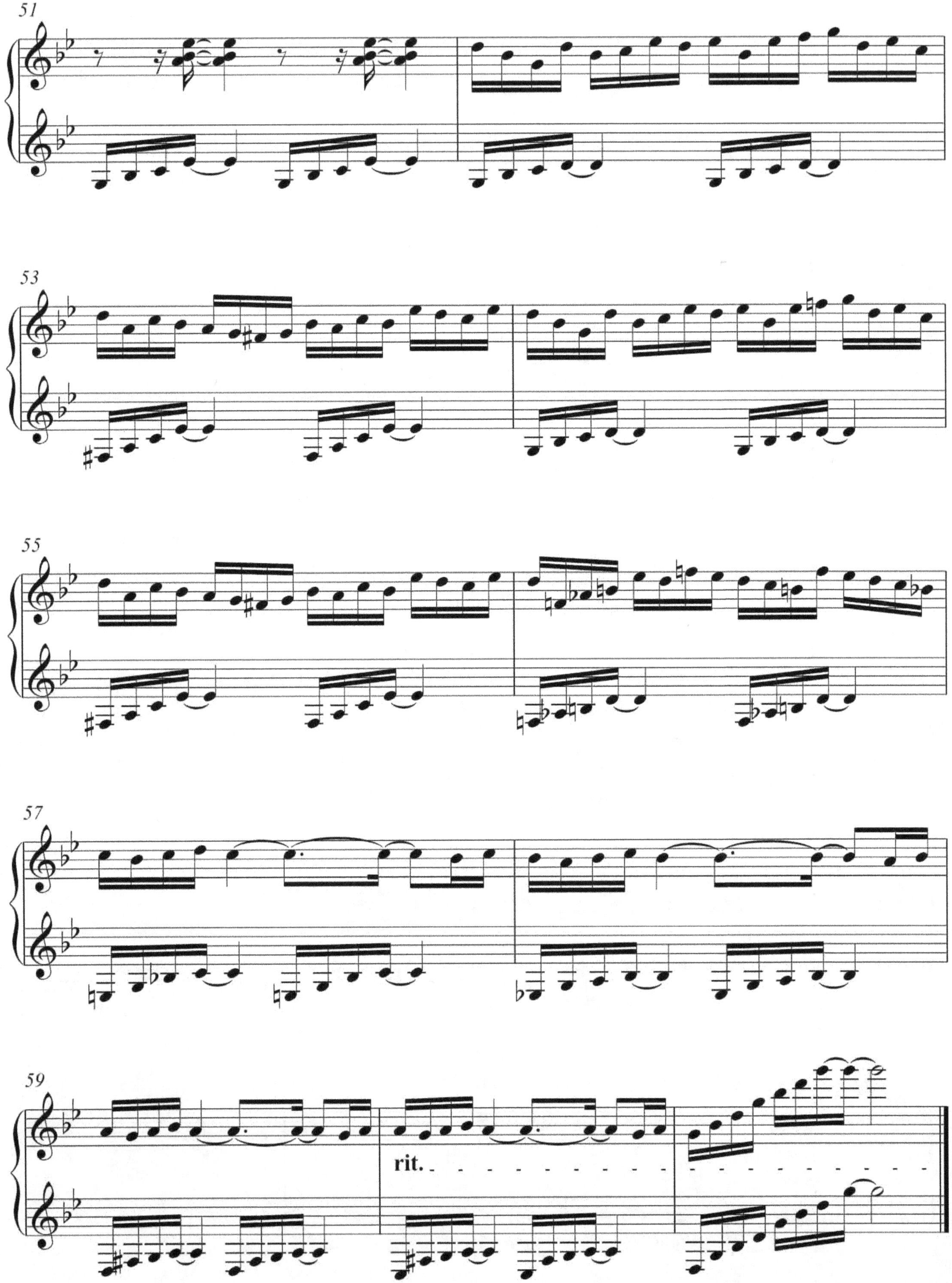
51
53
55
57
59
rit.

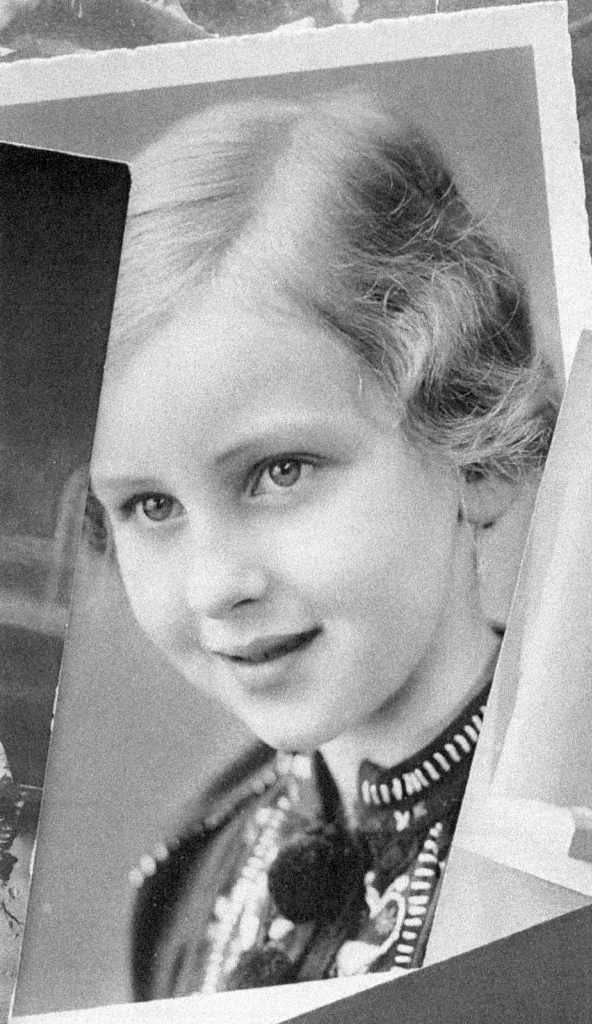

Beautiful Memories

Tito Abeleda

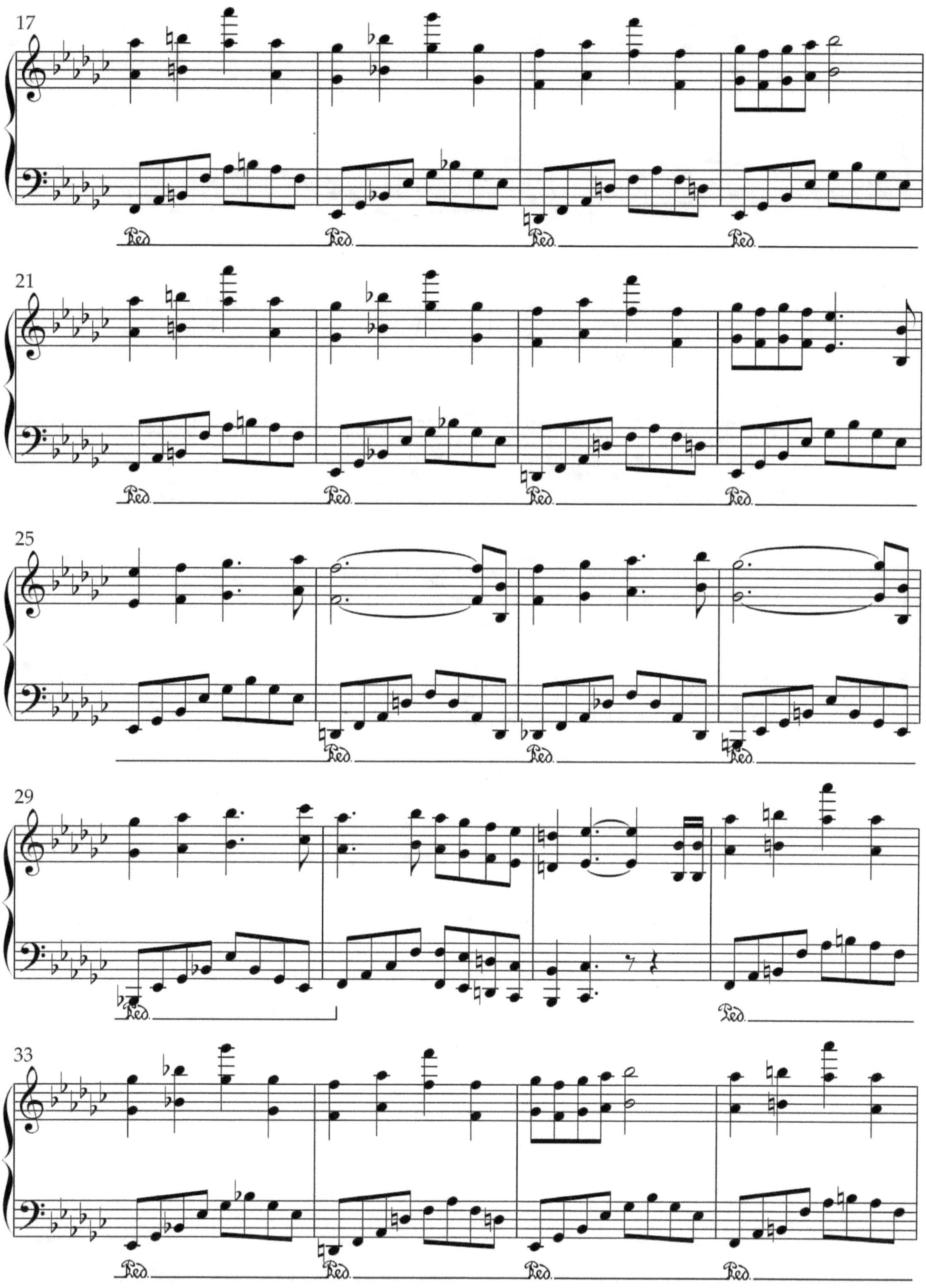
17
Ped.
21
Ped.
25
Ped.
29
Ped.
33
Ped.

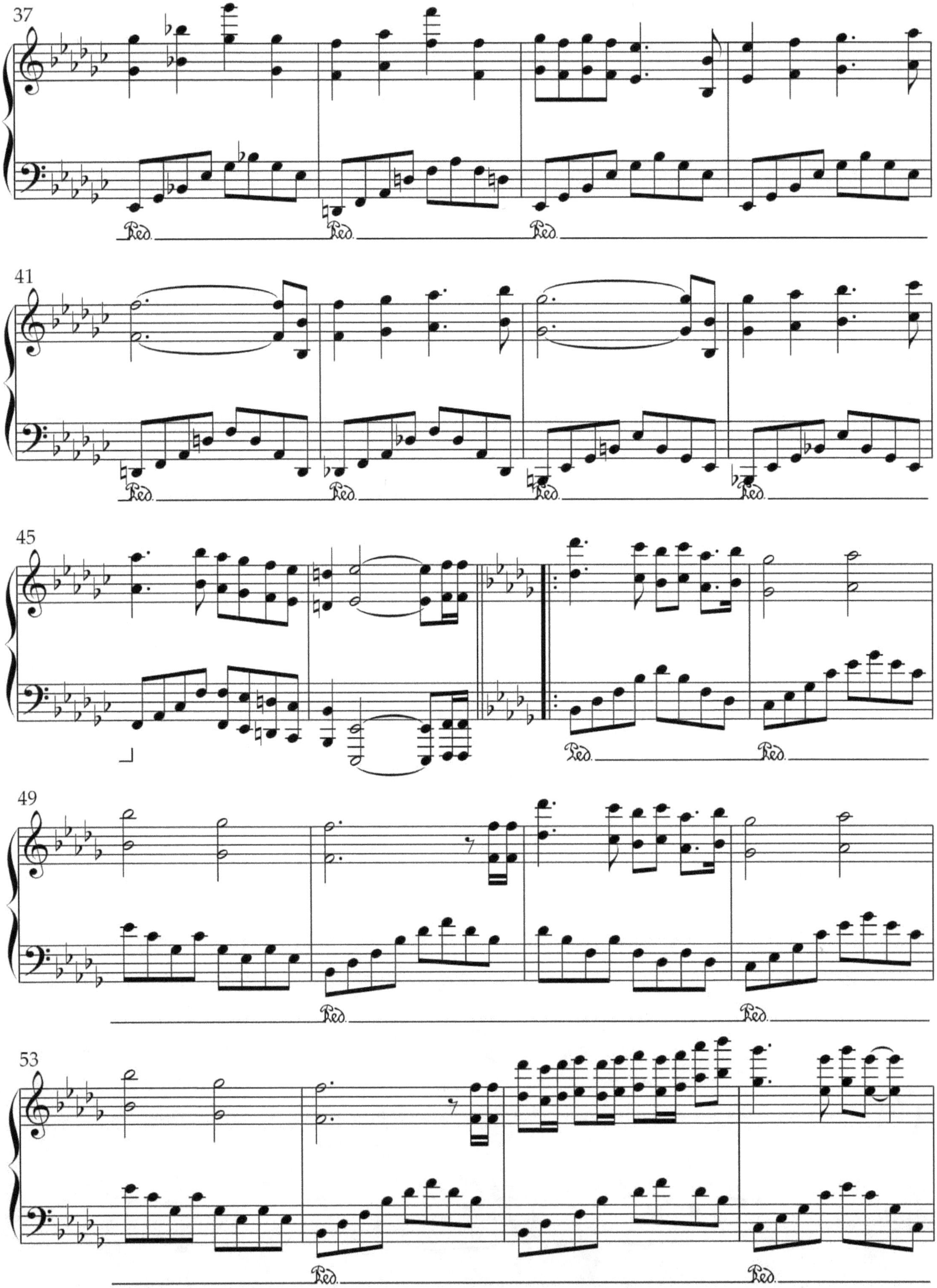
37
Ped.
Ped.
Ped.
41
Ped.
Ped.
Ped.
Ped.
45
Ped.
Ped.
49
Ped.
Ped.
53
Ped.
Ped.

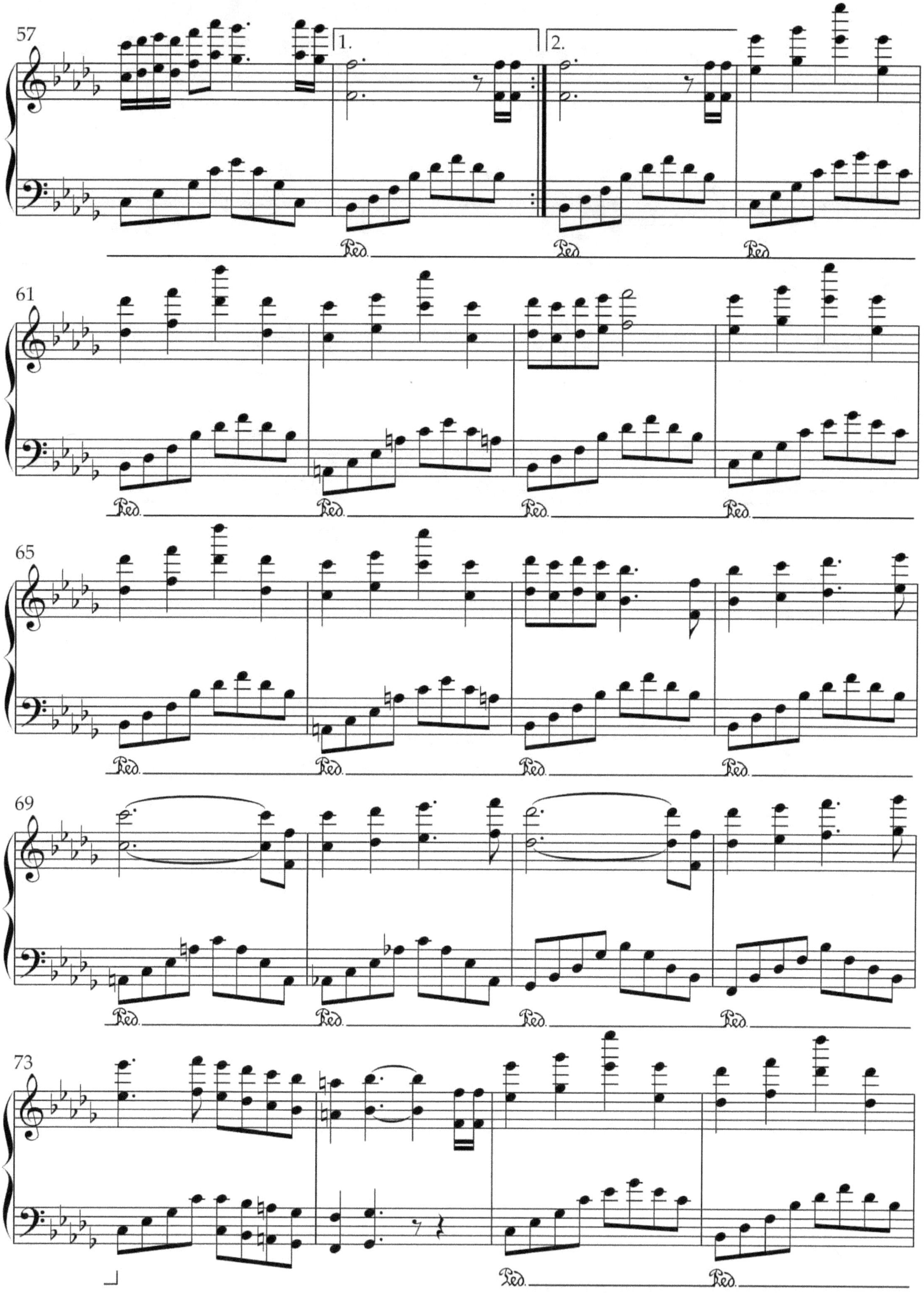
57
1.
2.
Red.
61
65
69
73

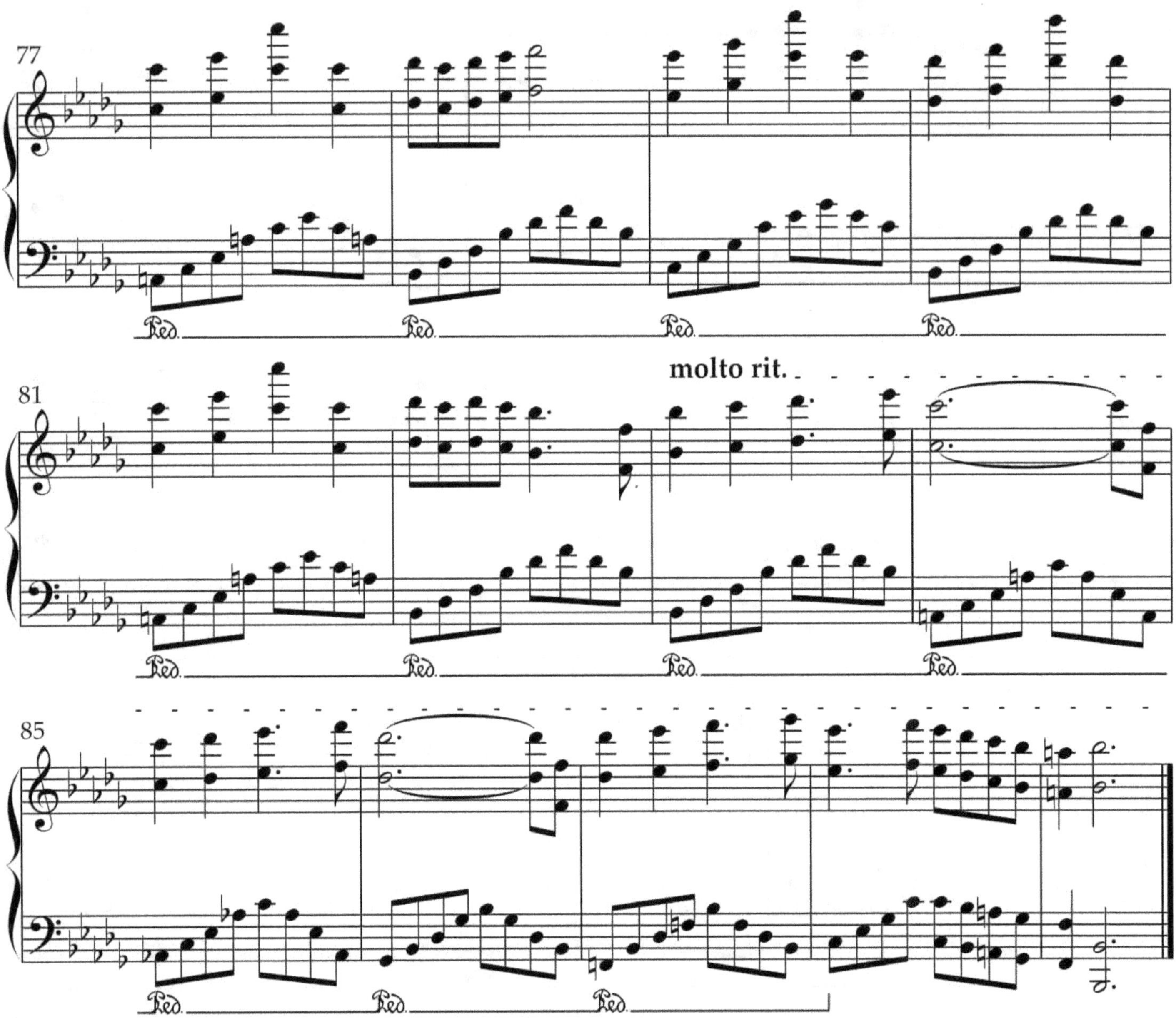
77
Red.
81
molto rit.
Red.
85
Red.

Silent Night, Holy Night

Music by Franz X. Gruber
Arrangement by Tito Abeleda

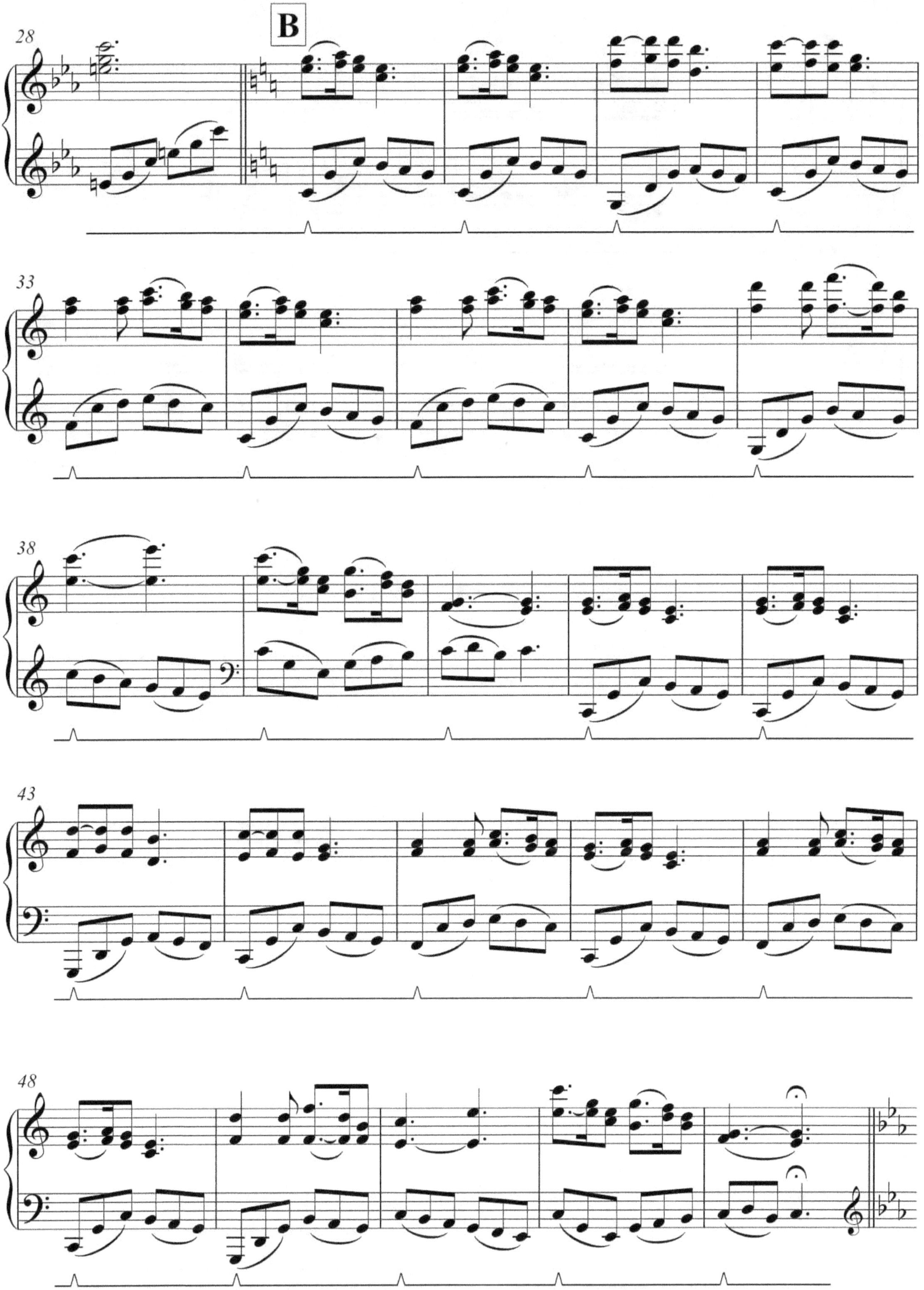
28
B
33
38
43
48

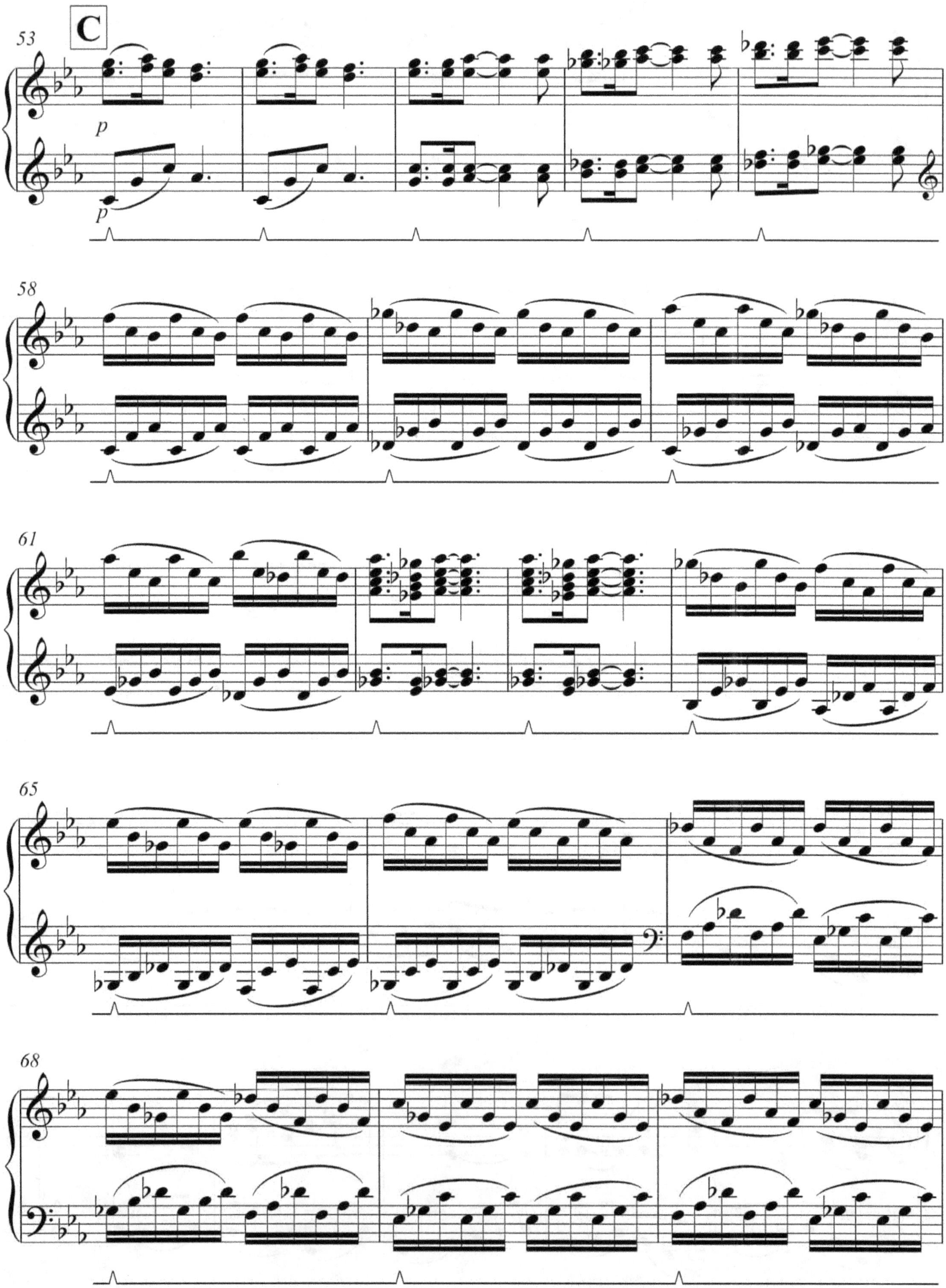
C
53
p
p
58
61
65
68

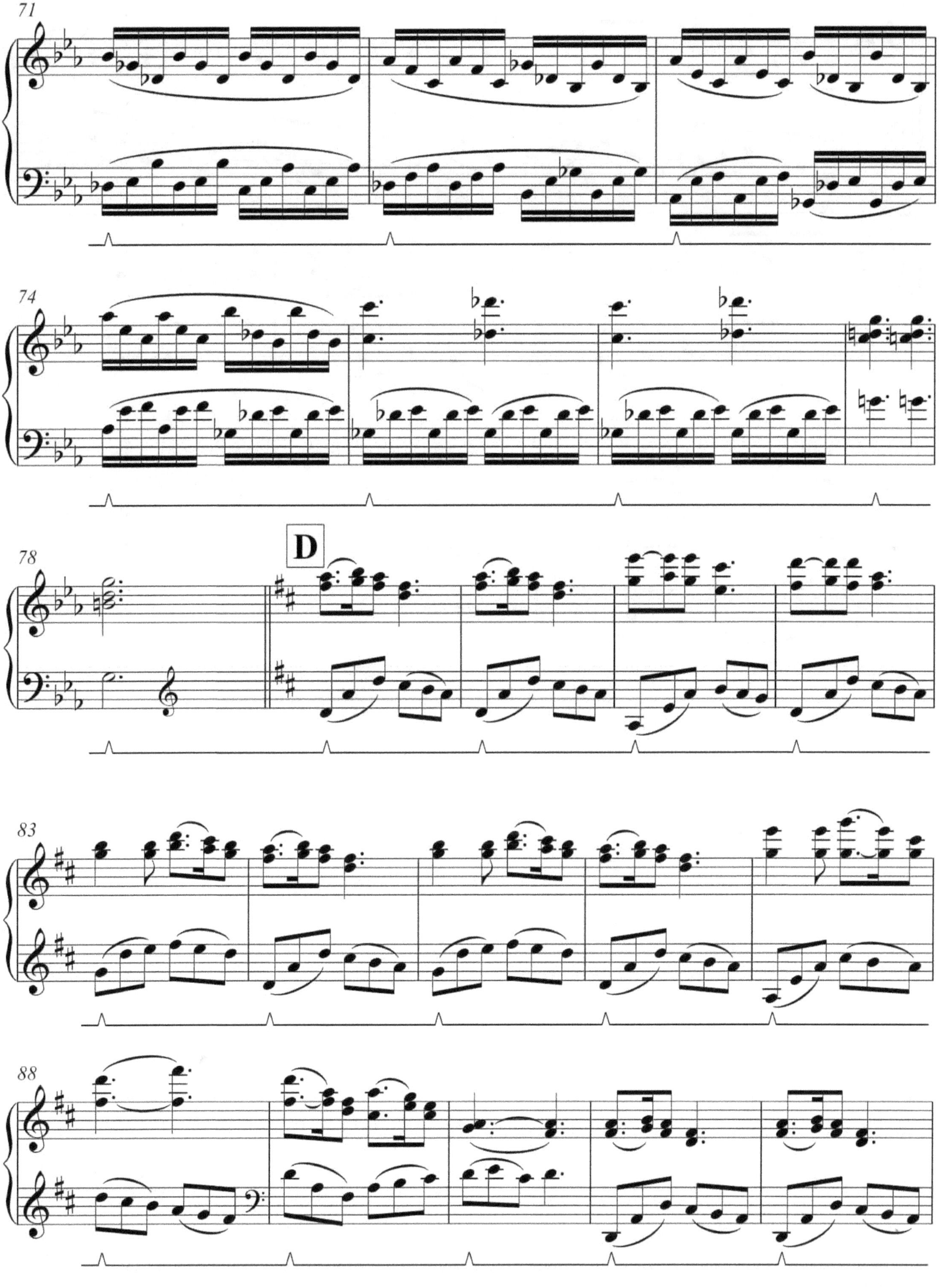
71
74
78
D
83
88

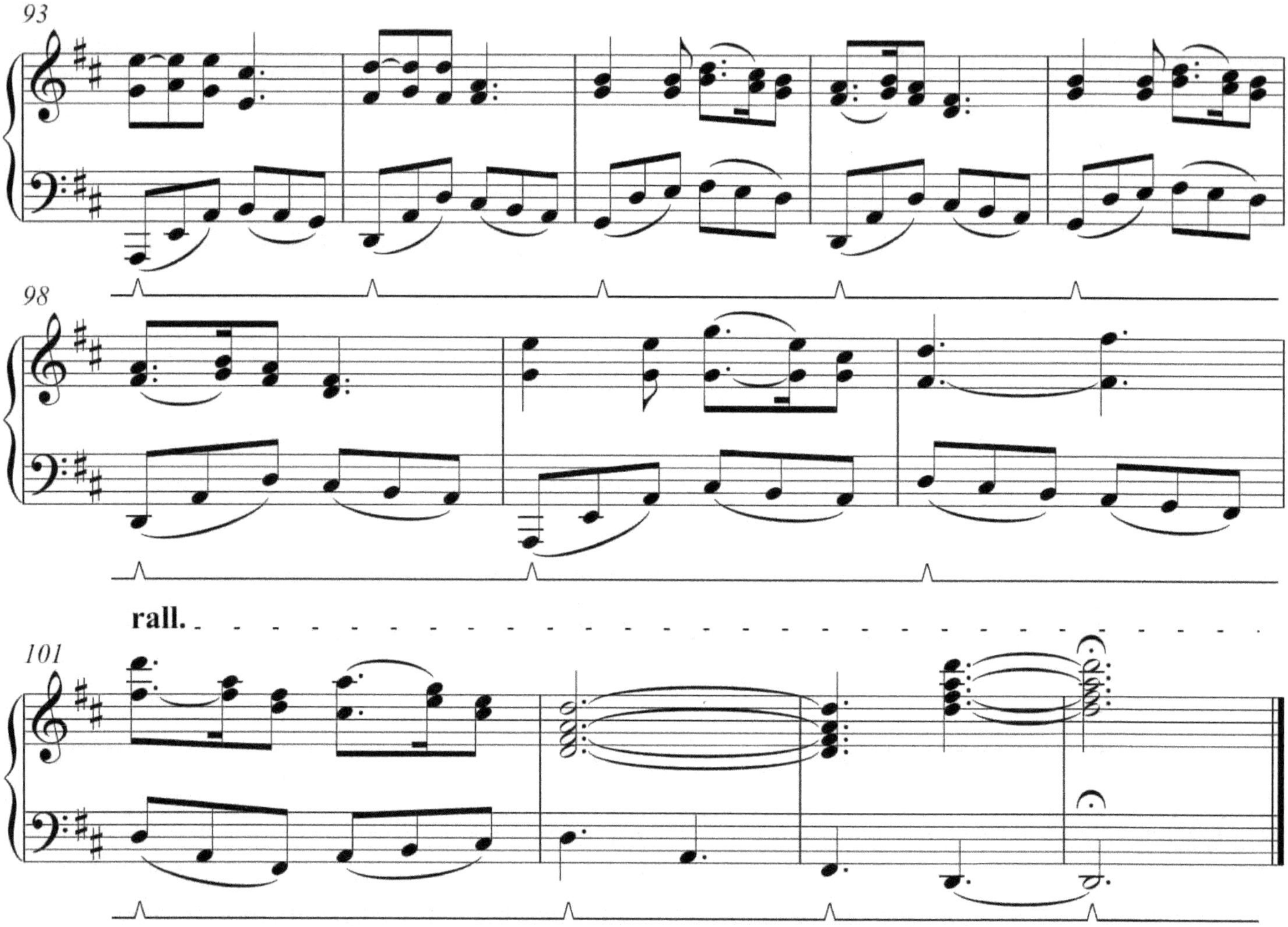
93
98
rall.
101

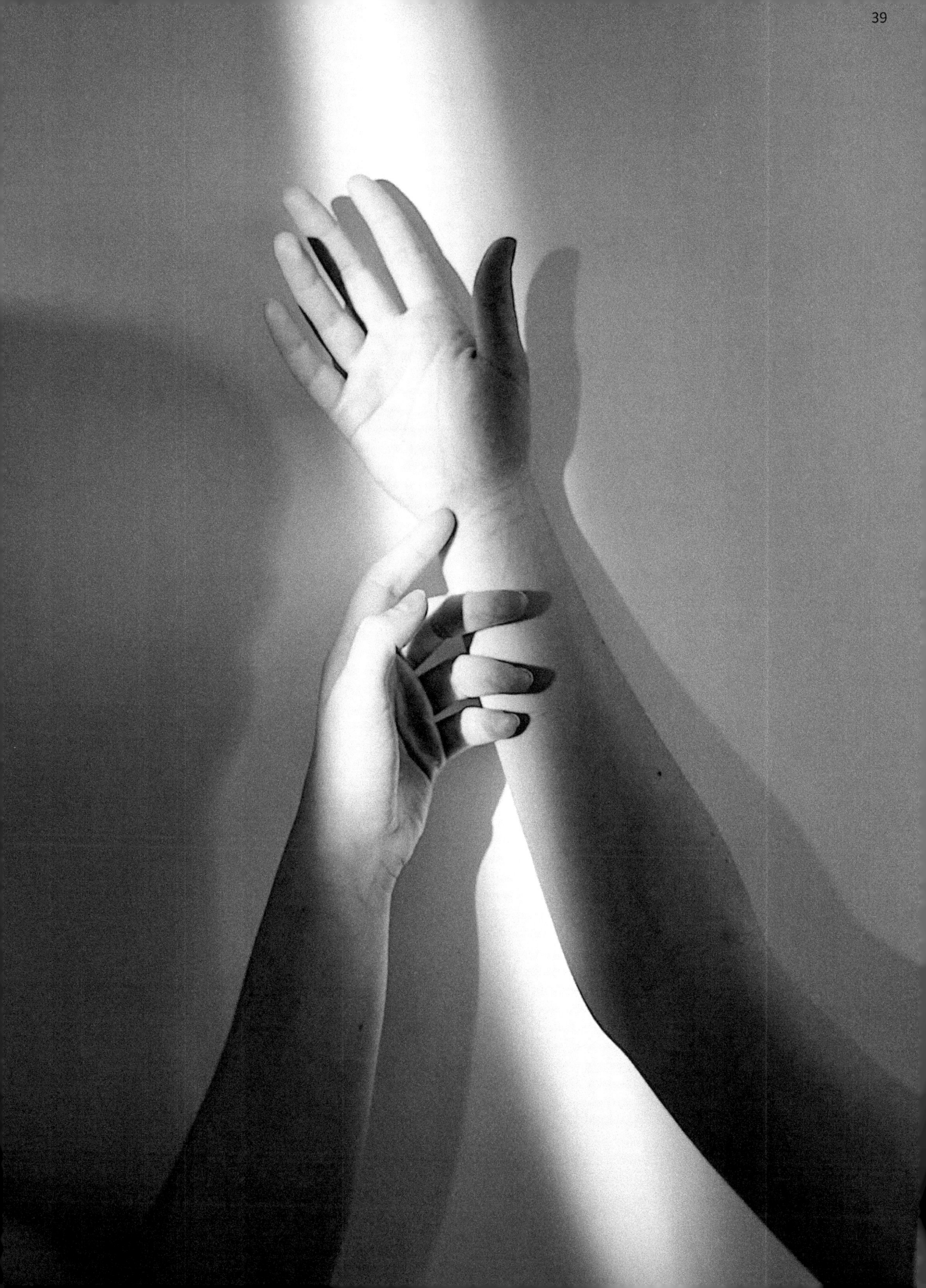

Forever Touched by Your Love

Tito Abeleda

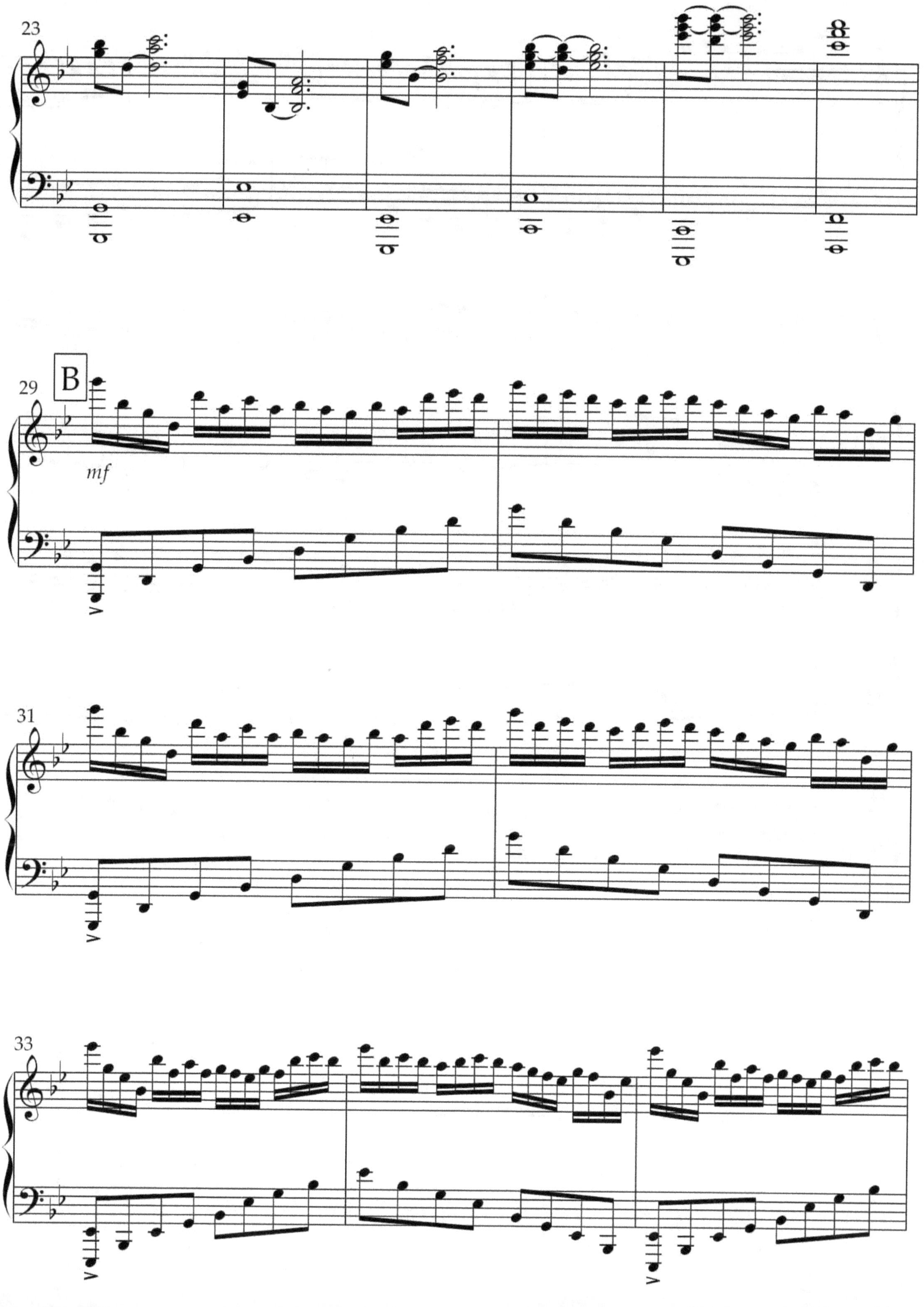
23
B
29
mf
31
33

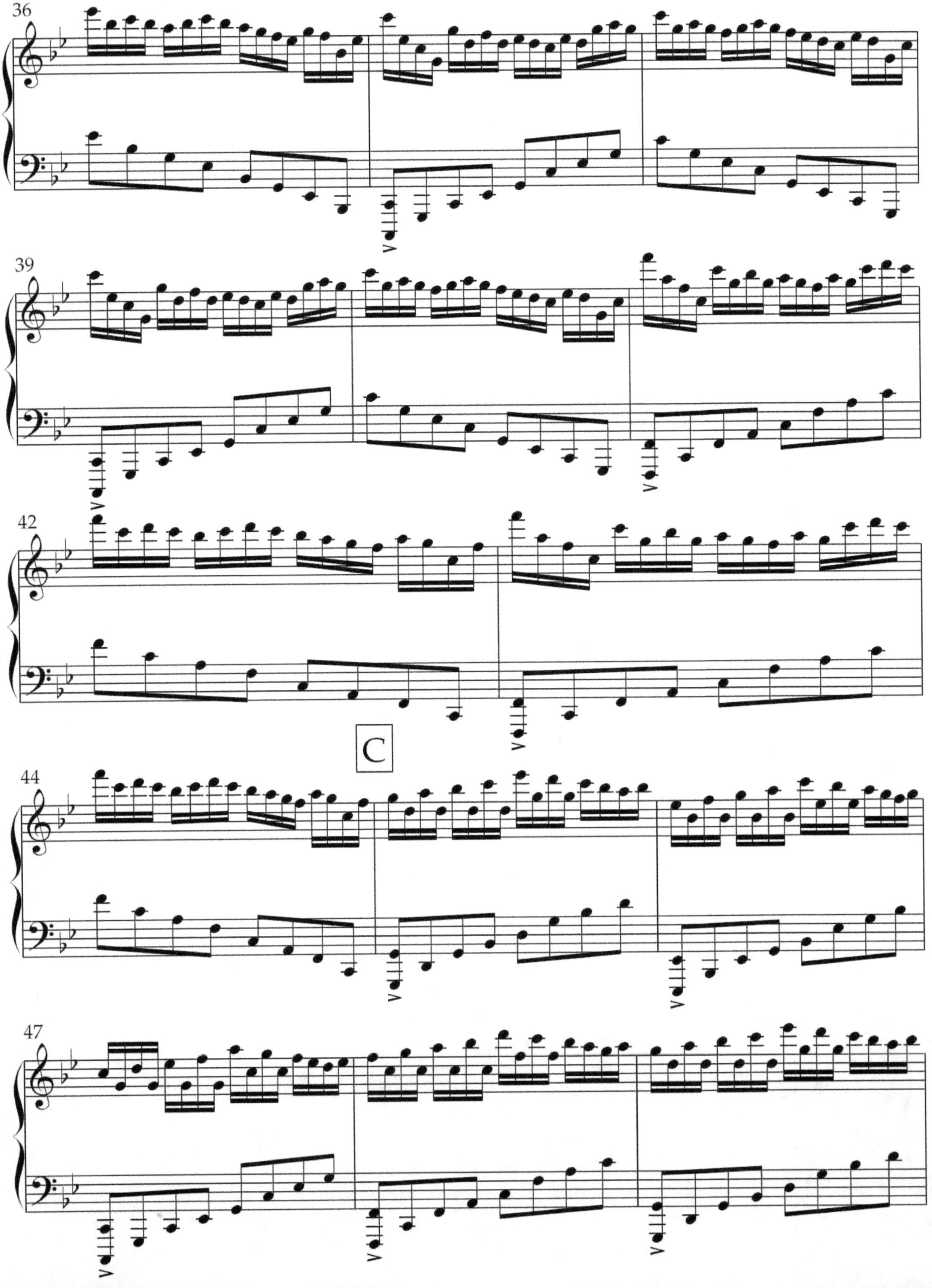
36
39
42
C
44
47

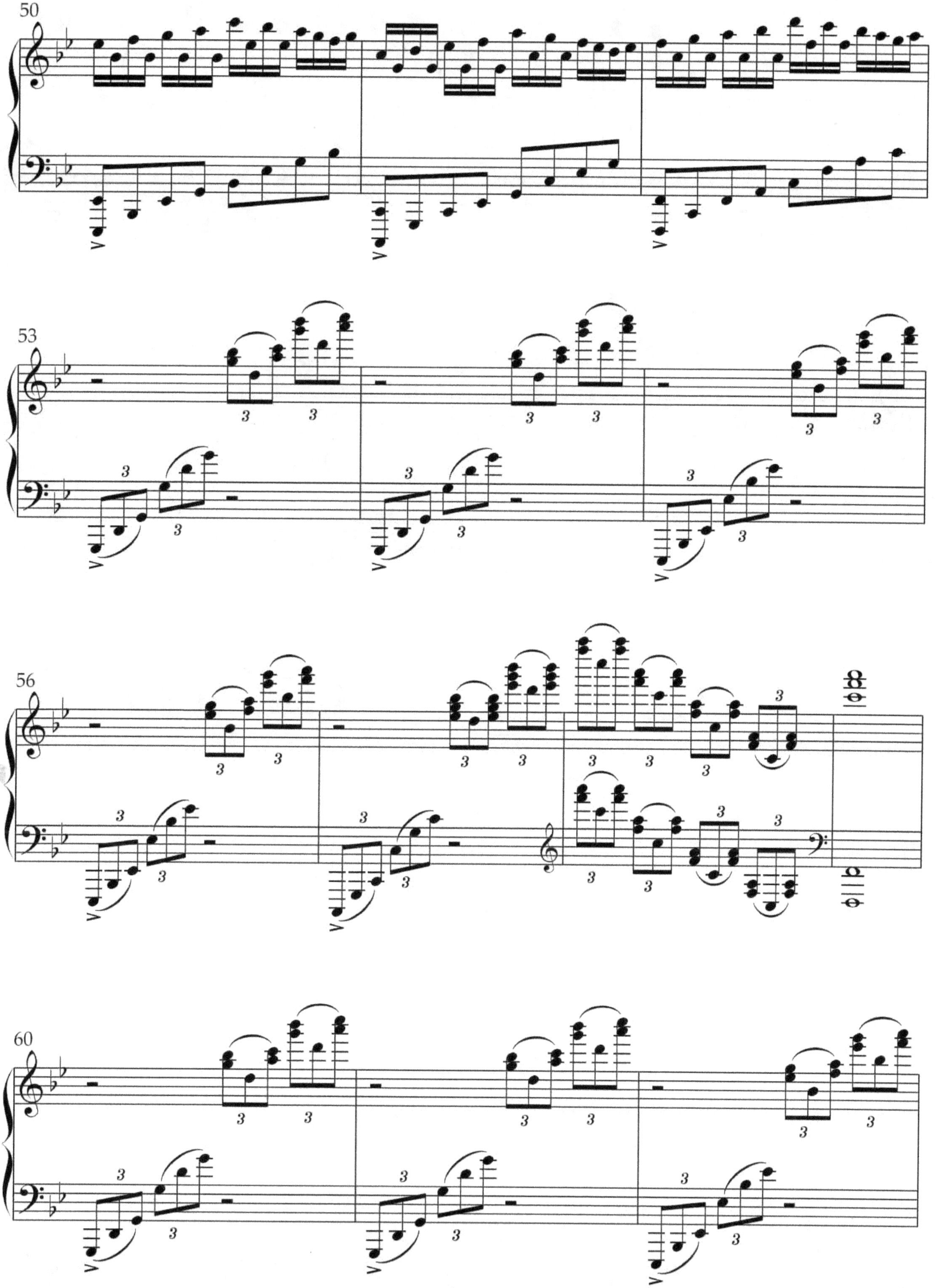
50
53
56
60

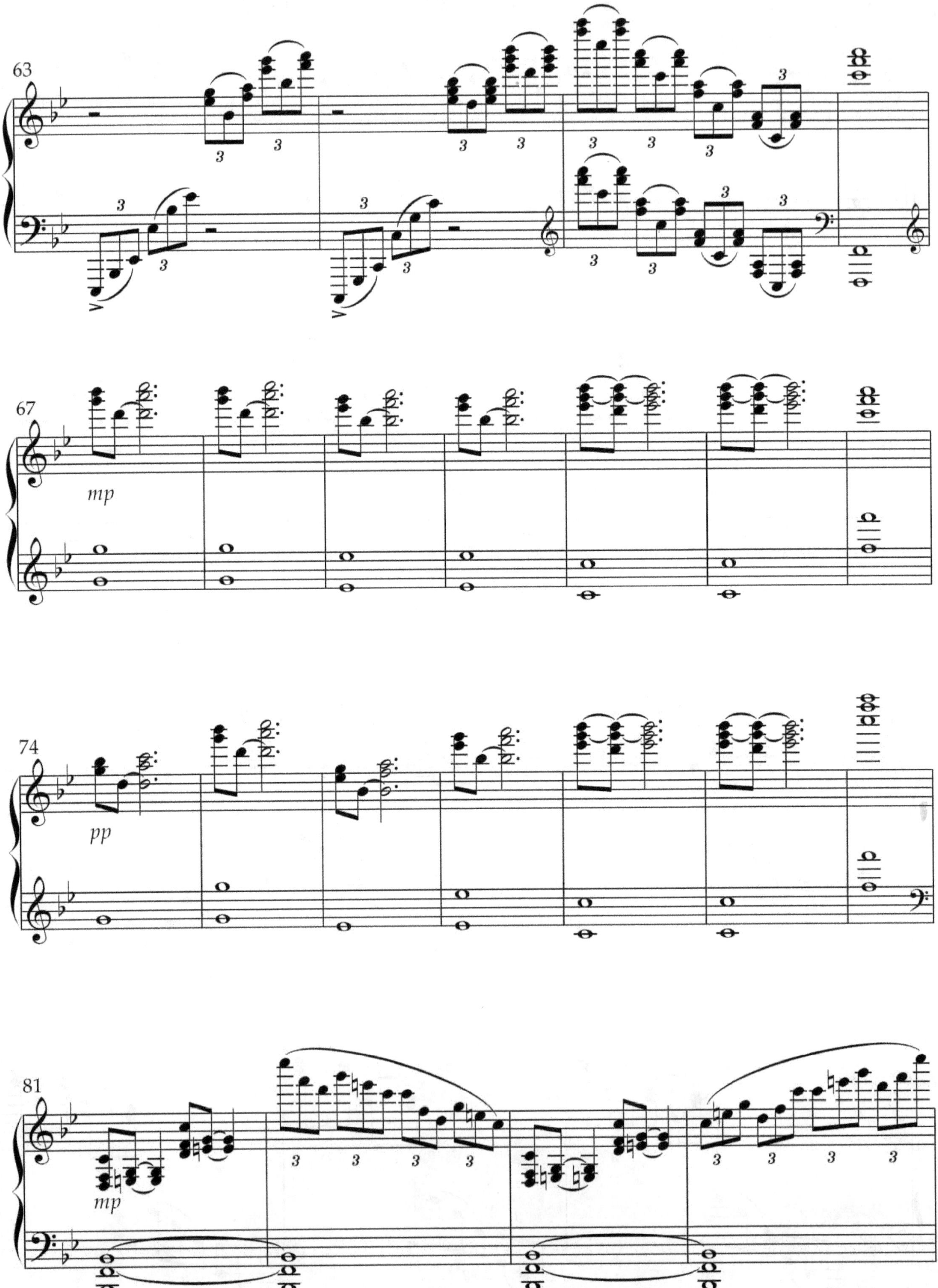
63
67
mp
74
pp
81
mp

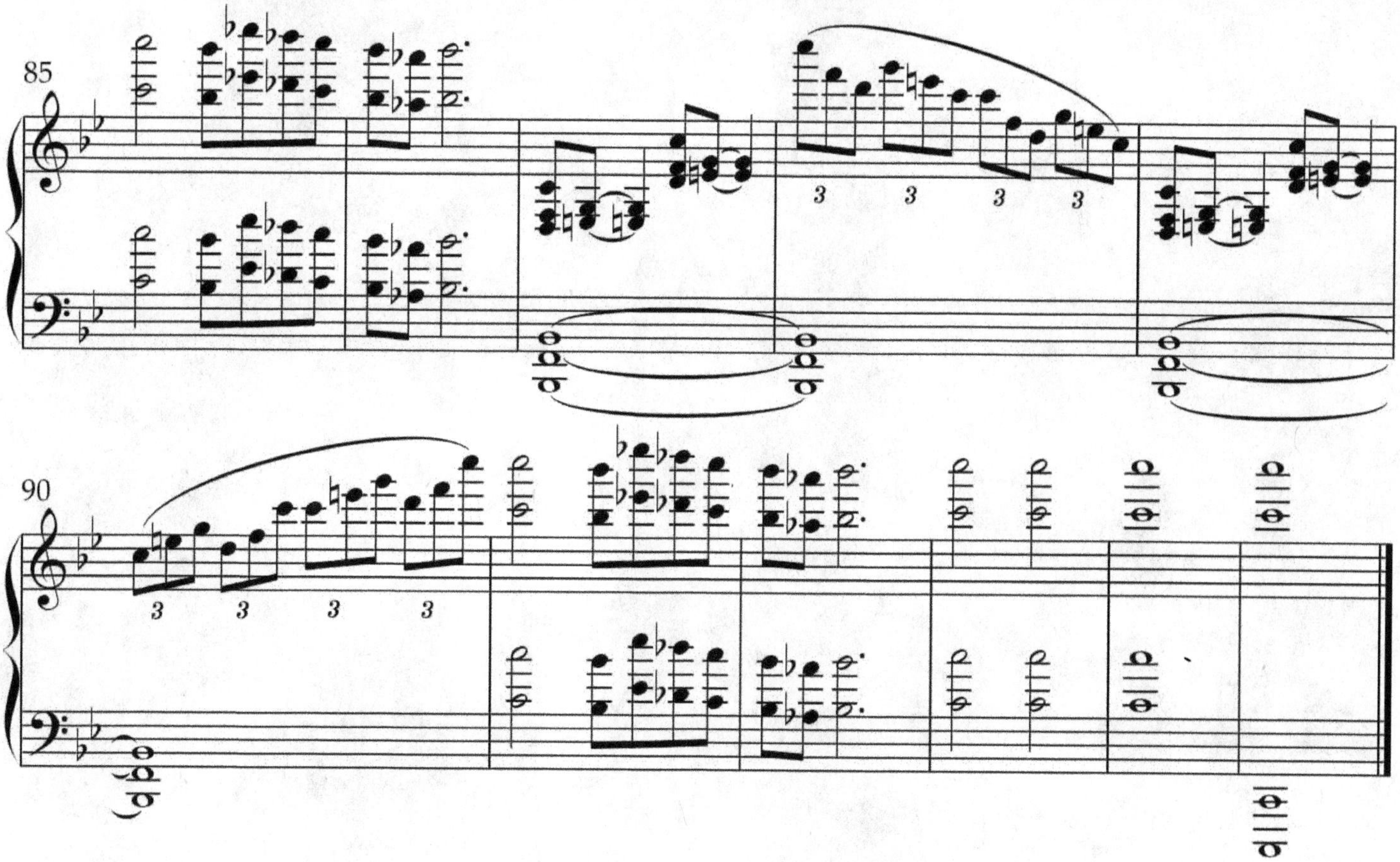
85
90

Running, Searching

Tito Abeleda

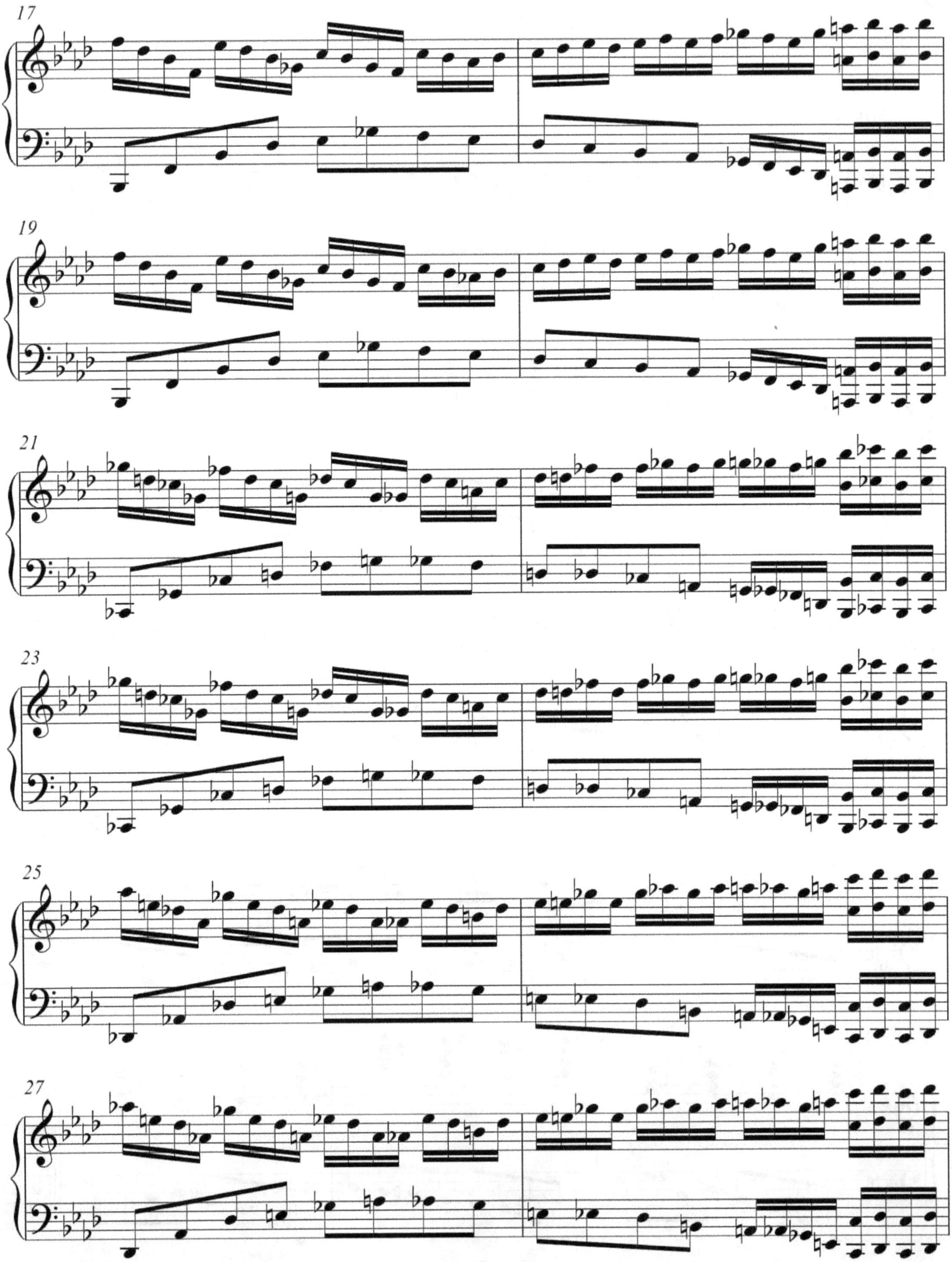
17
19
21
23
25
27

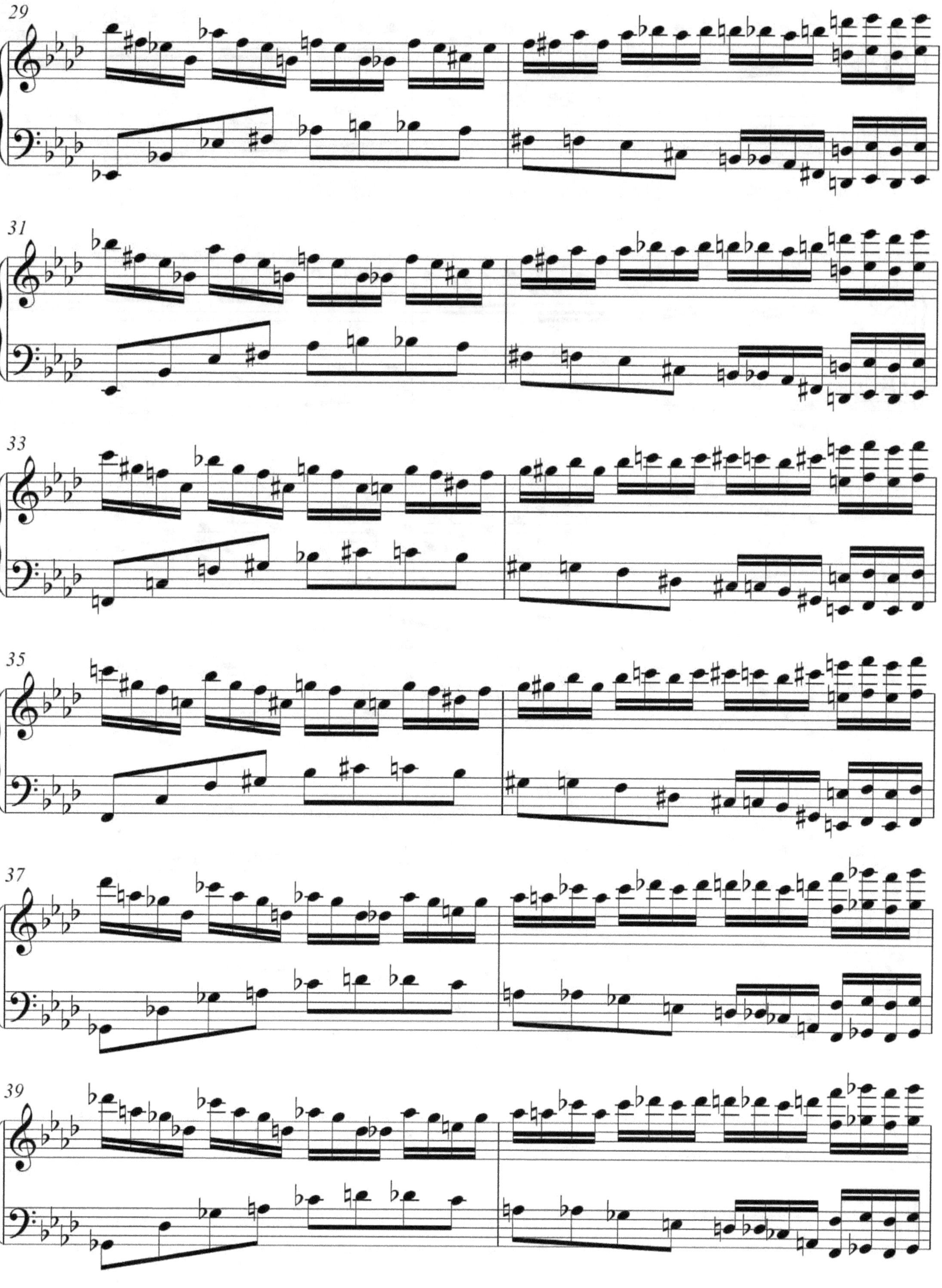
29
31
33
35
37
39

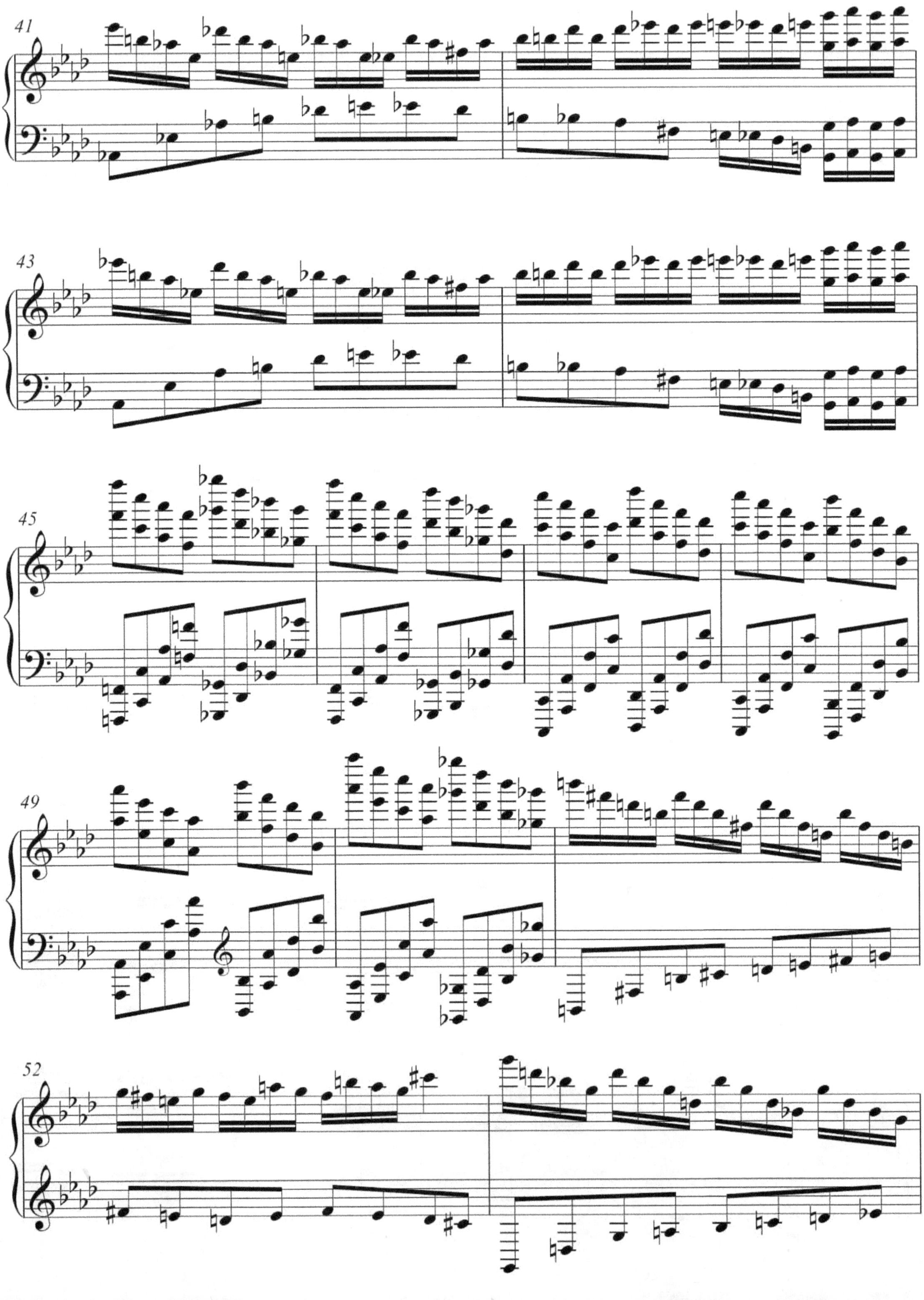
41
43
45
49
52

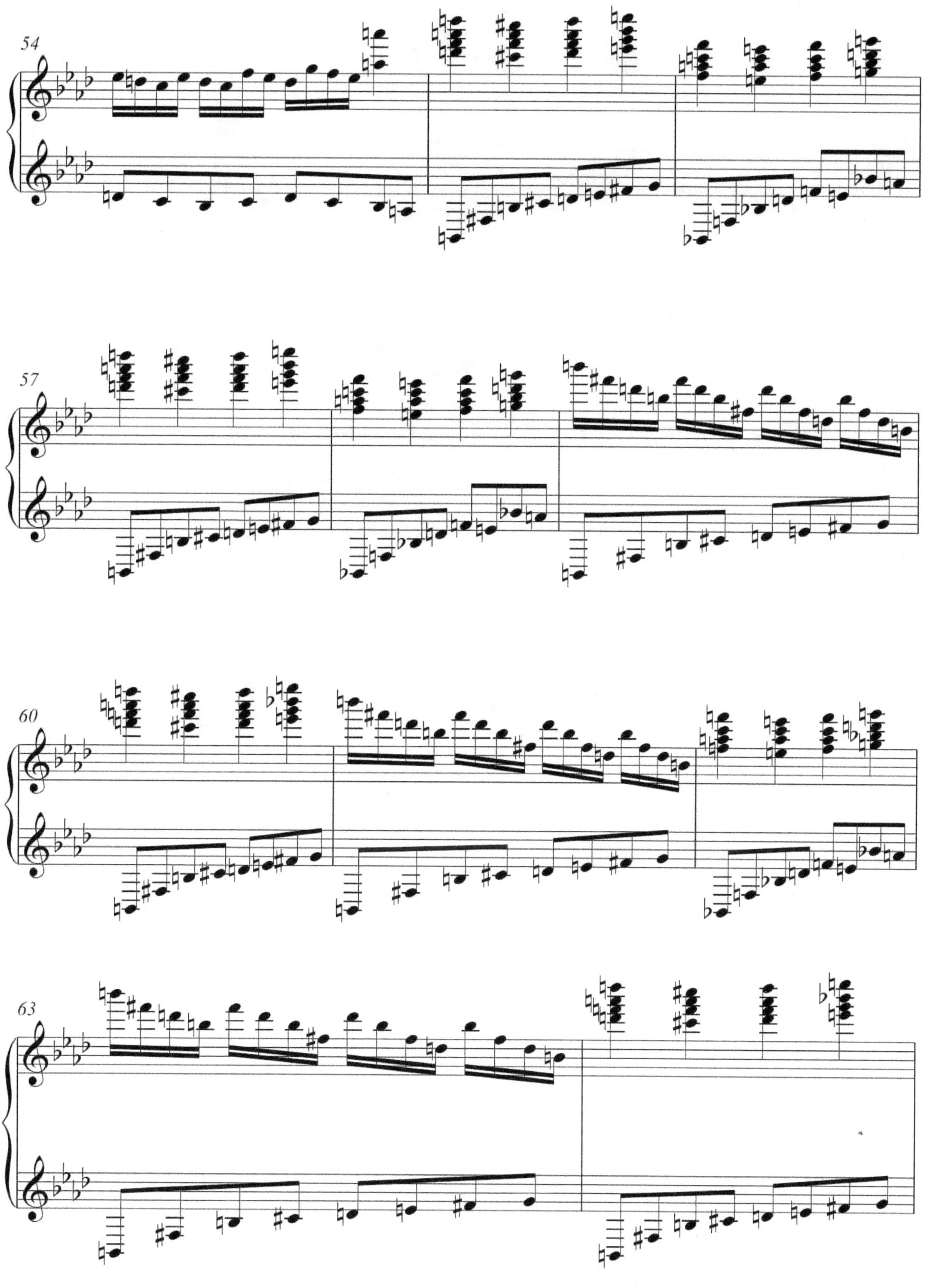
54
57
60
63

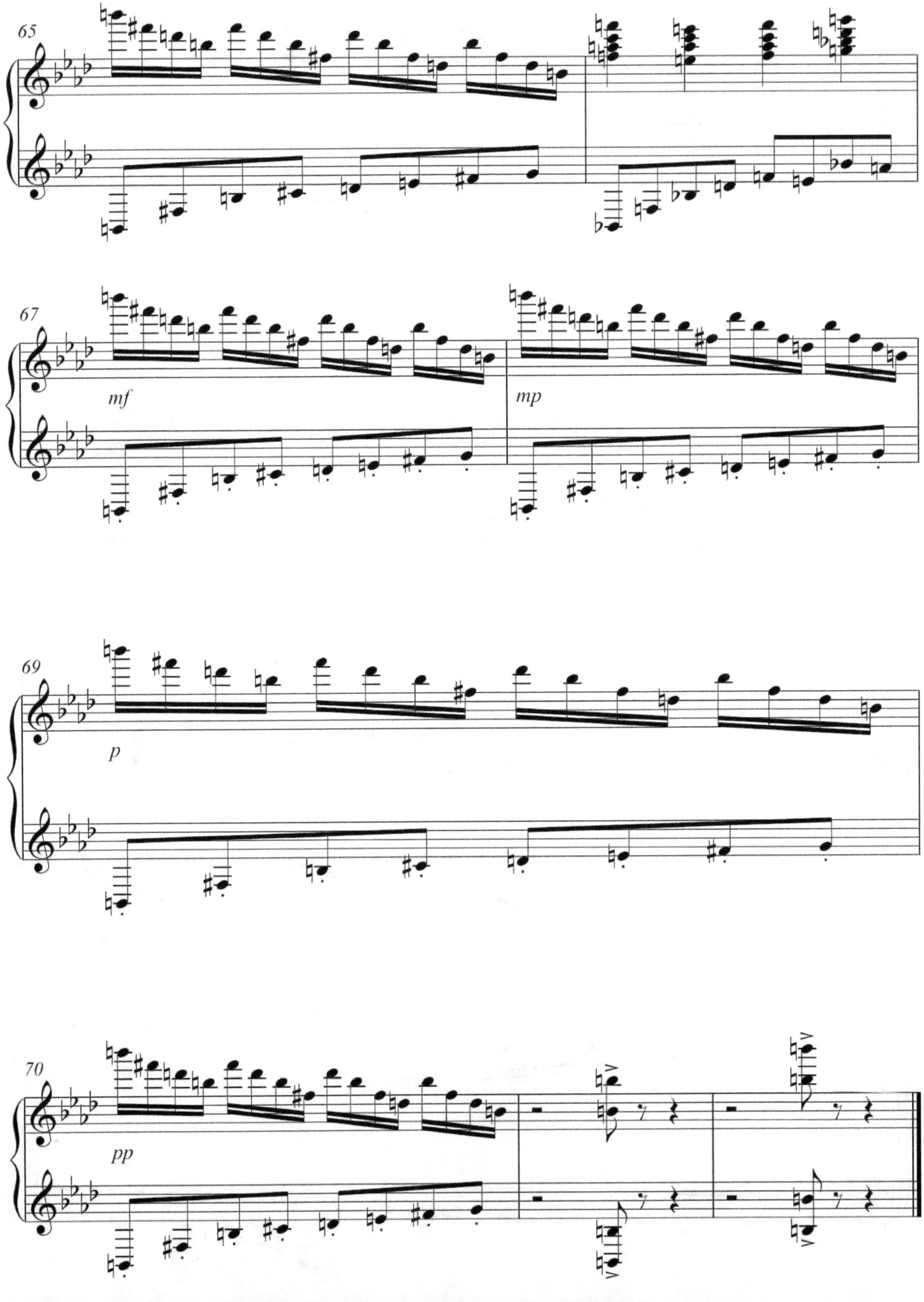
65
67
mf
mp
69
p
70
pp

Phoenix Rising

Tito Abeleda

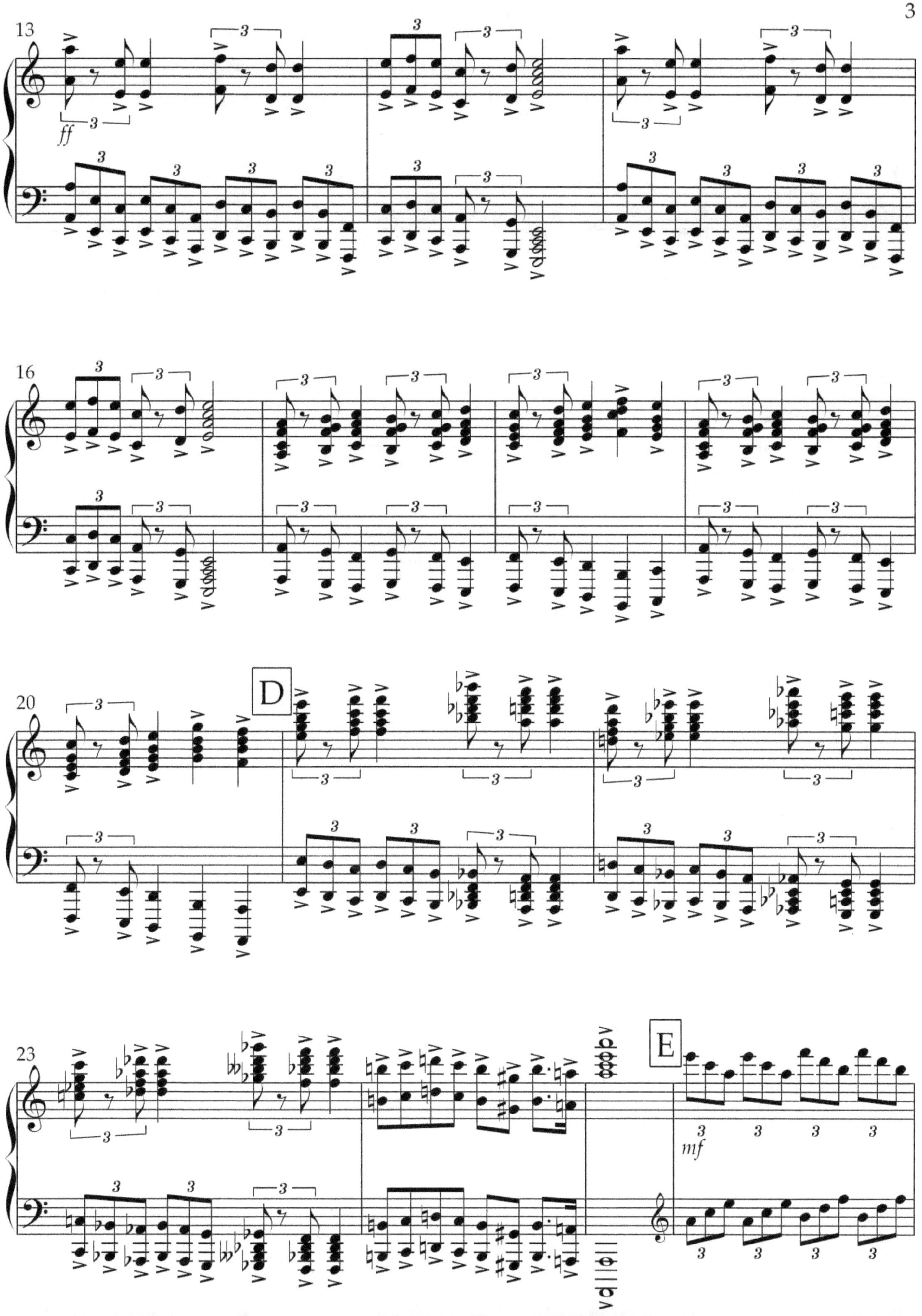
3
13
ff
16
20
D
23
E
mf

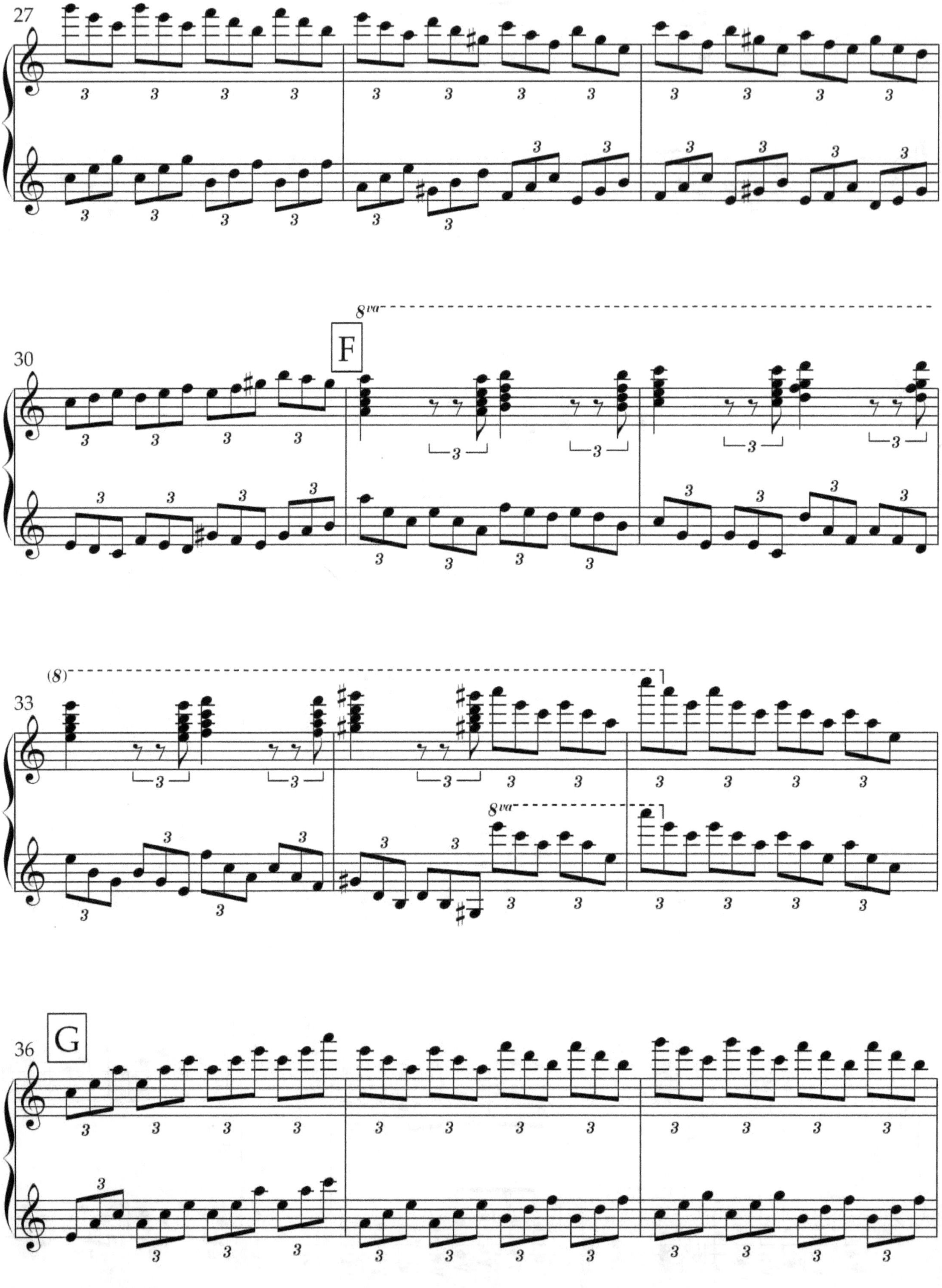
27
30
F
8va
33
(8)
8va
36
G

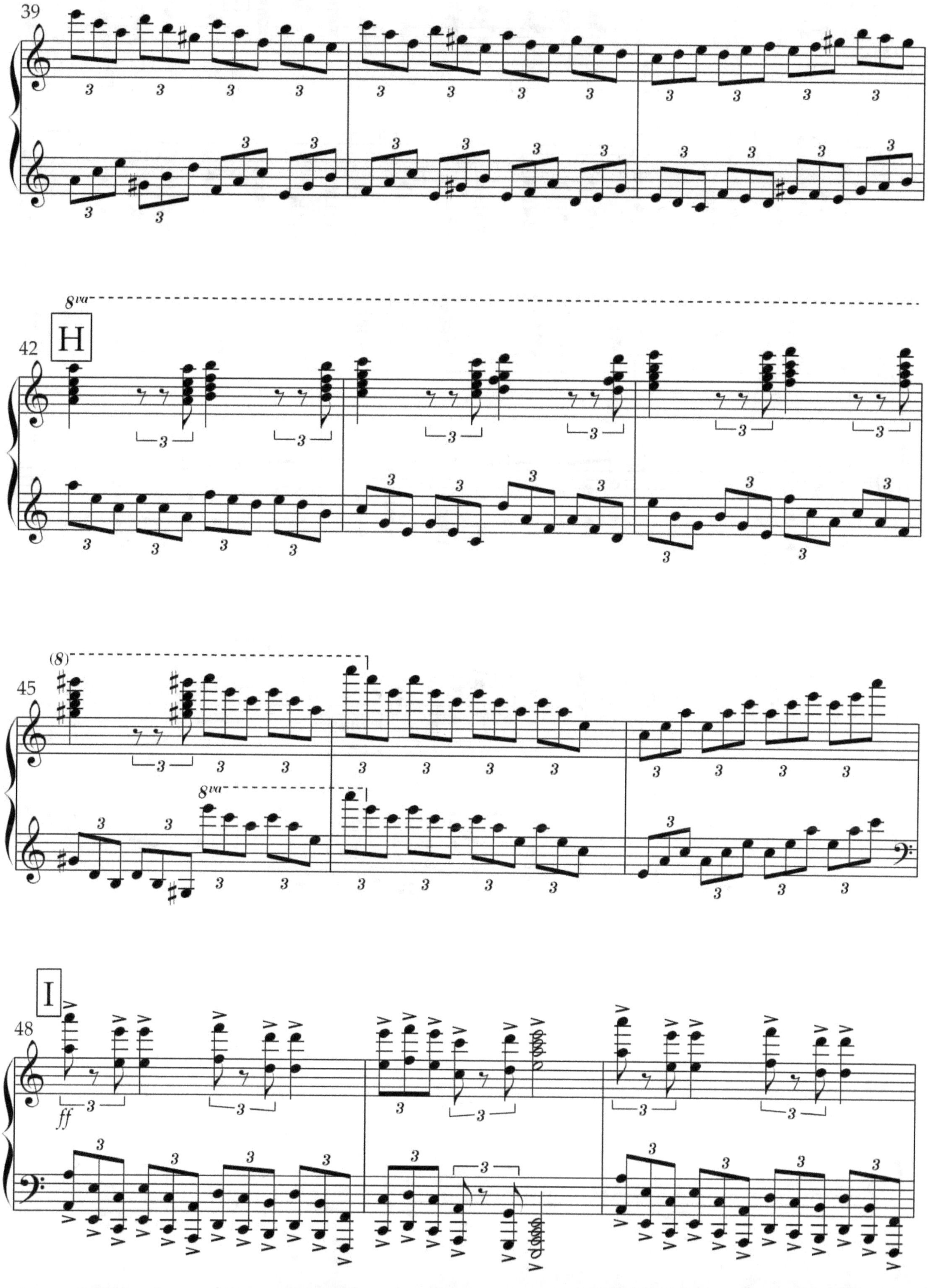
39
42
H
8va
45
(8)
8va
48
I
ff

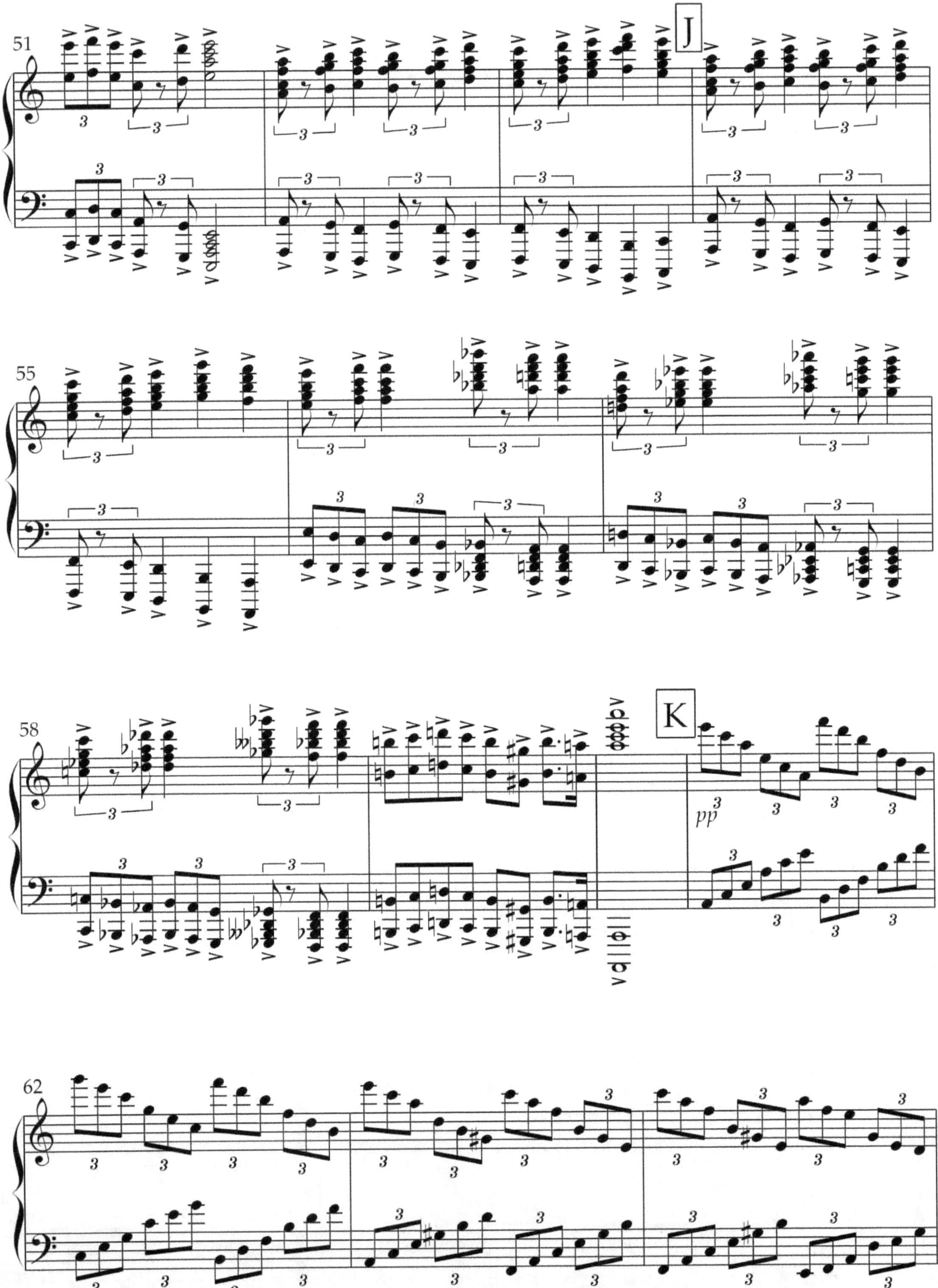
51
J
55
58
K
pp
62

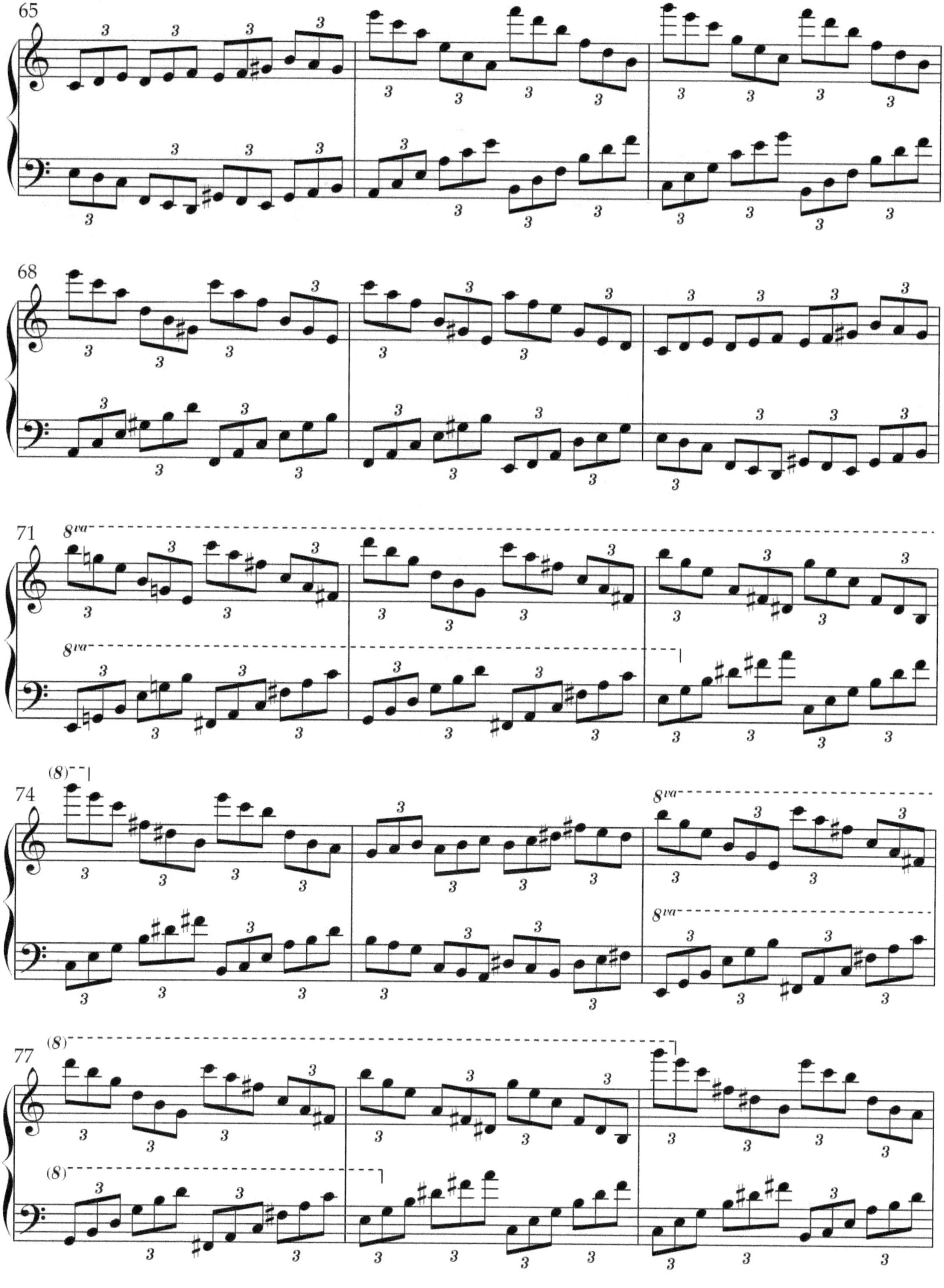
65
68
71
8va
8va
74
(8)
8va
8va
77
(8)
(8)

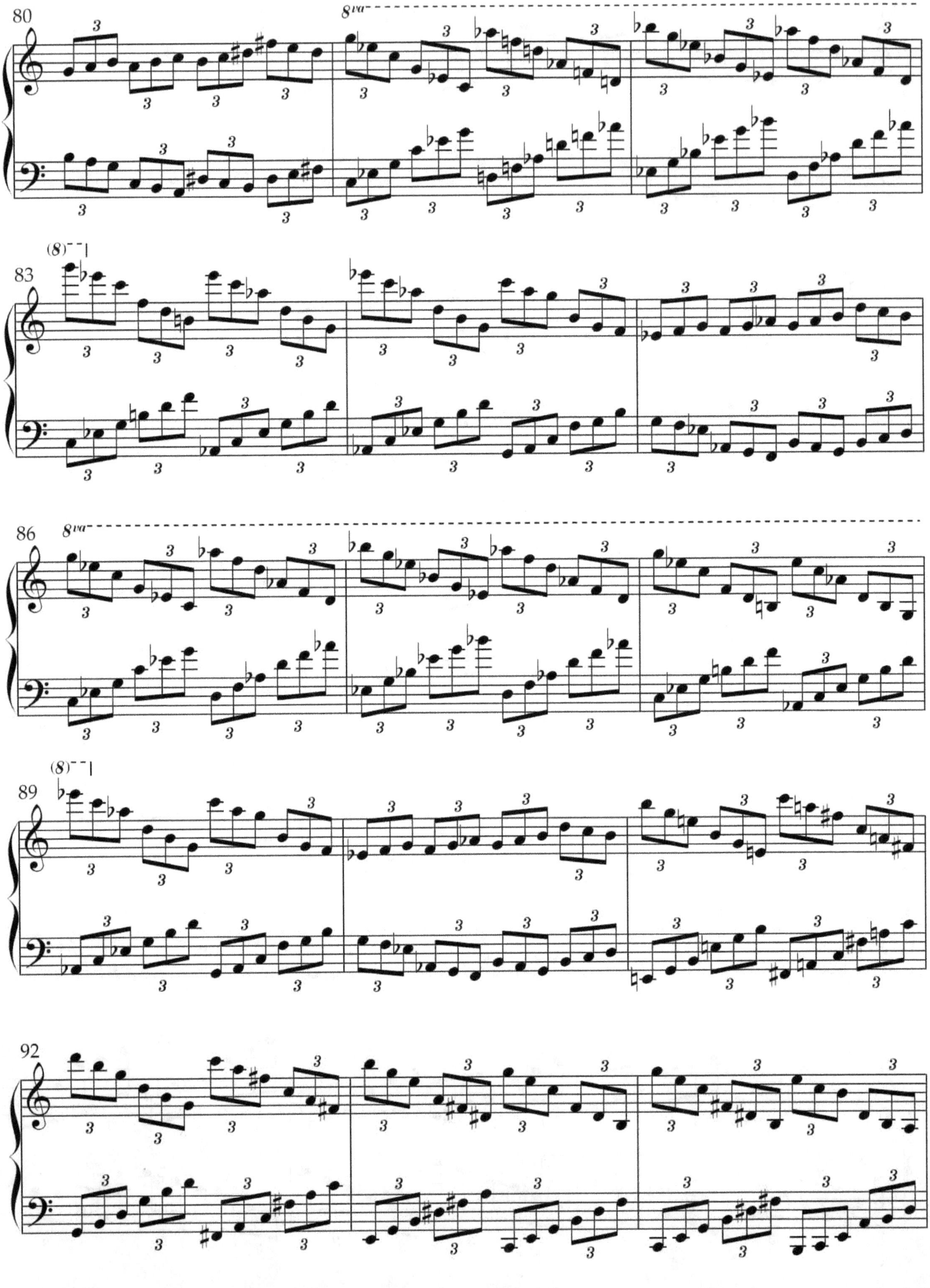
80
8va
83
(8)
86
8va
89
(8)
92

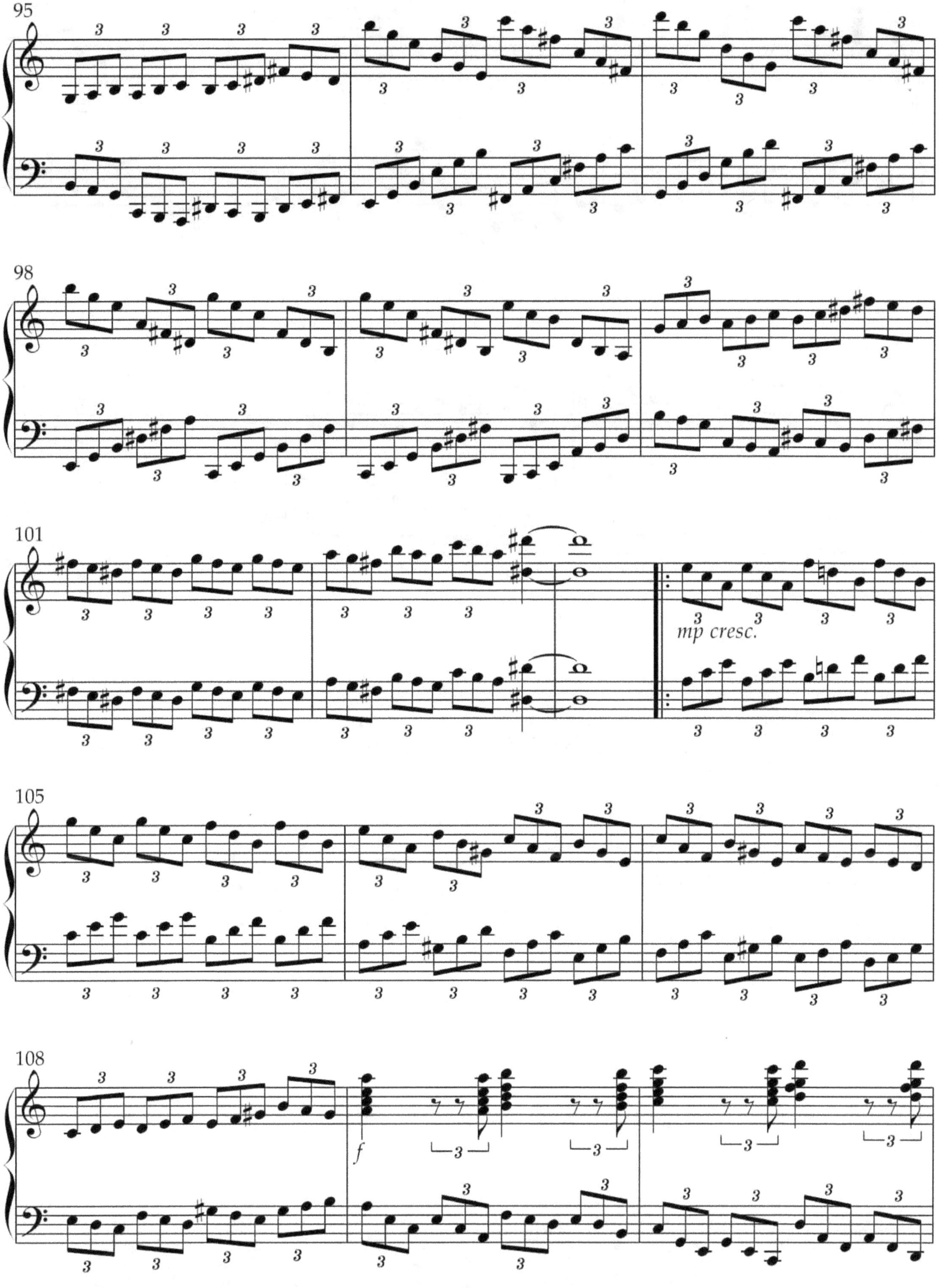
95
98
101
mp cresc.
105
108
f

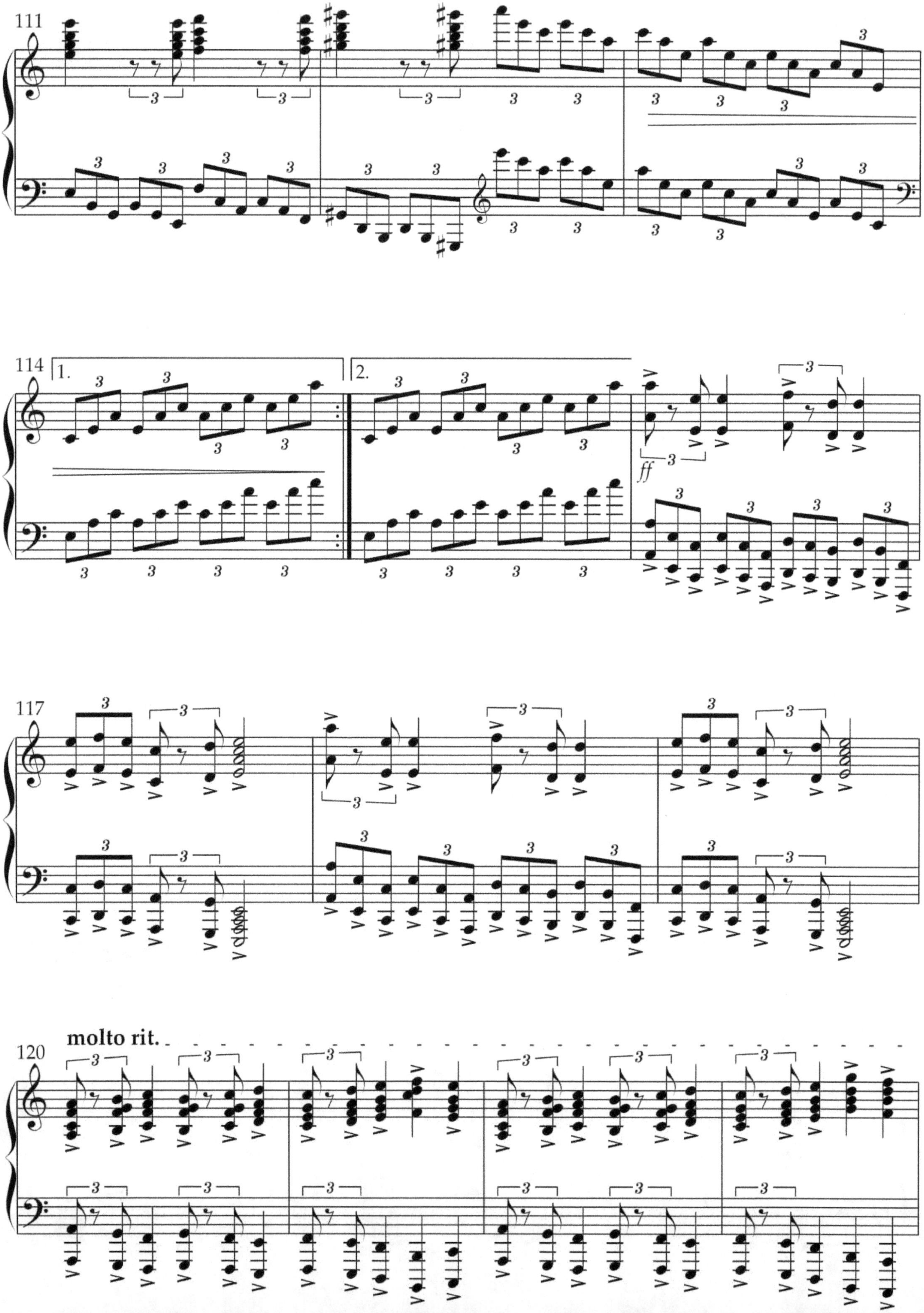
111
114
1.
2.
ff
117
120
molto rit.

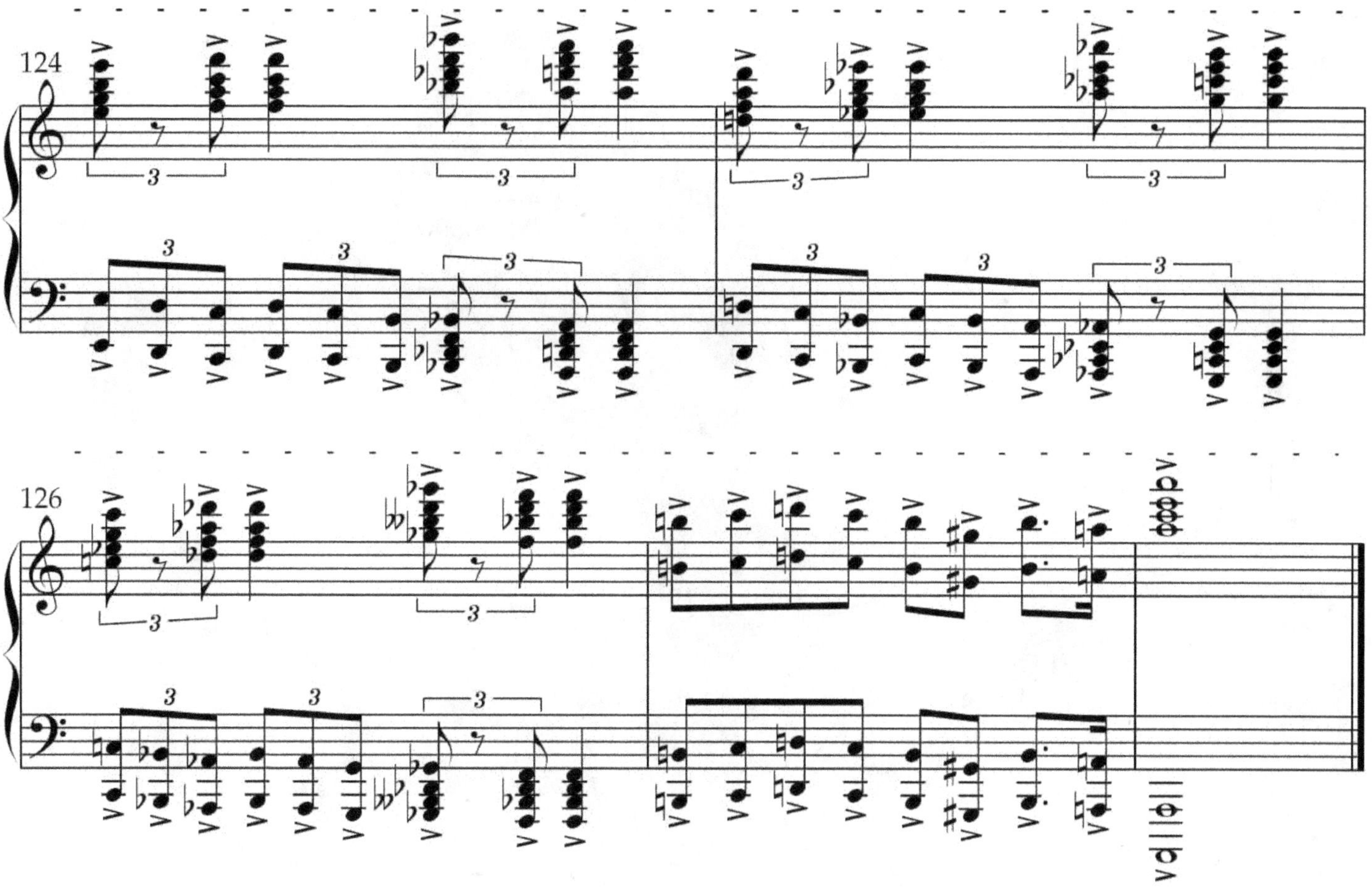
124
126

Tempus Fugit

Tito Abeleda

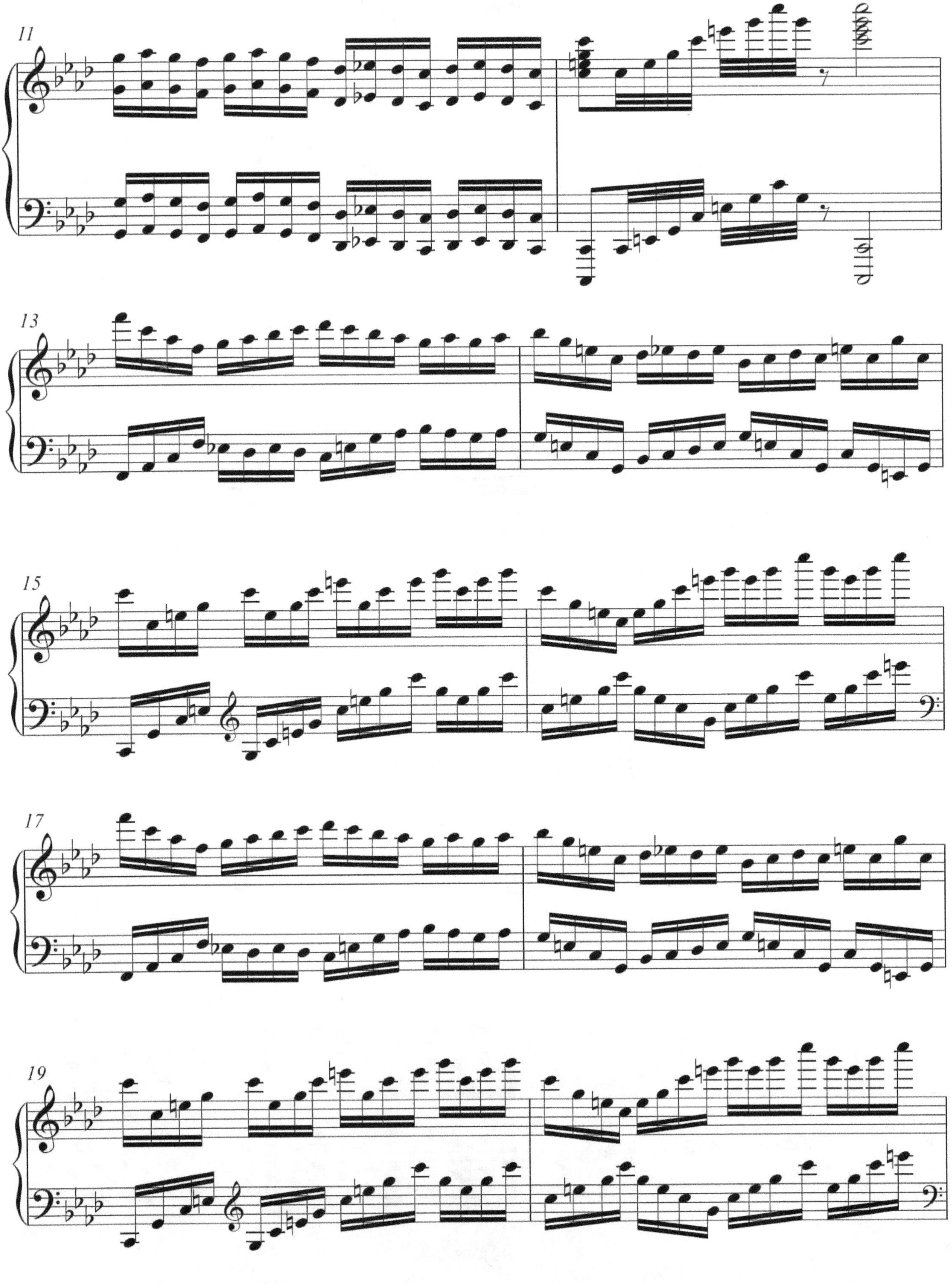
11
13
15
17
19

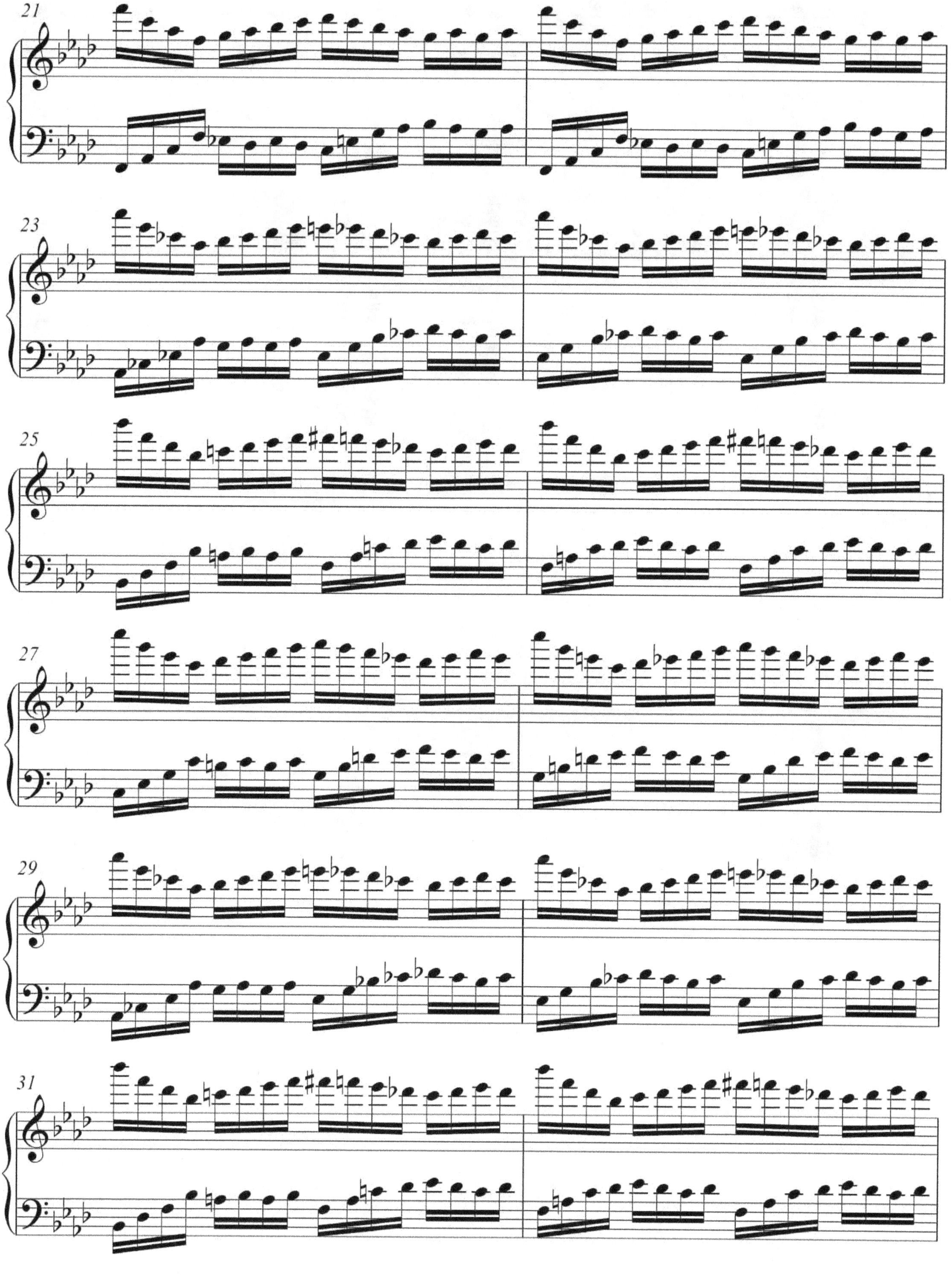
21
23
25
27
29
31

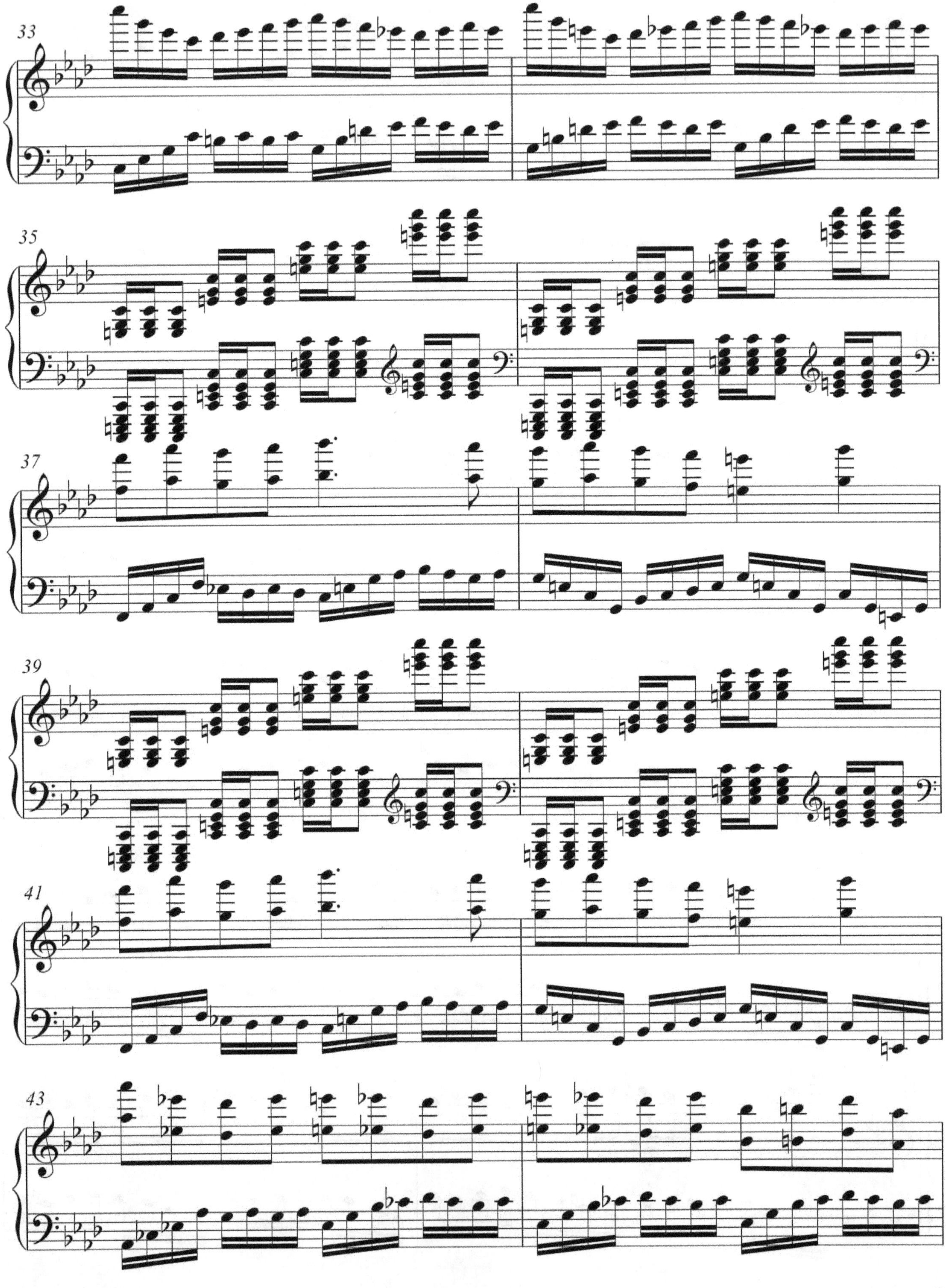
33
35
37
39
41
43

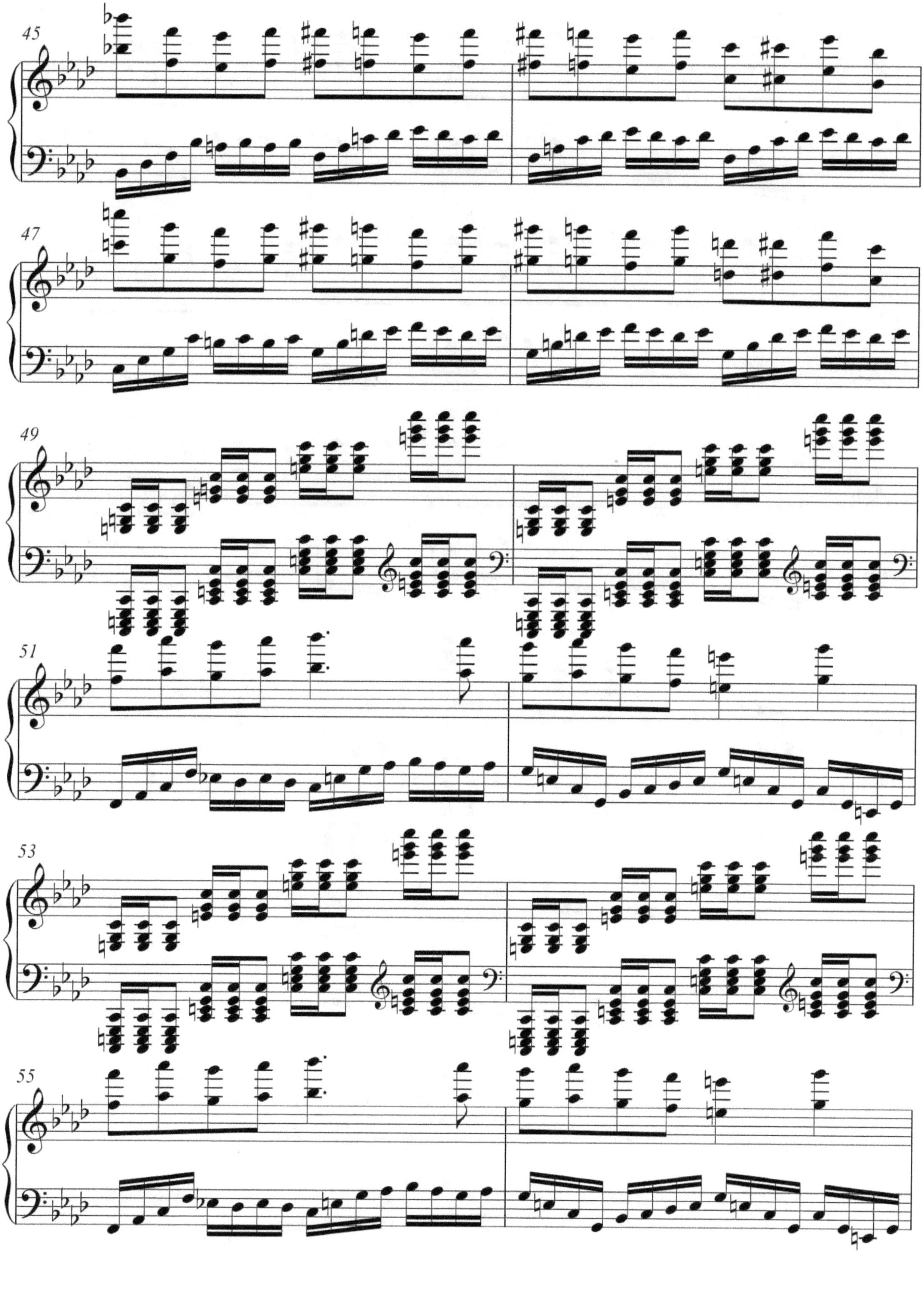
45
47
49
51
53
55

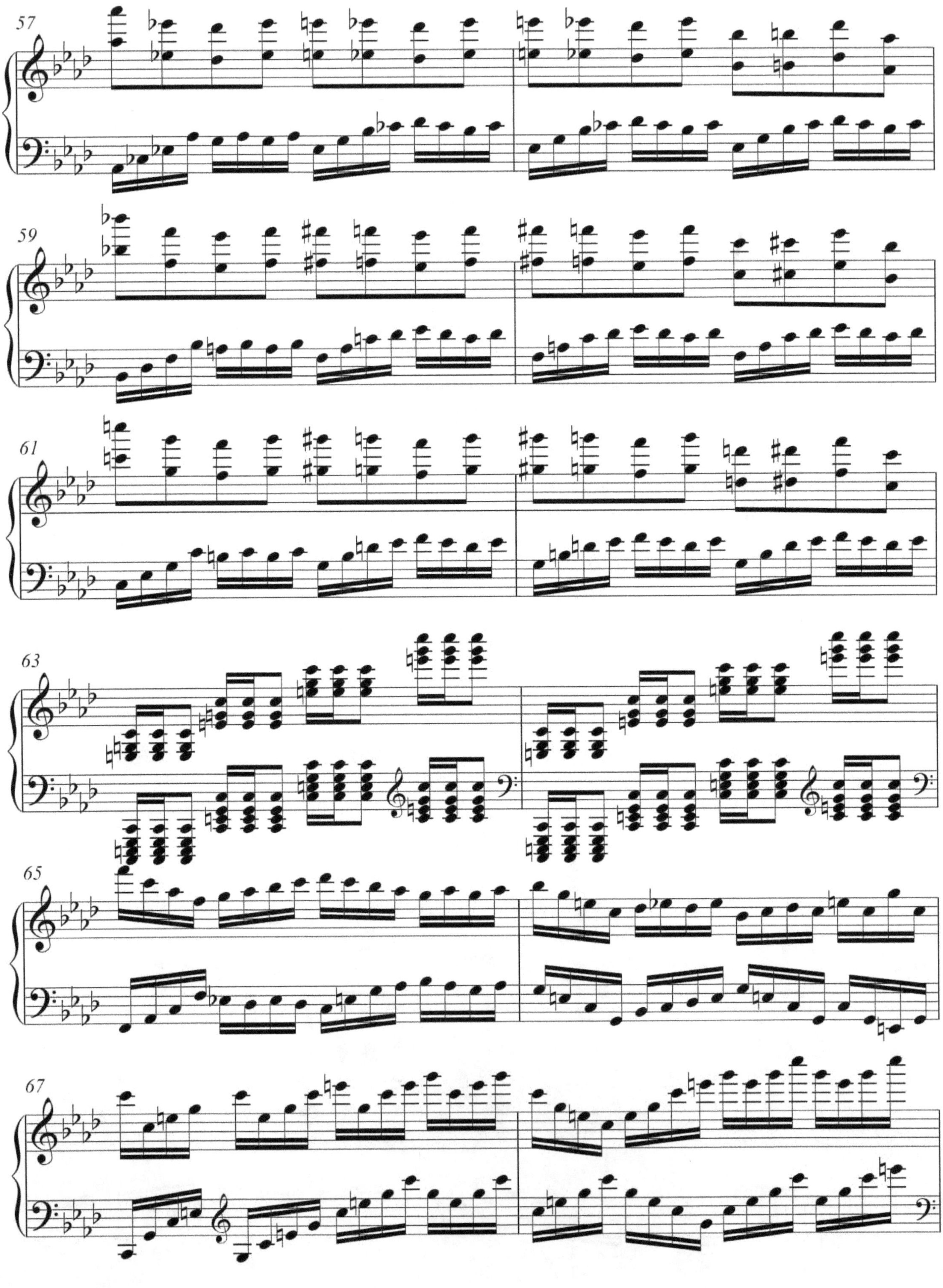

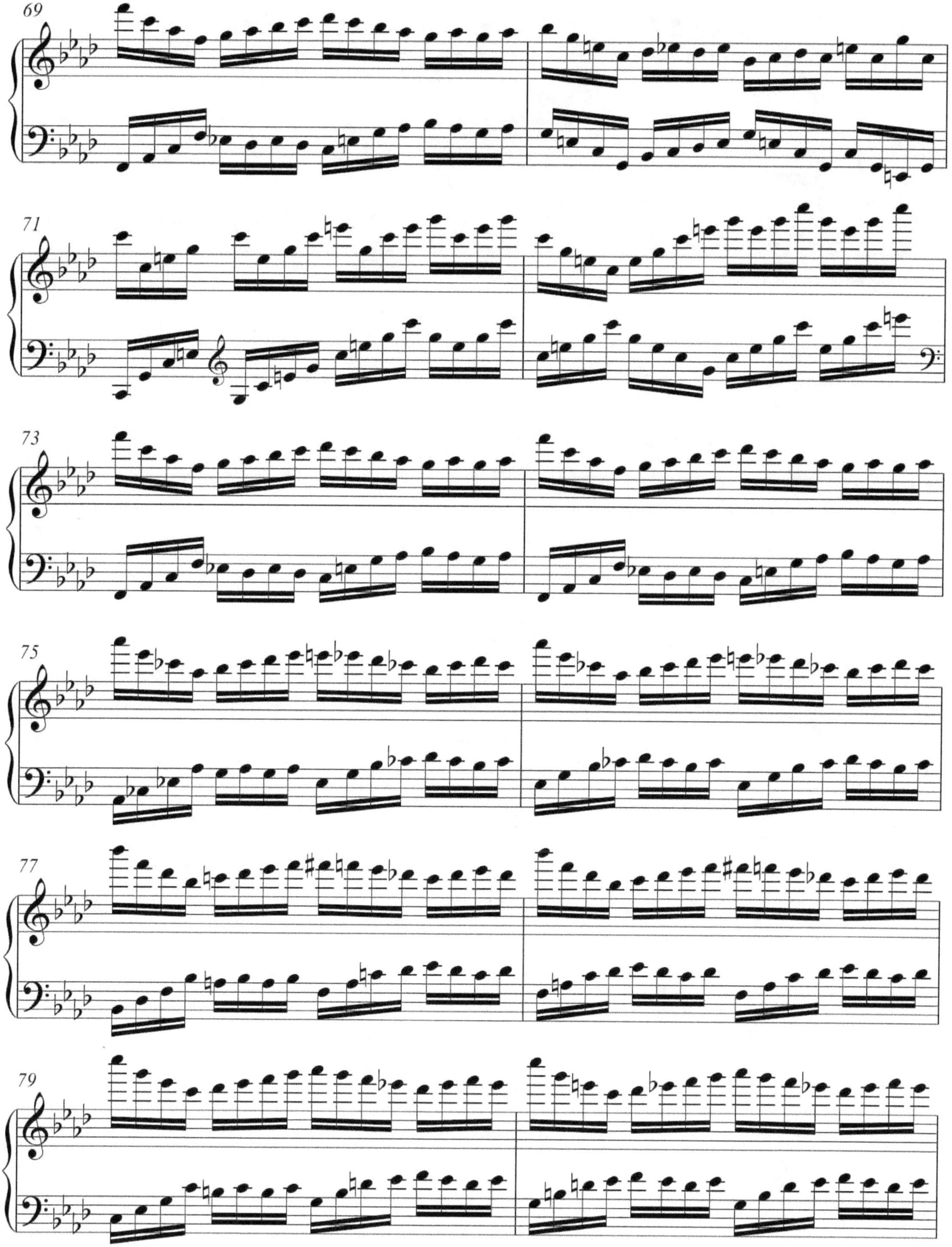
69
71
73
75
77
79

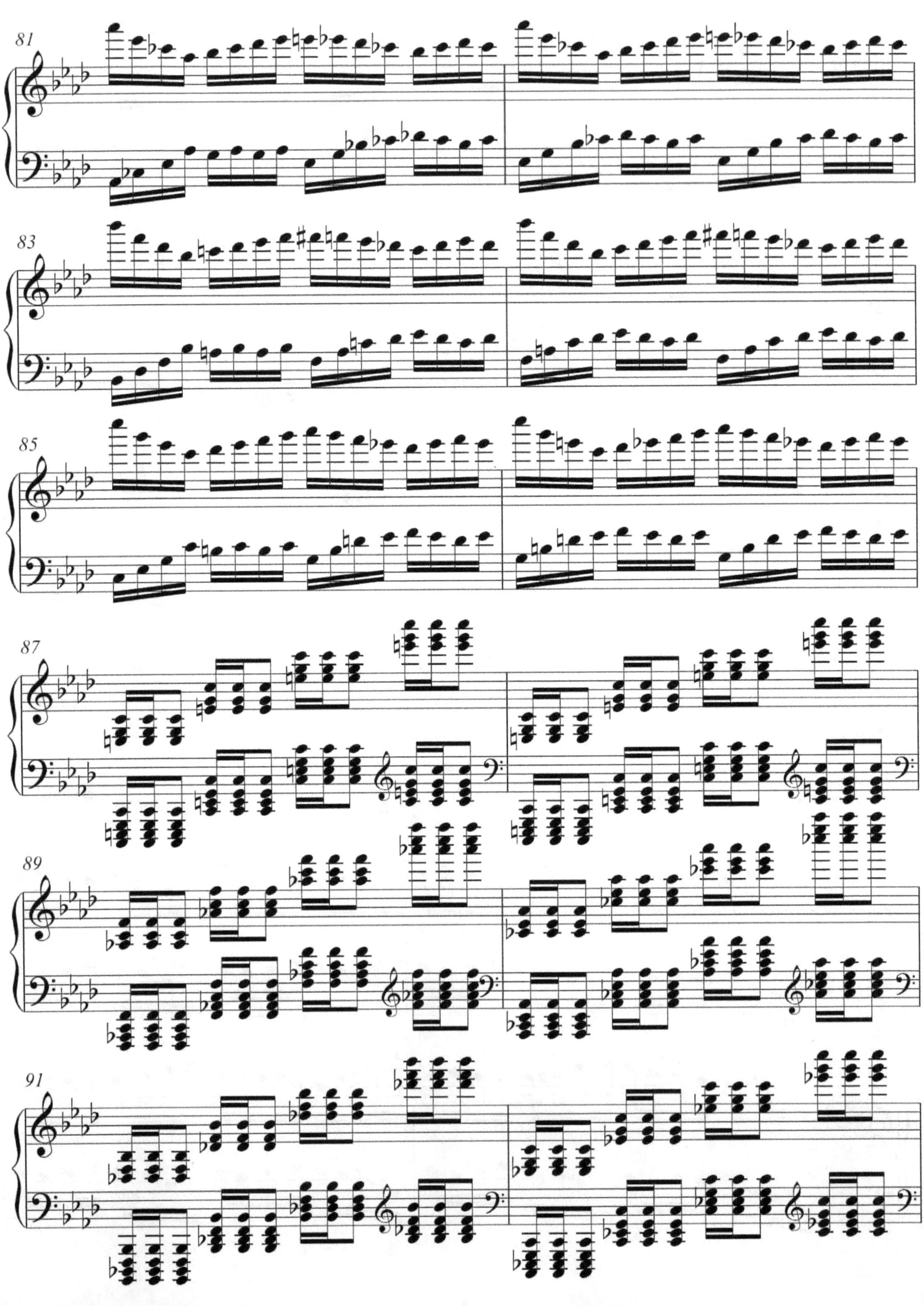
81
83
85
87
89
91

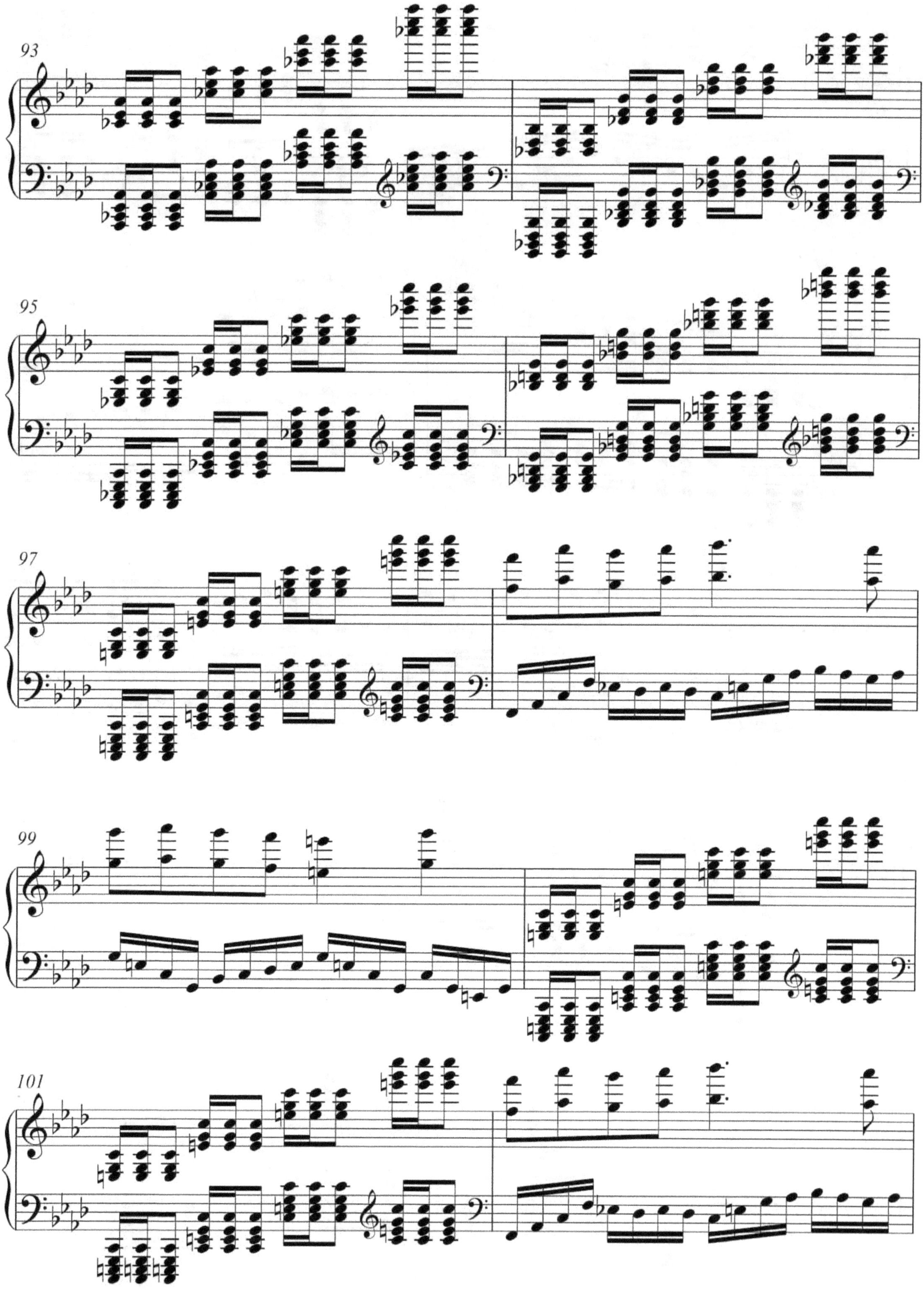
93
95
97
99
101

74

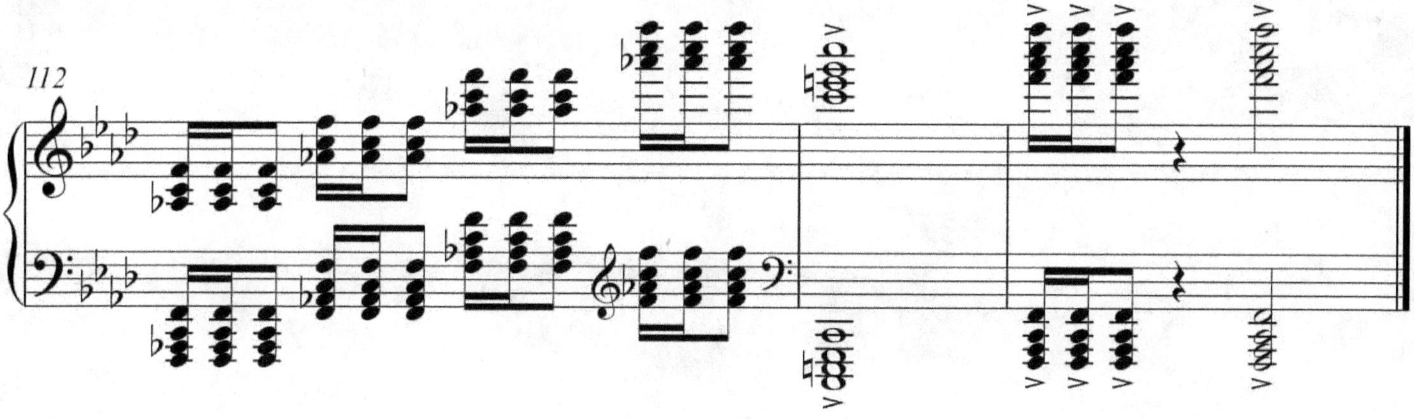
112

O Holy Night

Music by Adolphe C. Adam
Arrangement by Tito Abeleda

Andante ♩=80

p Legato con moto

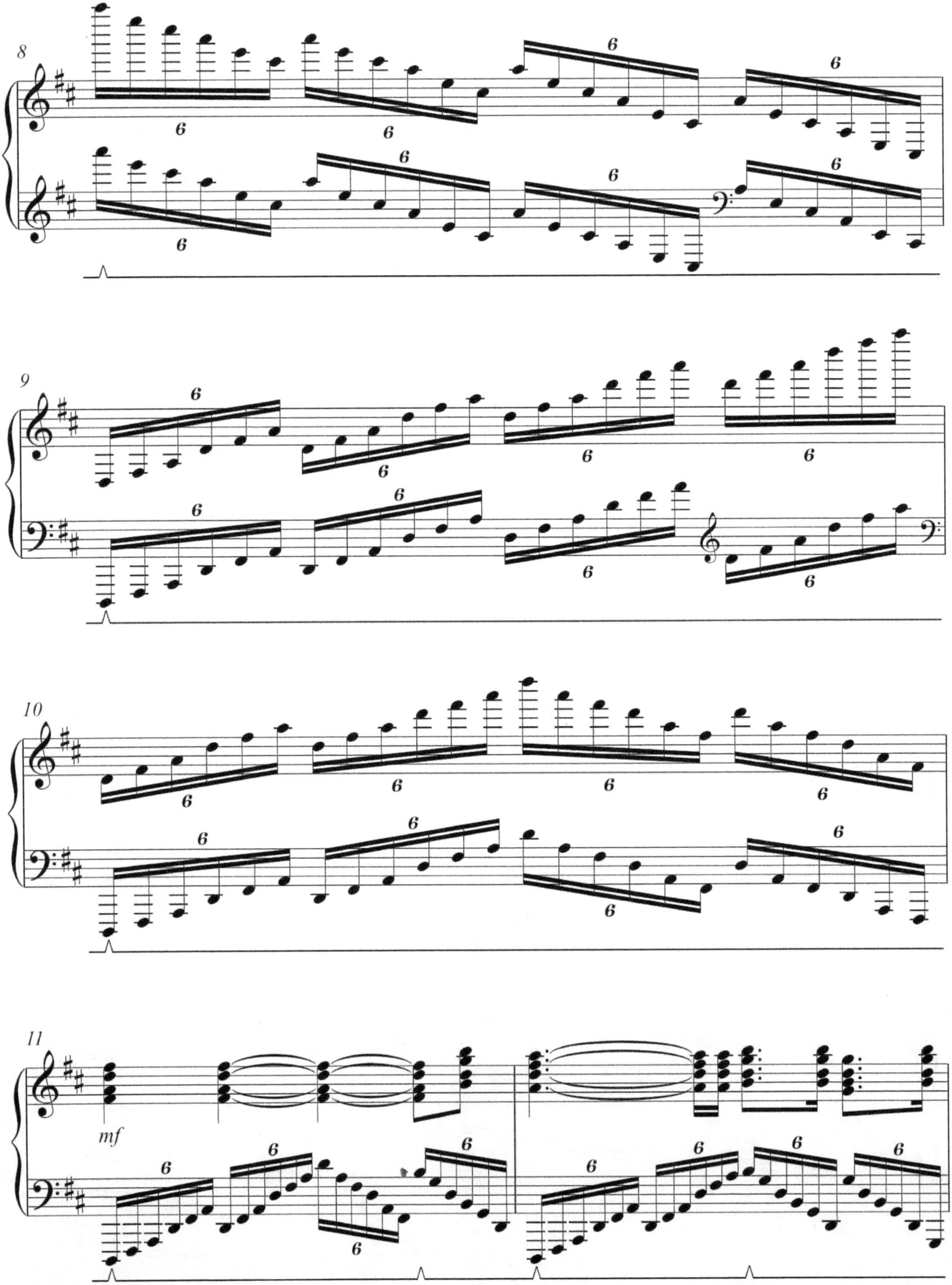
8
9
10
11
mf

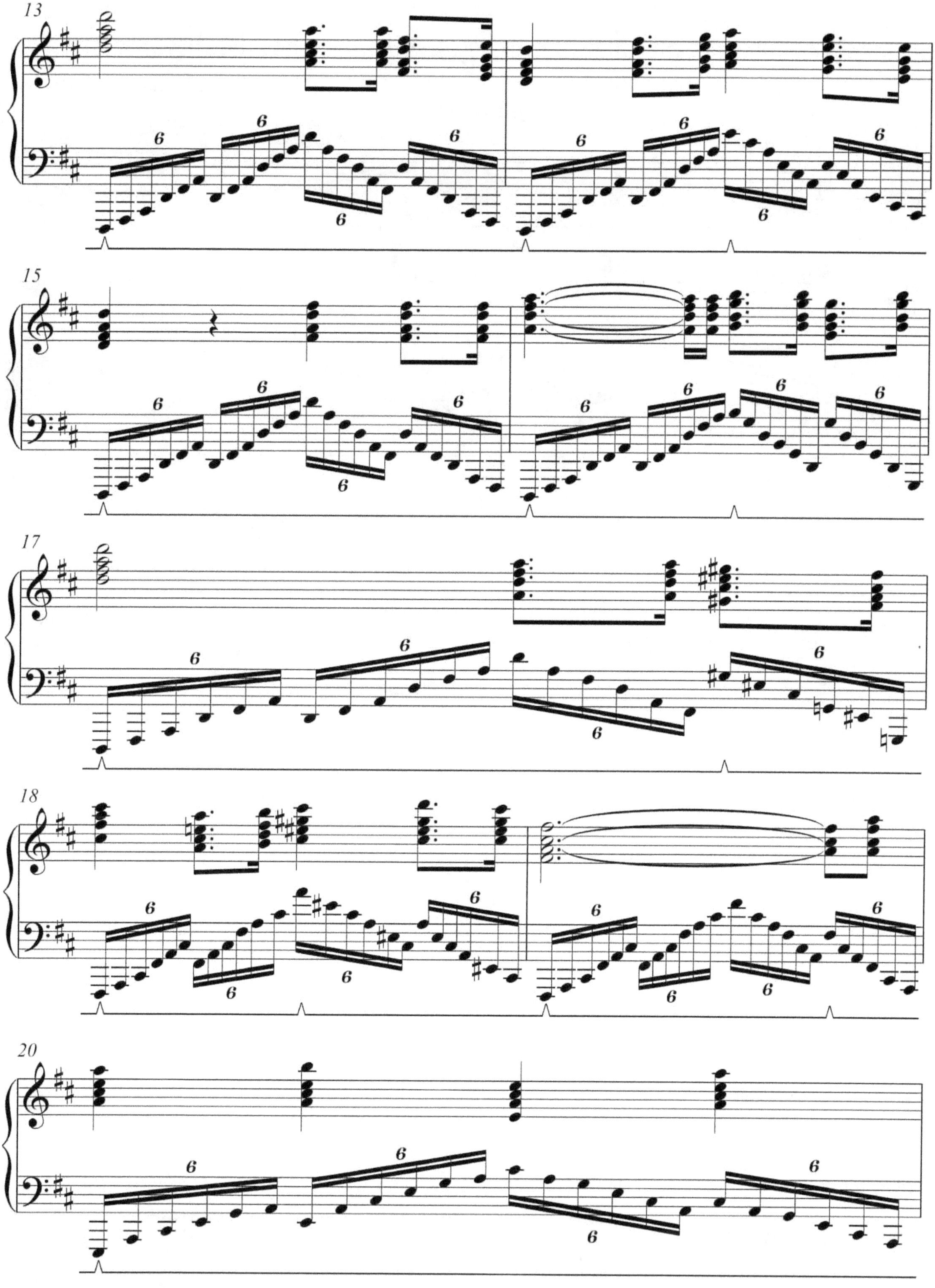
13
15
17
18
20

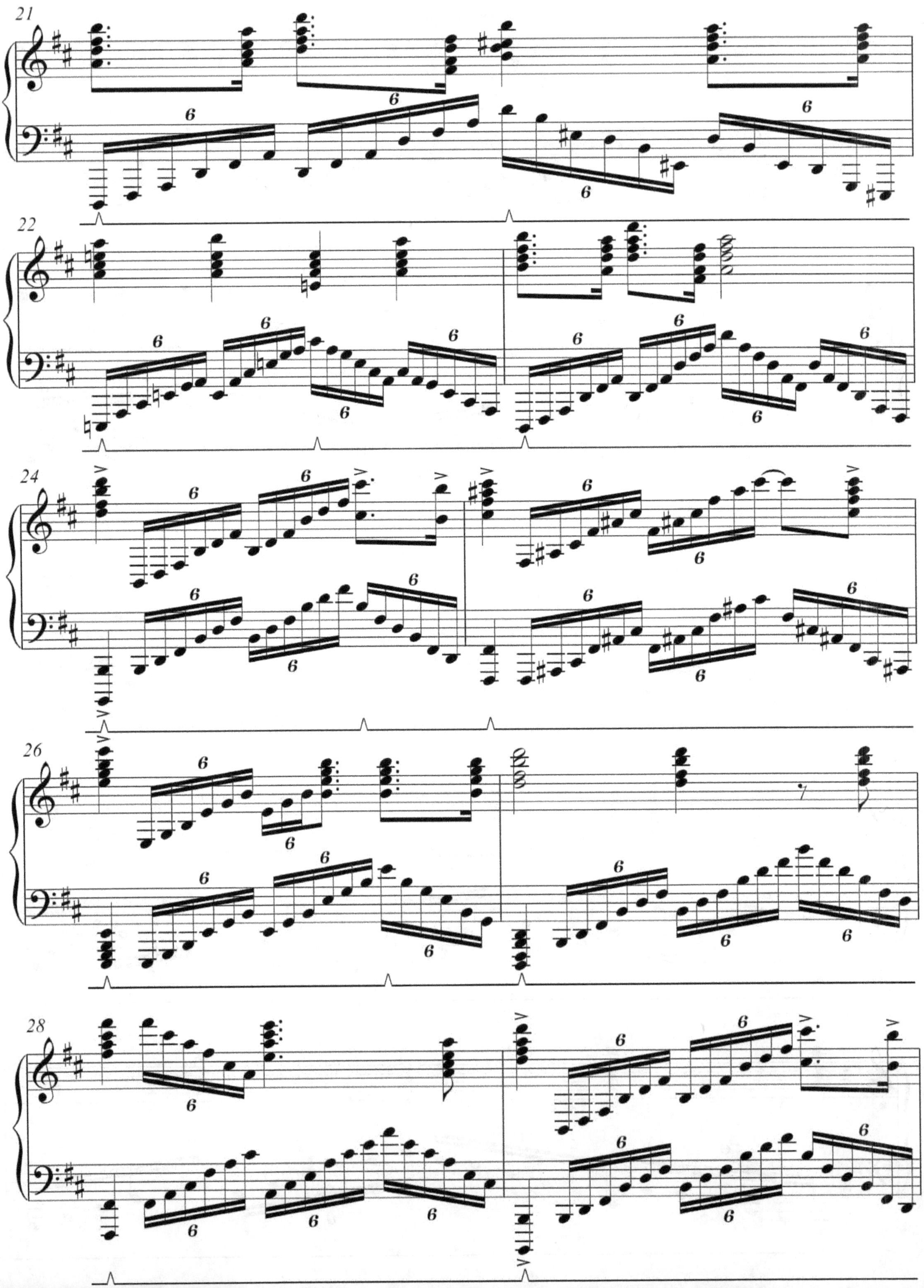
21
22
24
26
28

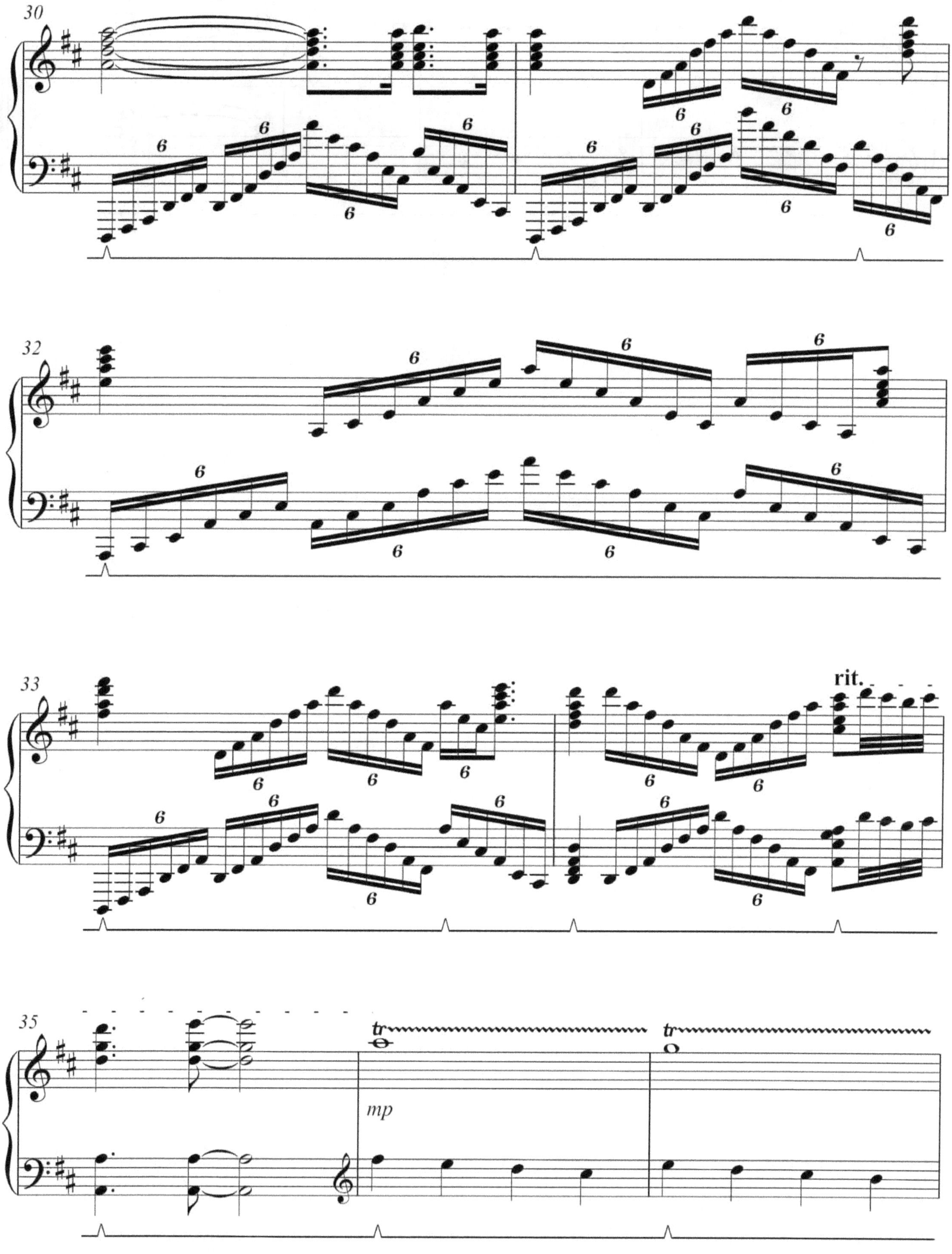
30
32
33
rit.
35
mp
tr
tr

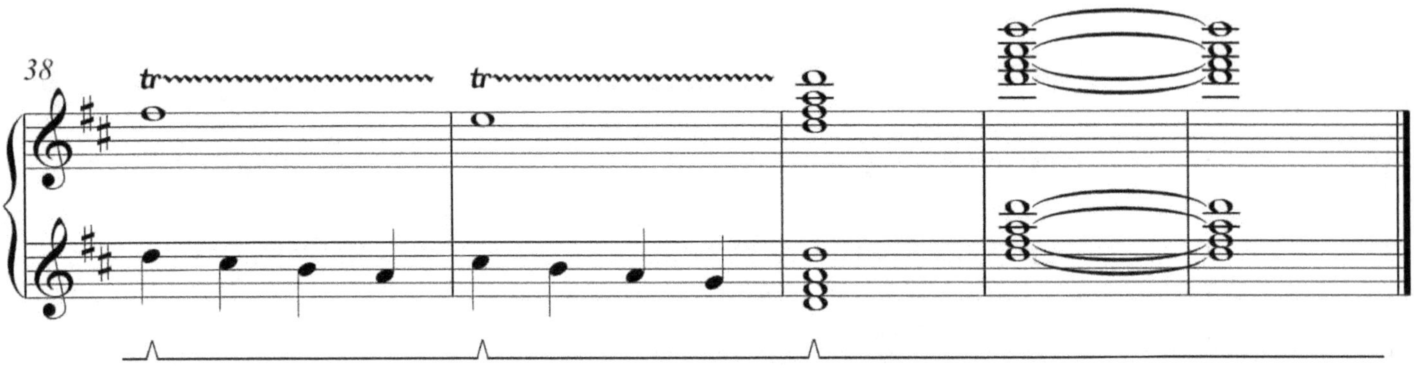
38
tr
tr

Descensus ad Infero
(Score)

Tito Abeleda

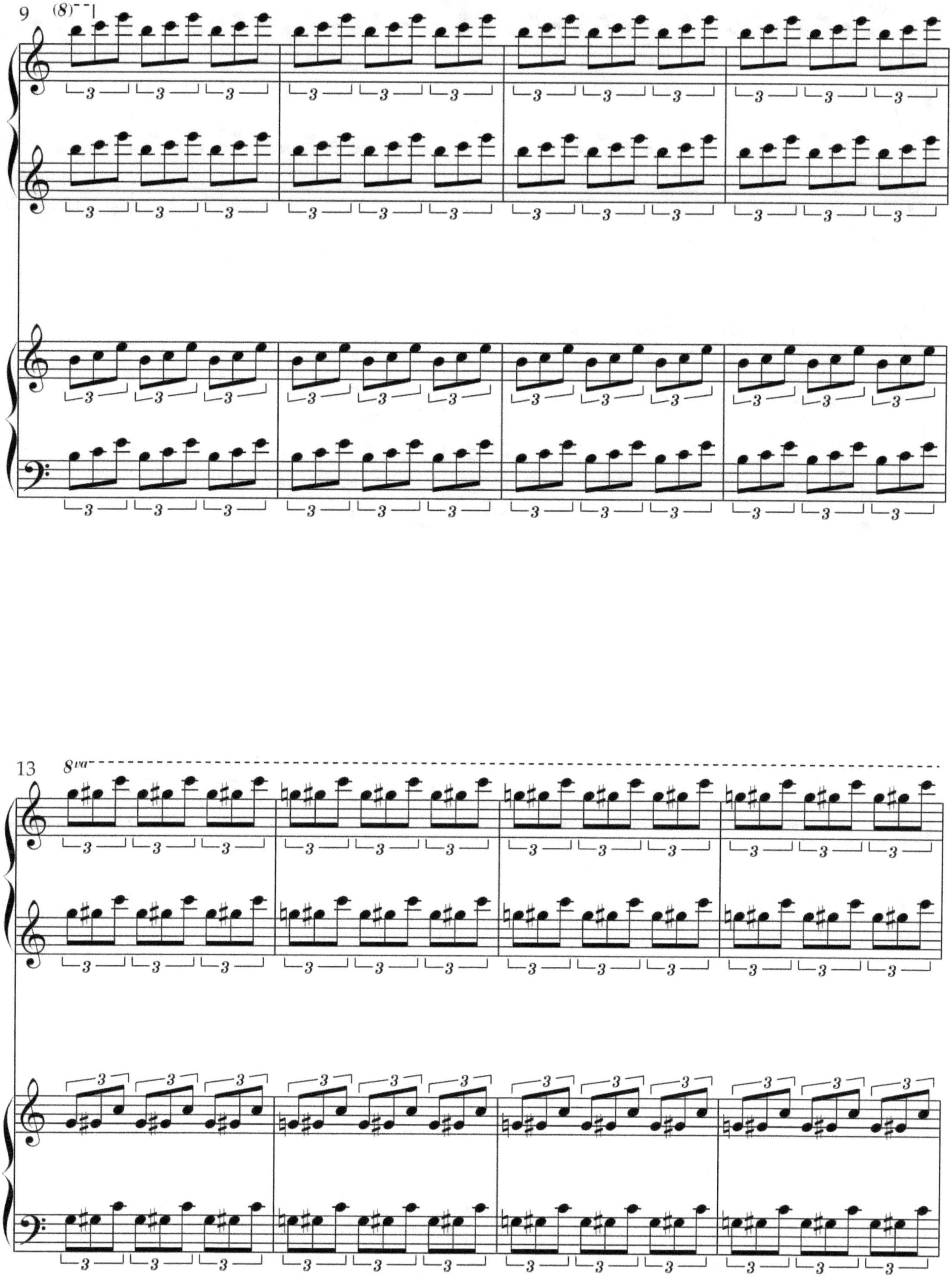
9
(8)
13
8va

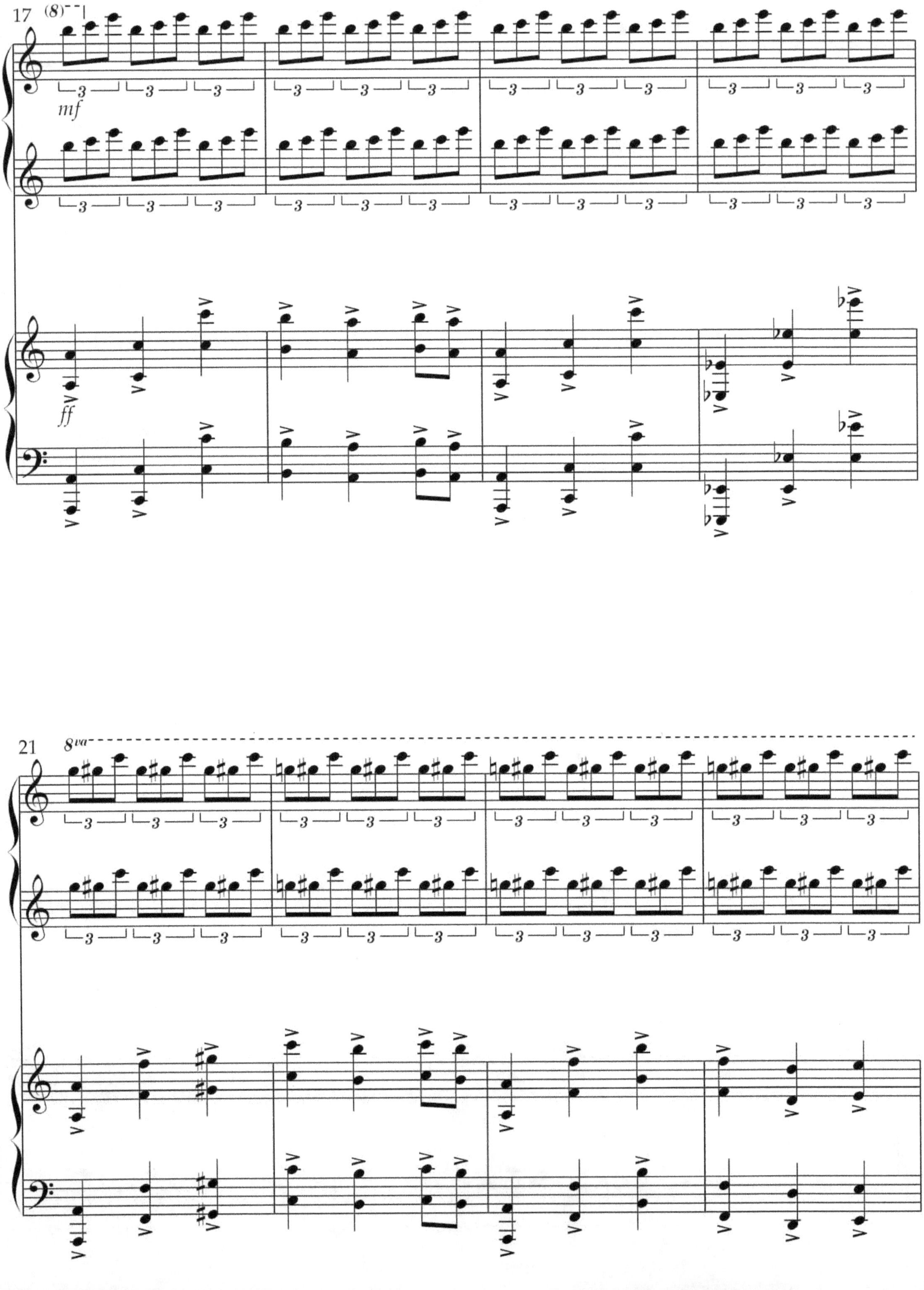
17
(8)
mf
ff
21
8va

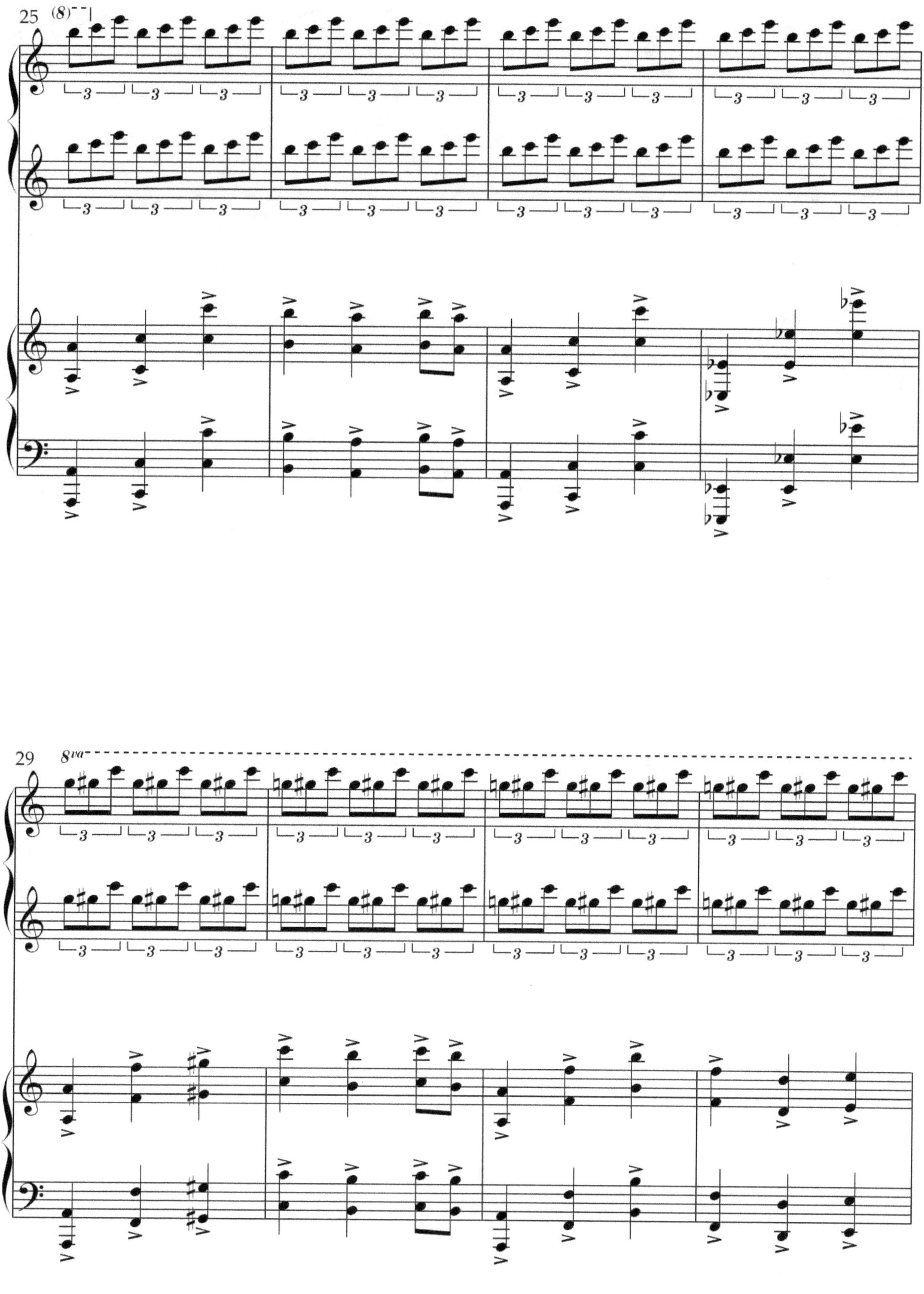
25
(8)
29
8va

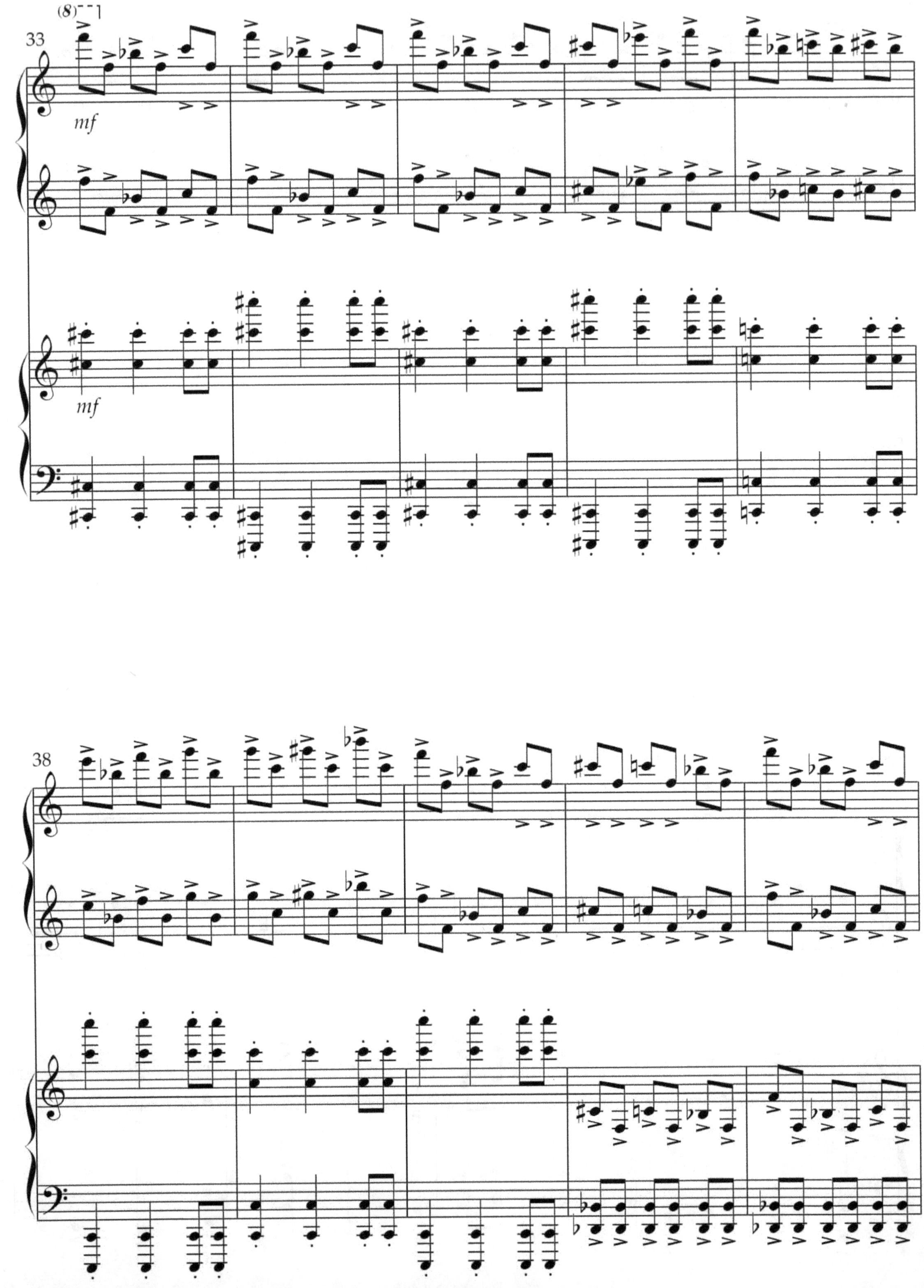
(8)
33
mf
mf
38

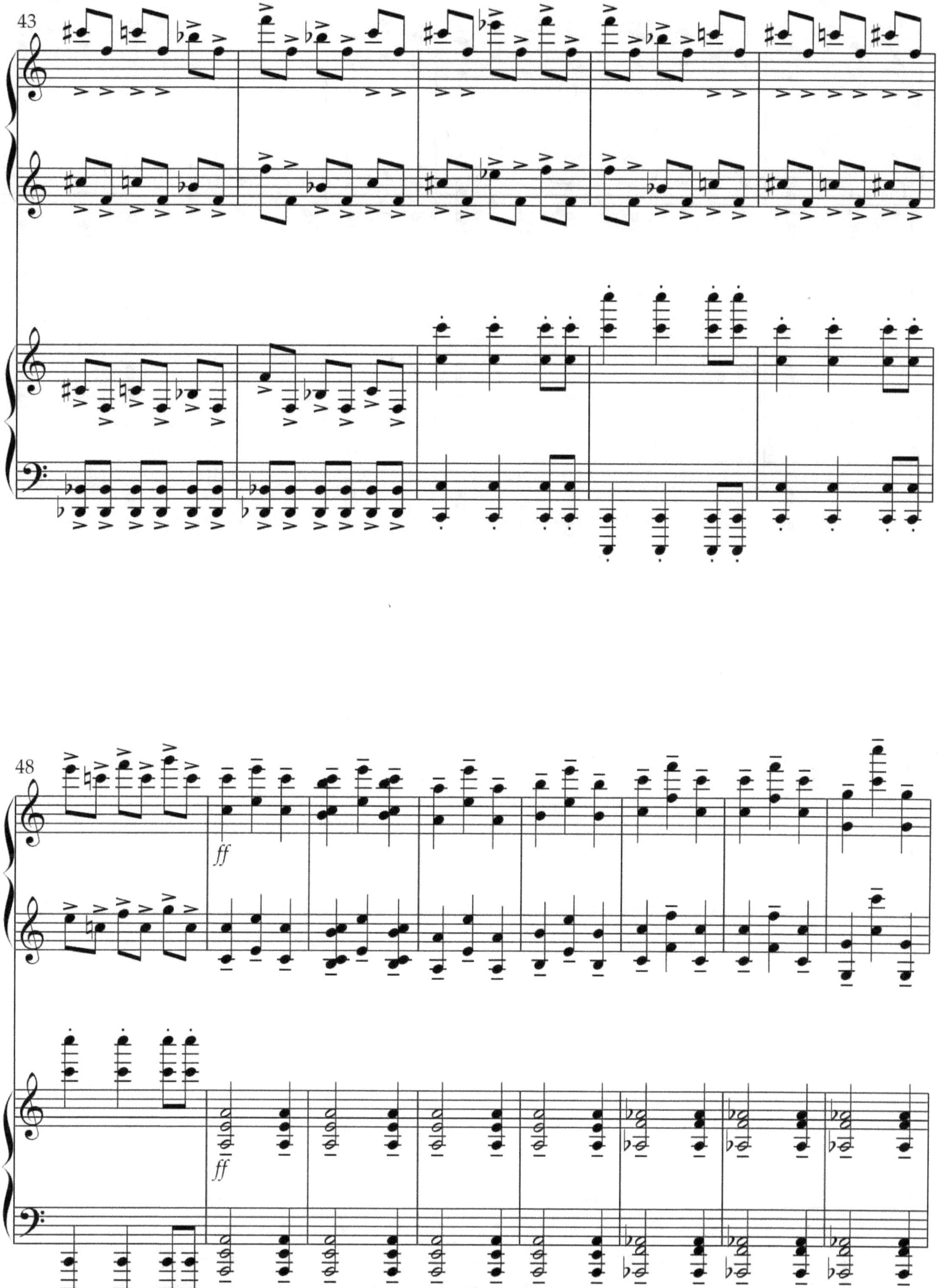
43
48
ff
ff

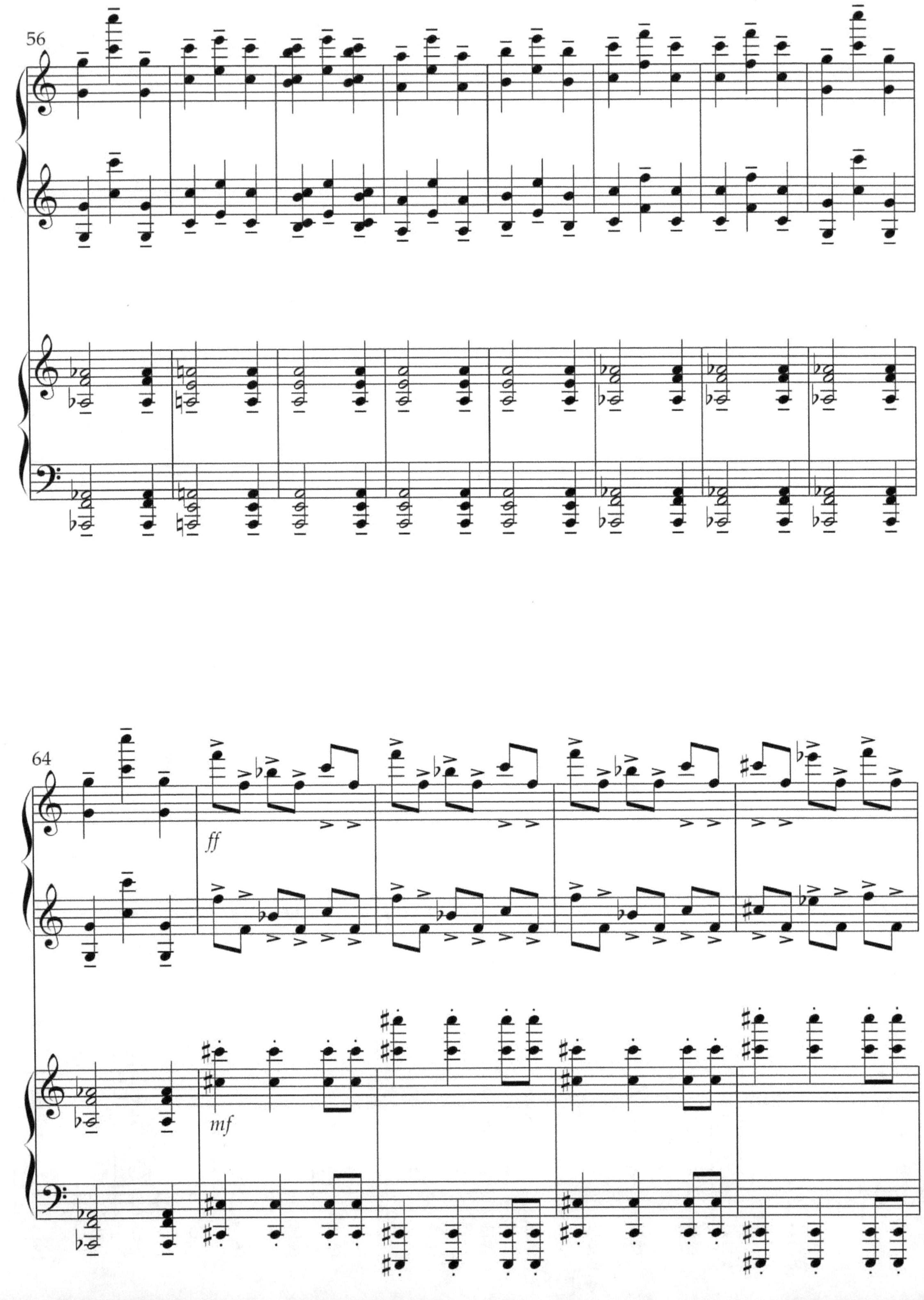
56
64
ff
mf

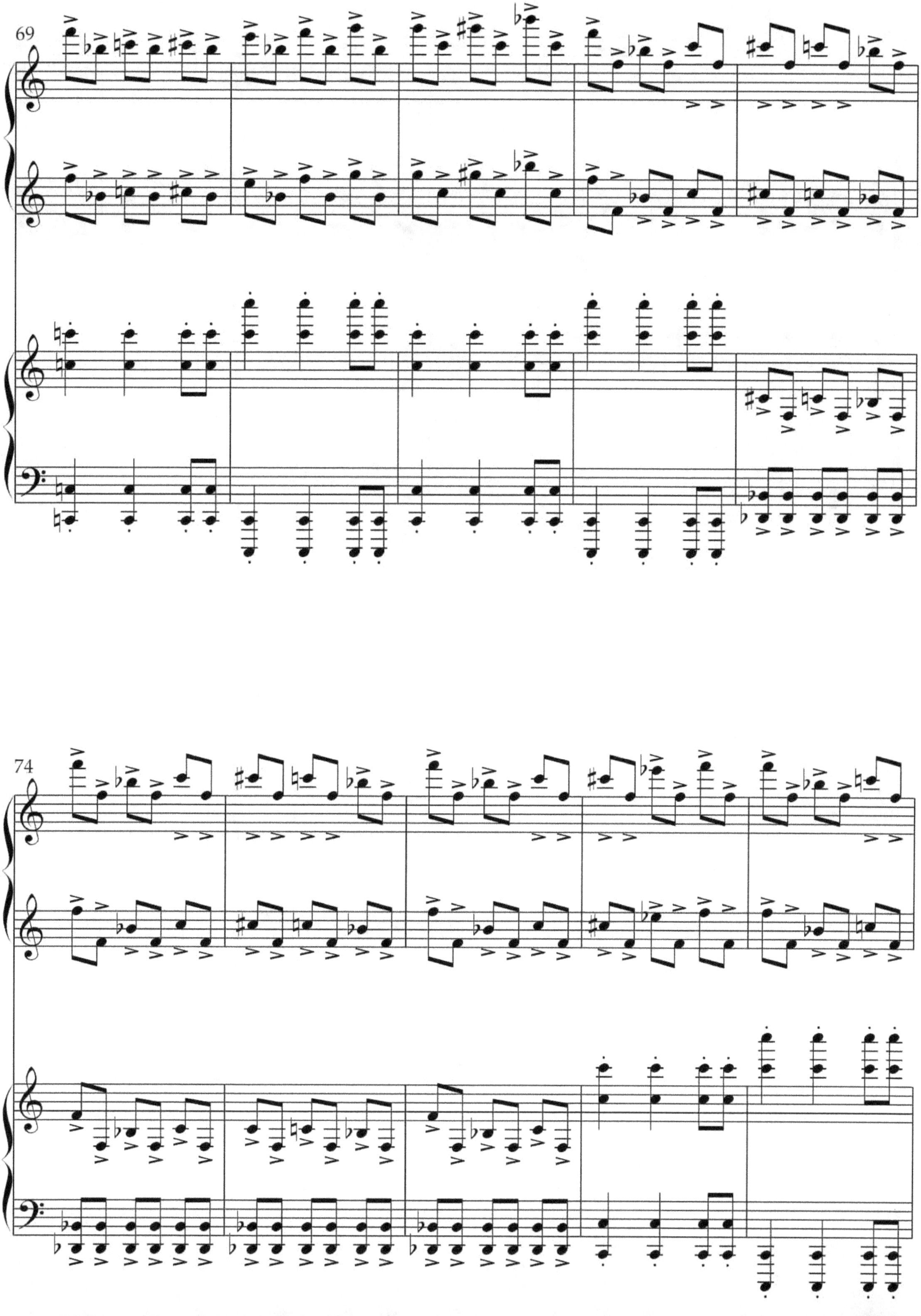
69
74

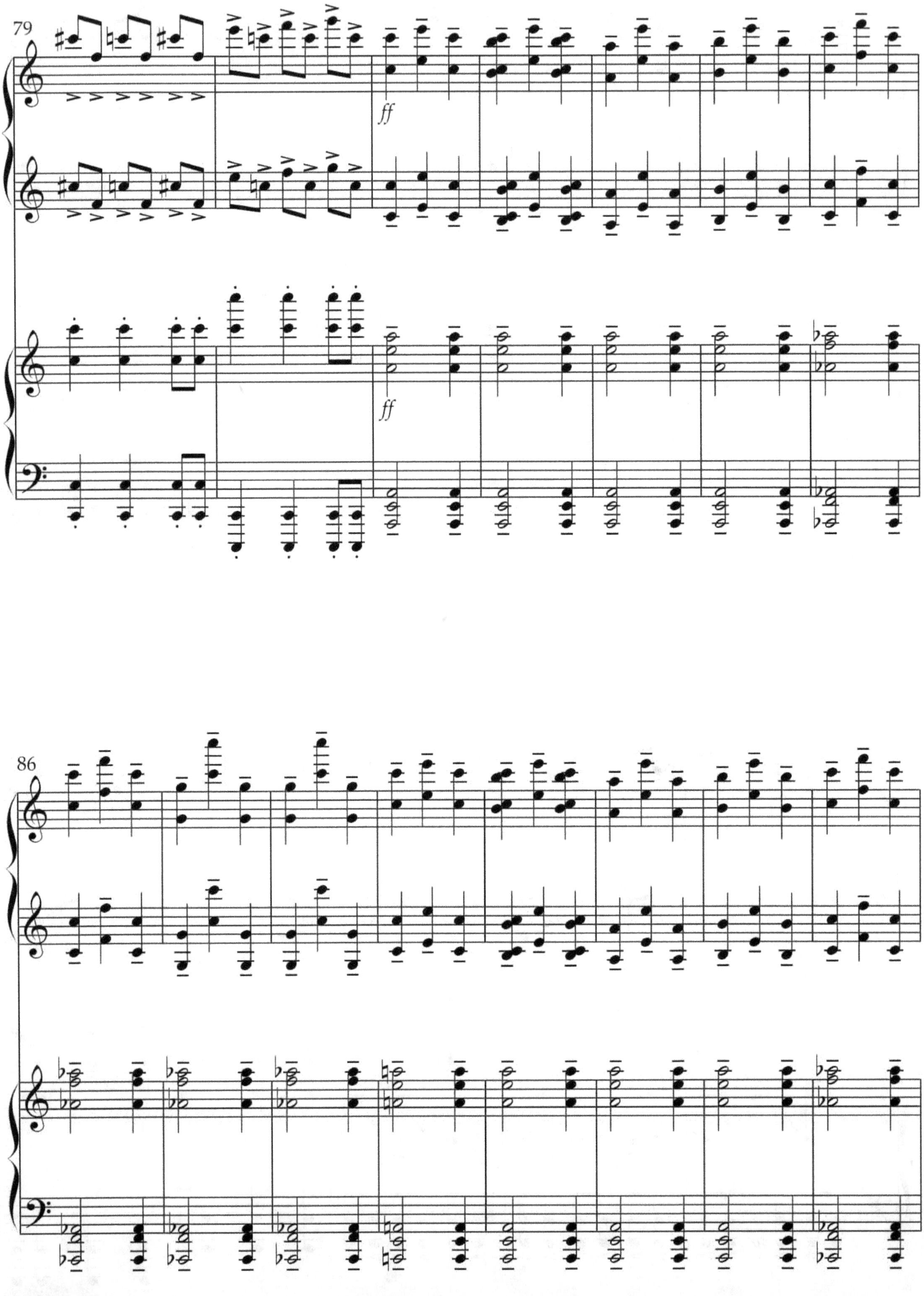
79
ff
ff
86

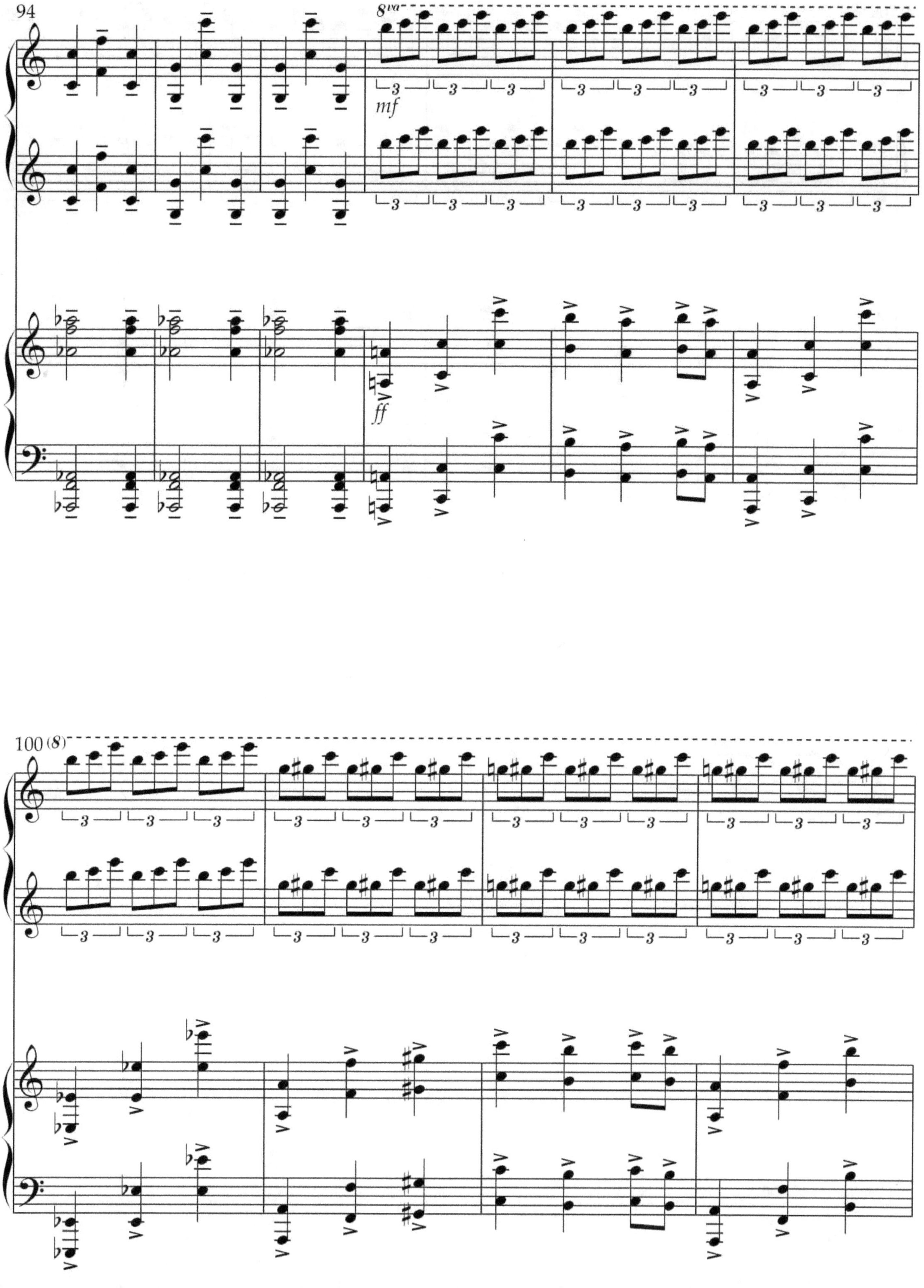
94
8va
mf
ff
100 (8)

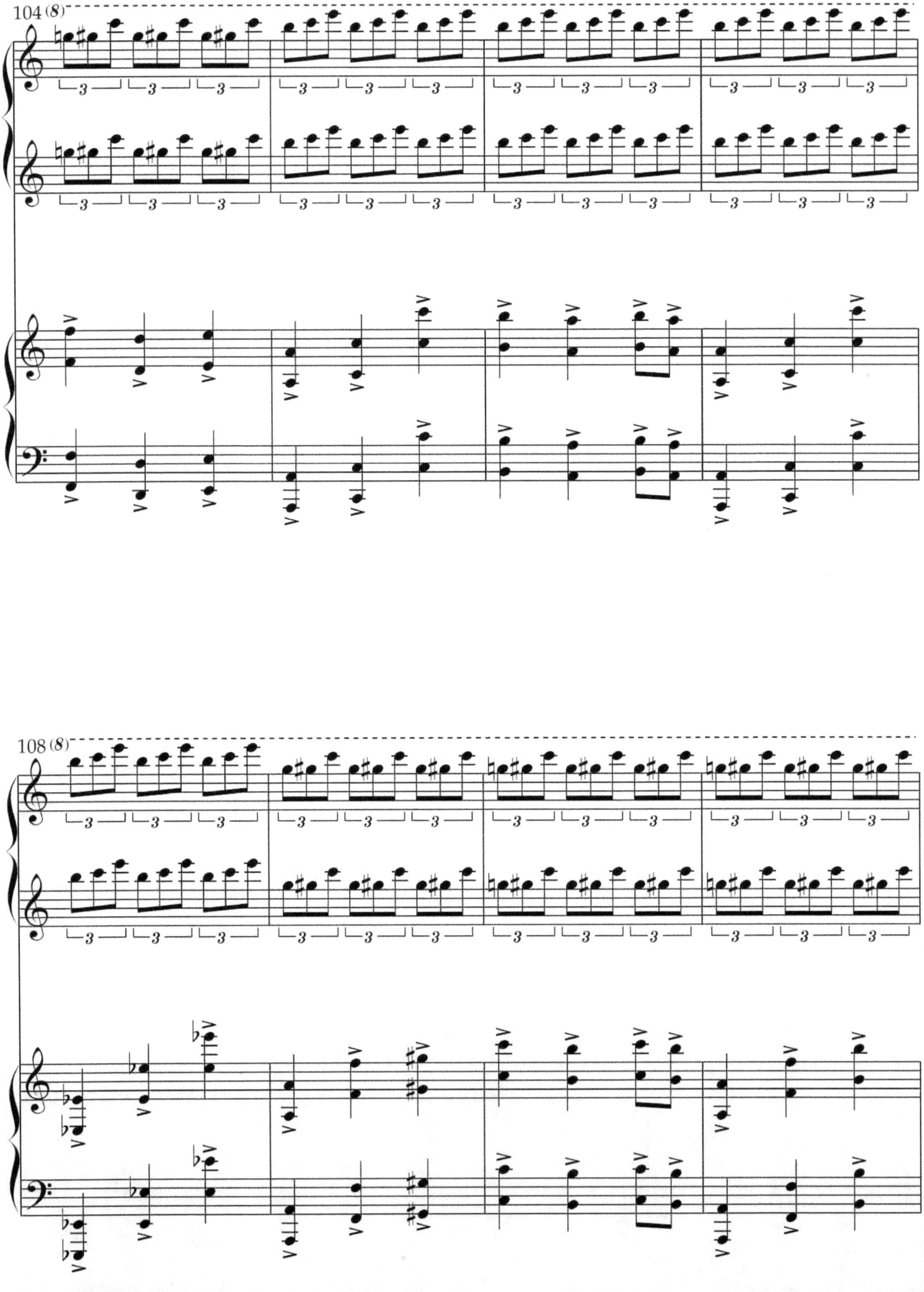
104 (8)
108 (8)

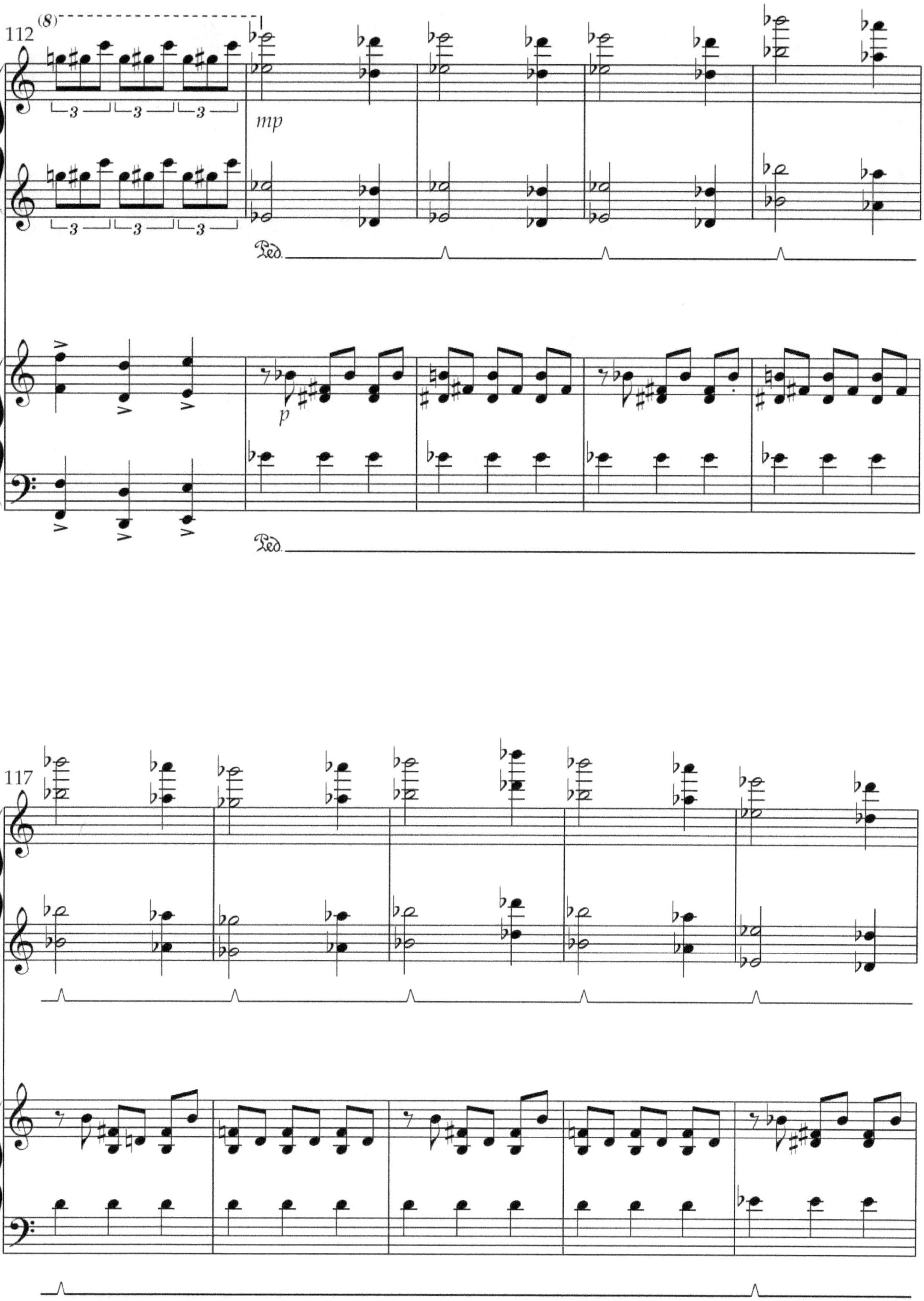
112
(8)
3
mp
Ped.
p
Ped.
117

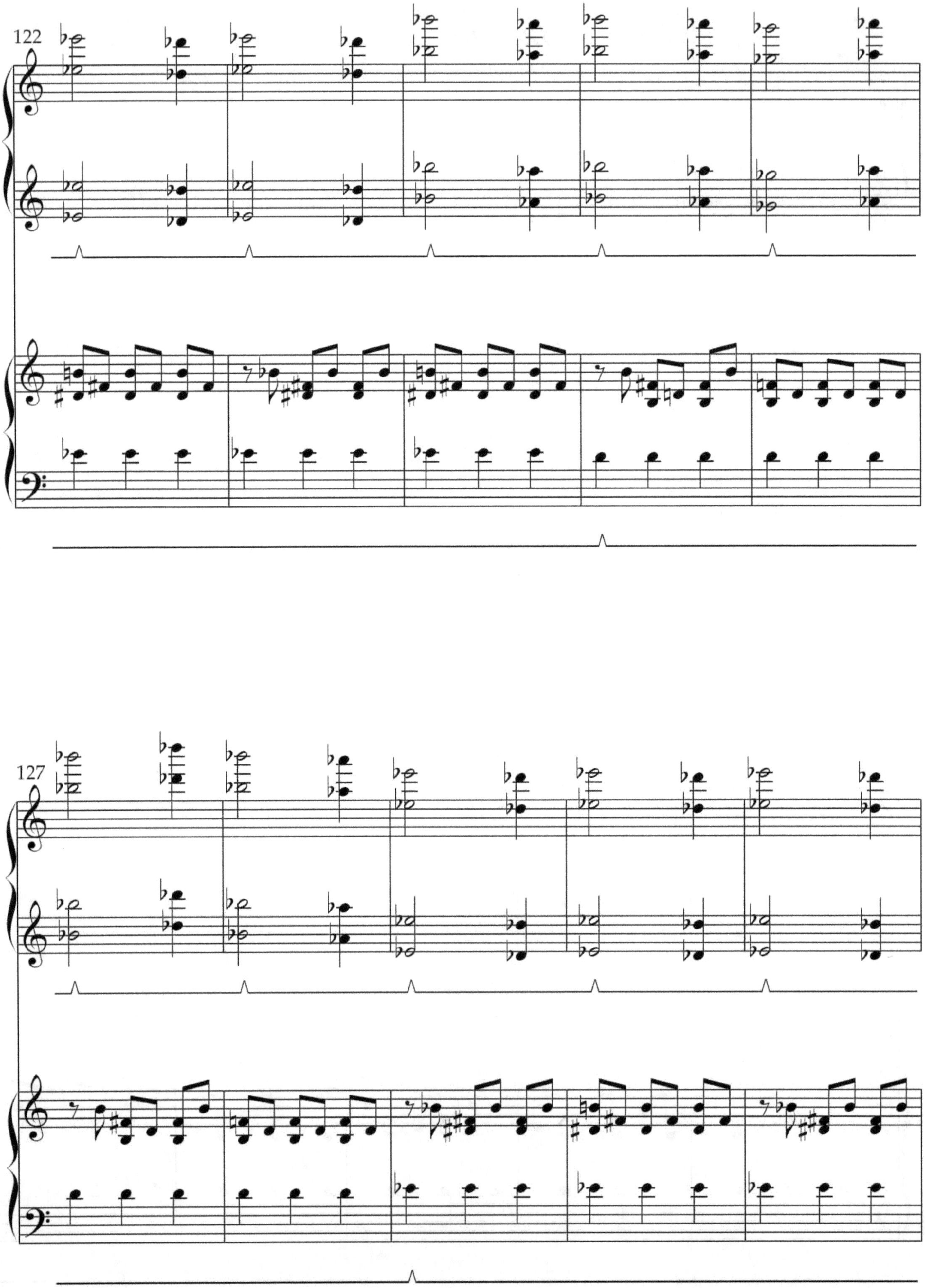
122
127

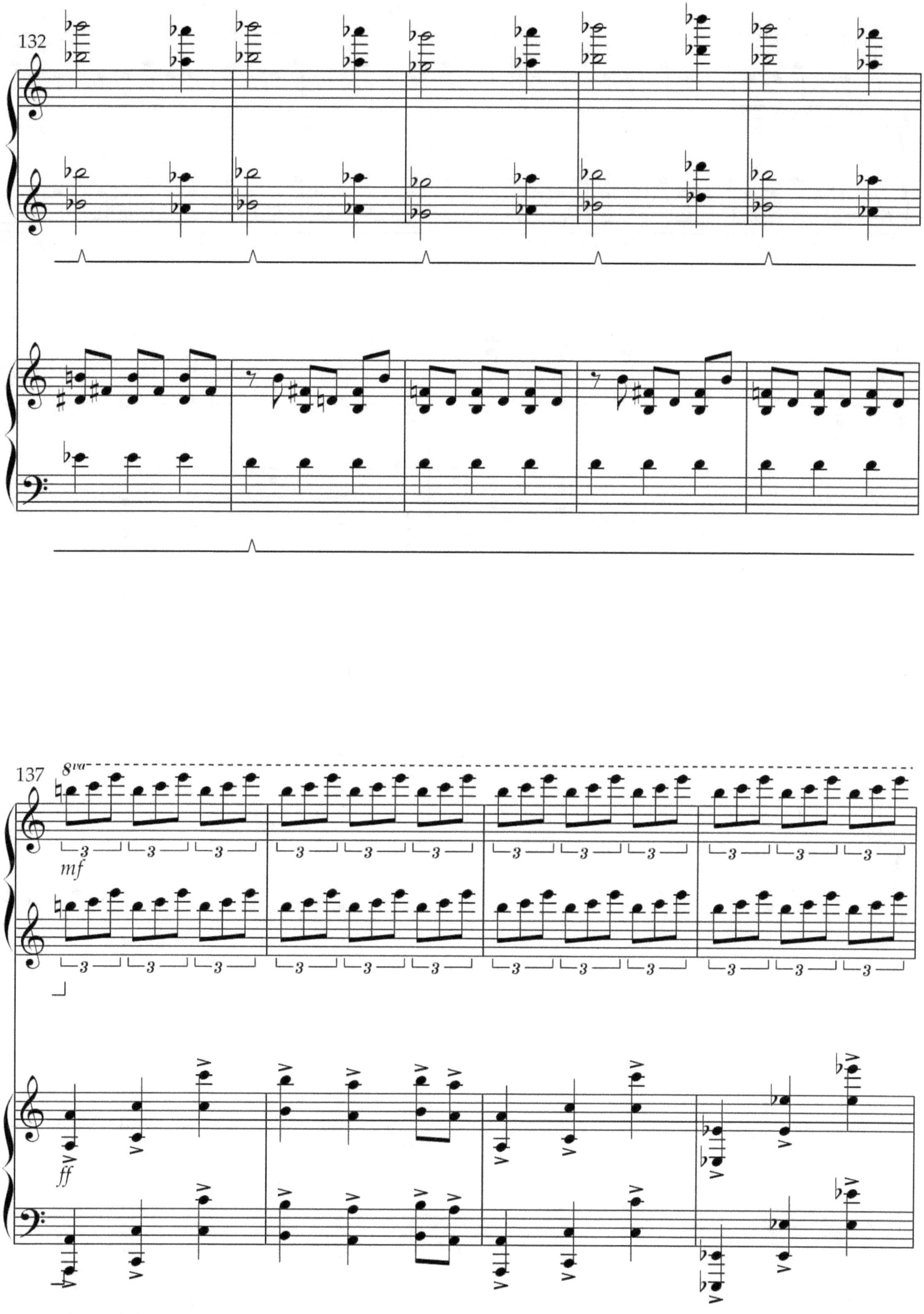
132
137
8va
mf
ff

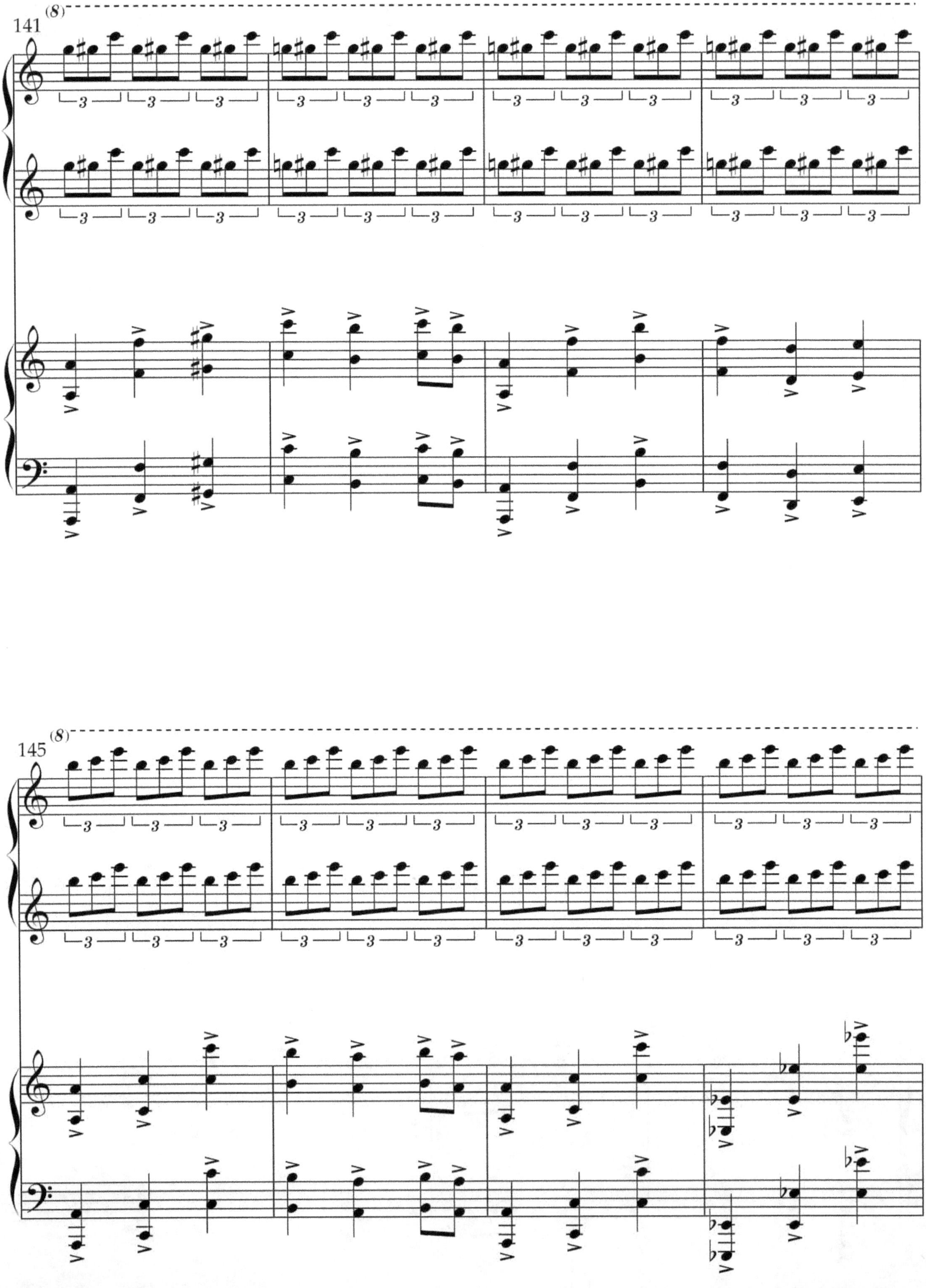
141
(8)
145
(8)

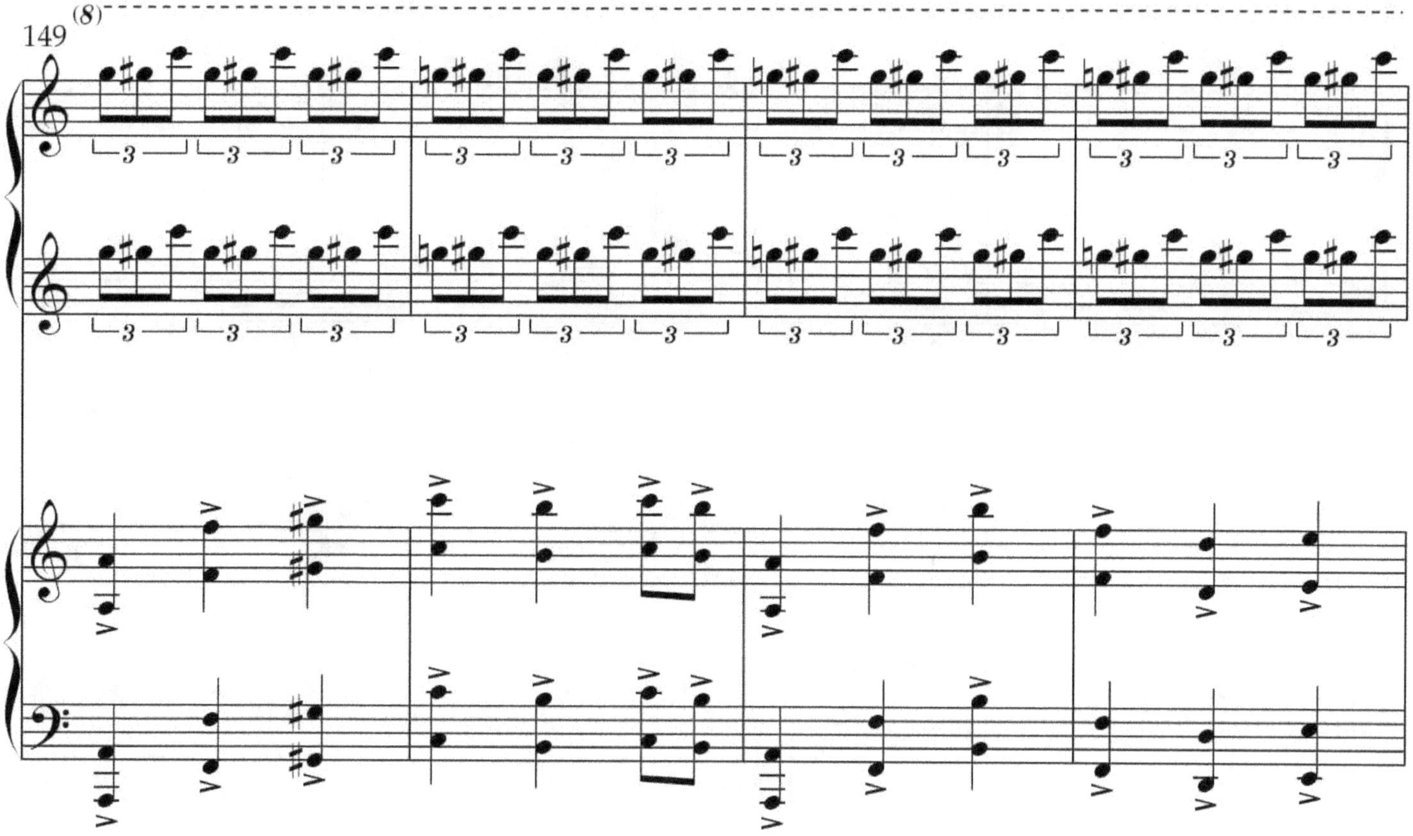
149
(8)
3

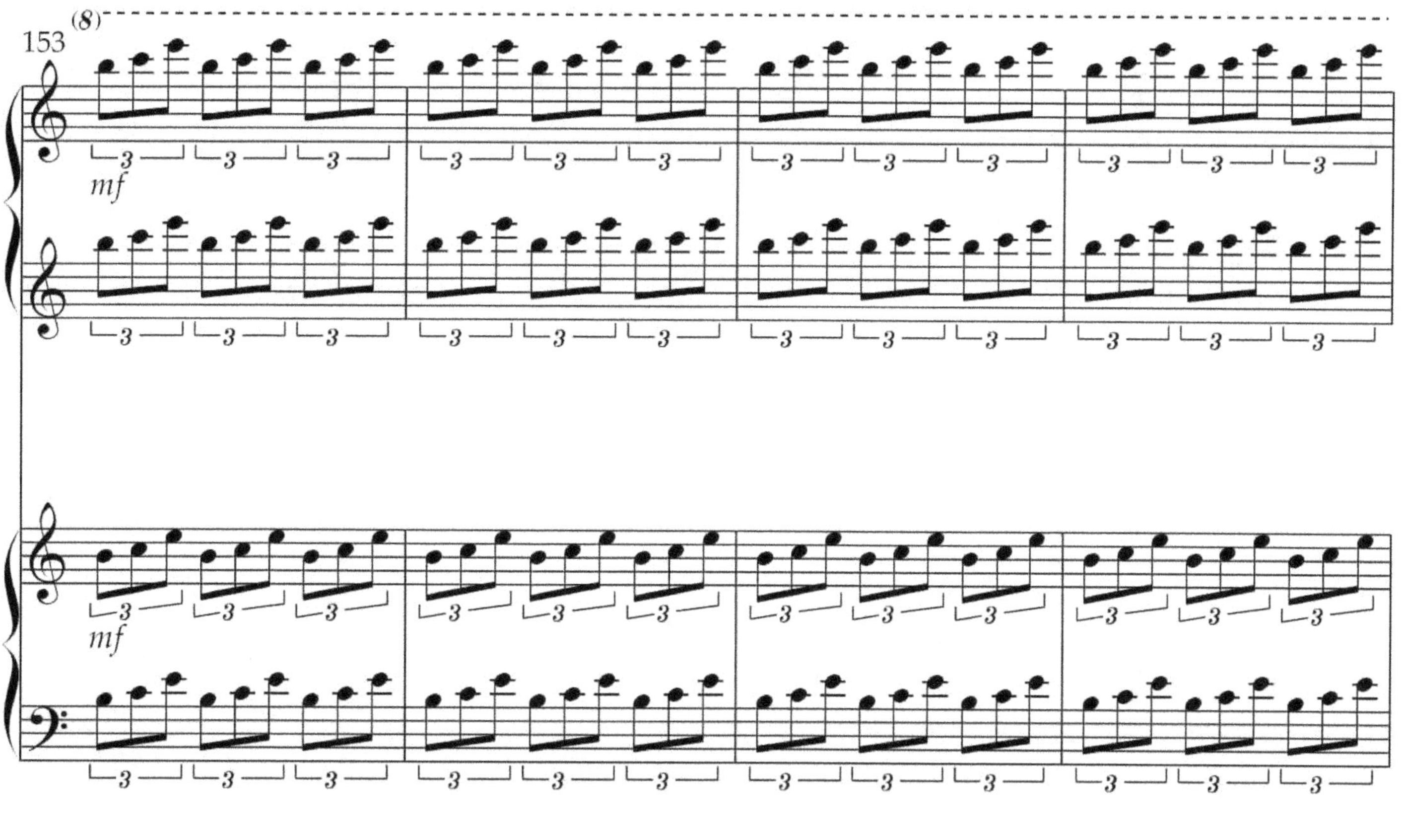
153
(8)
3
mf
mf

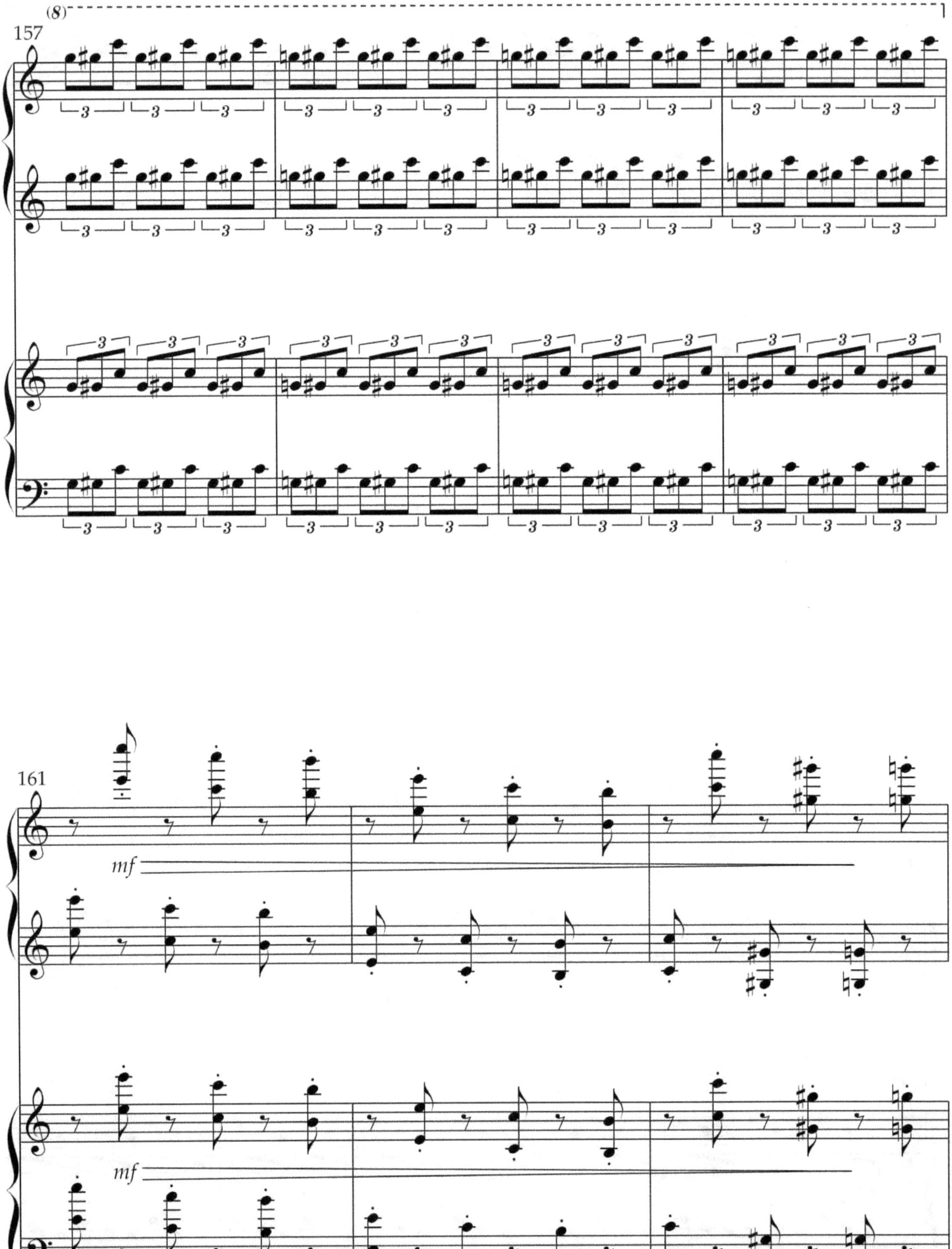
(8)
157
161
mf
mf

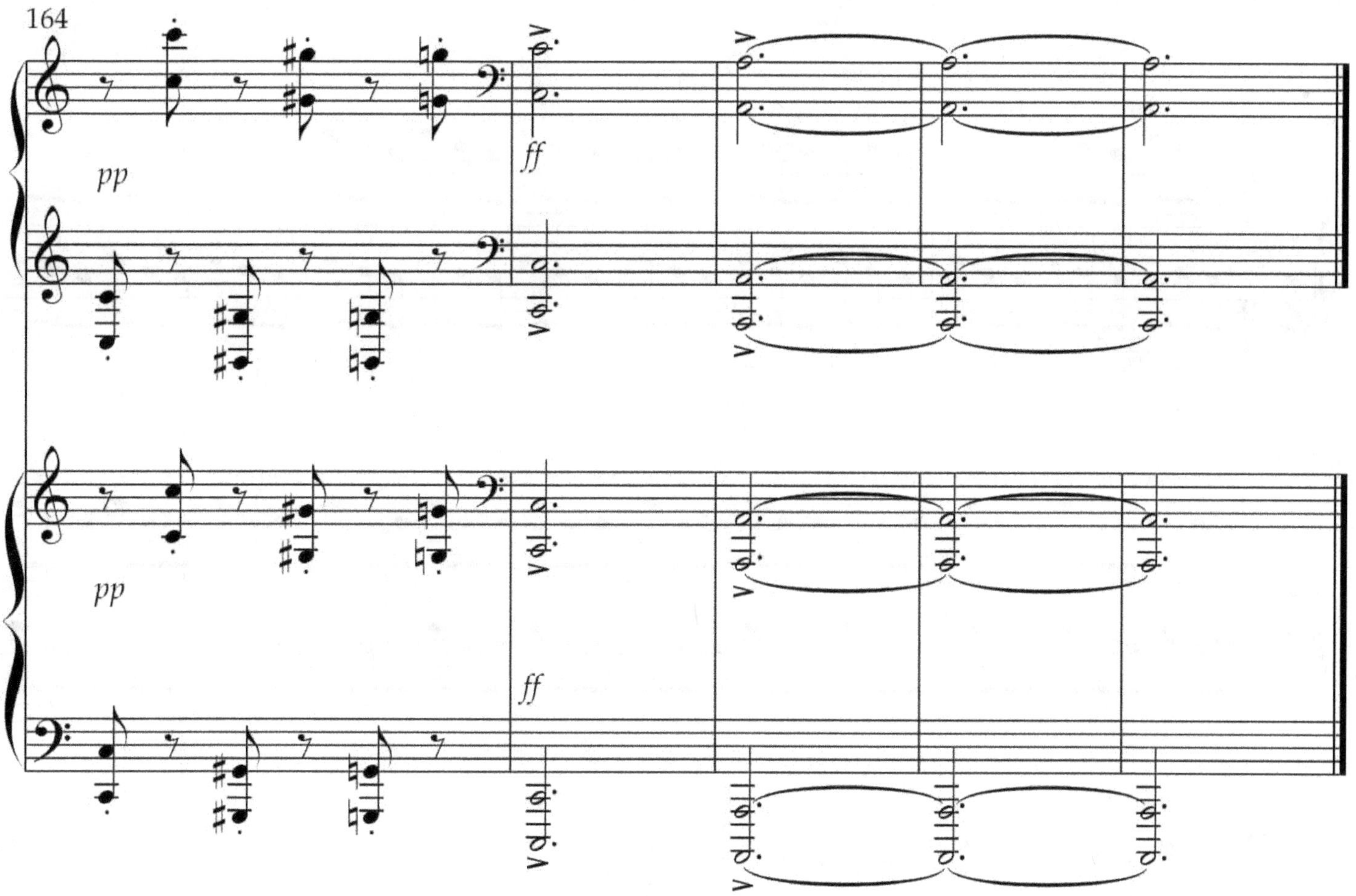
164
pp
ff
pp
ff

Descensus ad Infero

Piano 1

Tito Abeleda

Piano

Piano

Piano

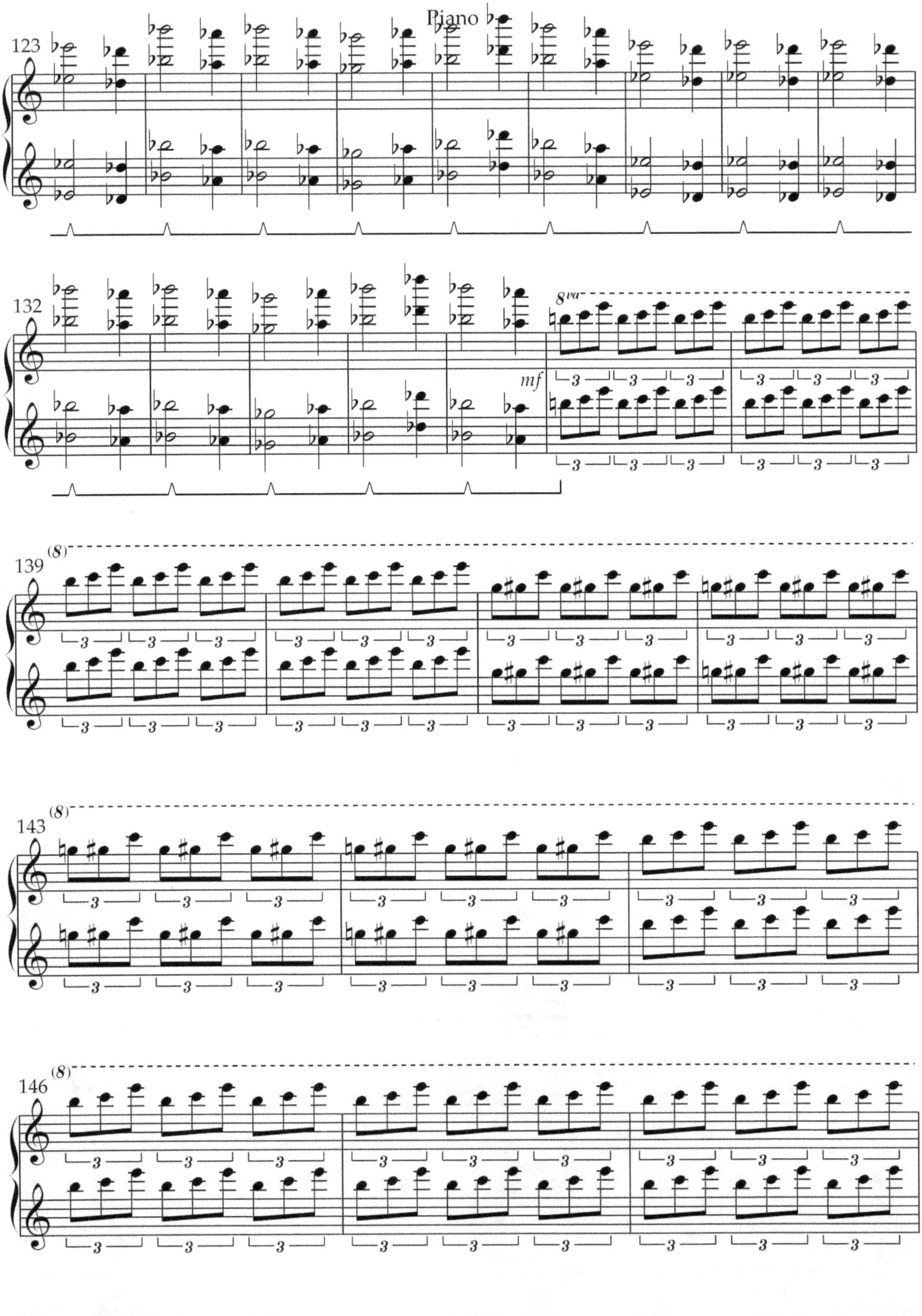
123
132
mf
8va
139
(8)
143
(8)
146
(8)

Piano

Descensus ad Infero

Piano 2

Tito Abeleda

Terrifying ♩ = 131

Piano

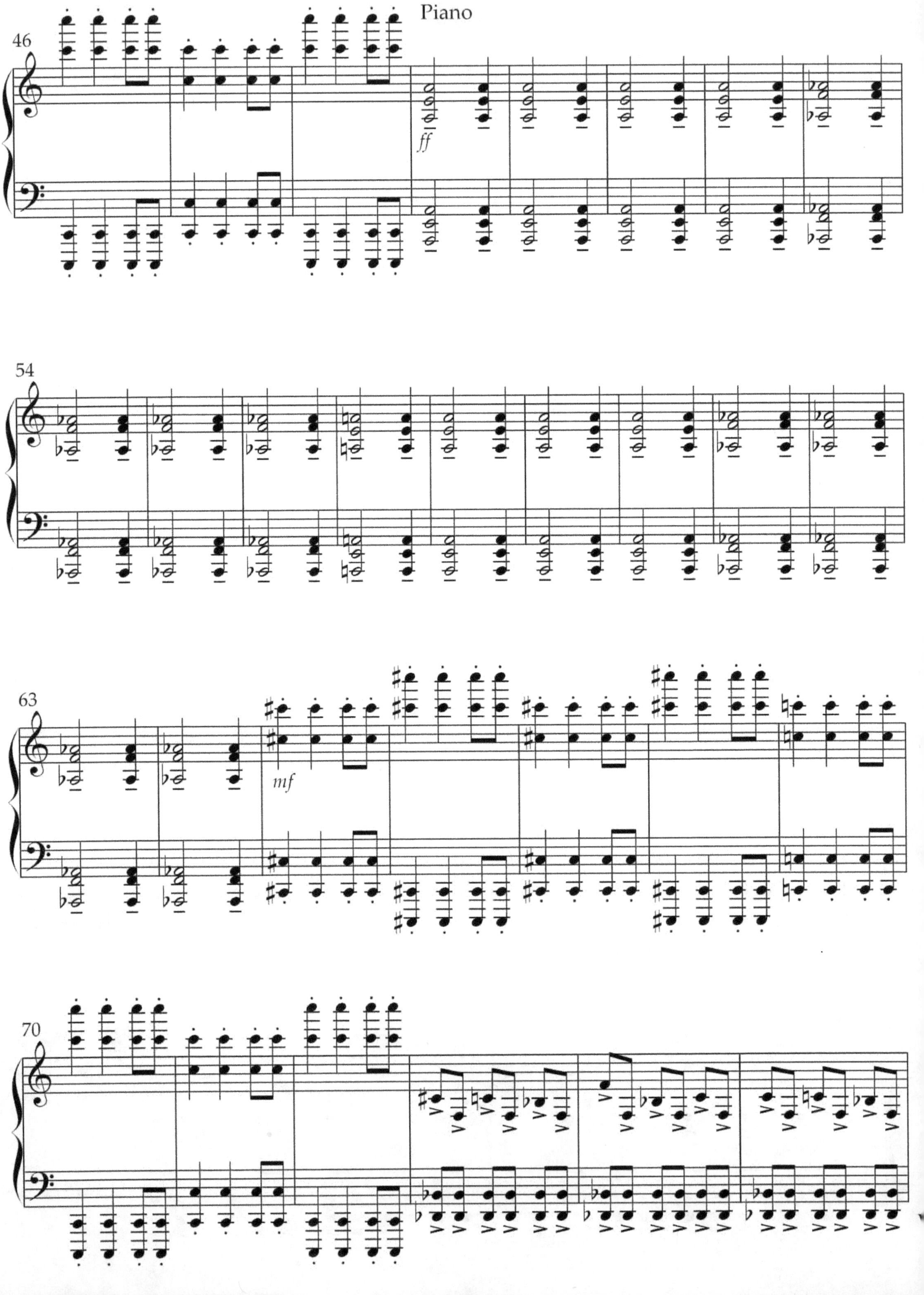
Piano
46
ff
54
63
mf
70

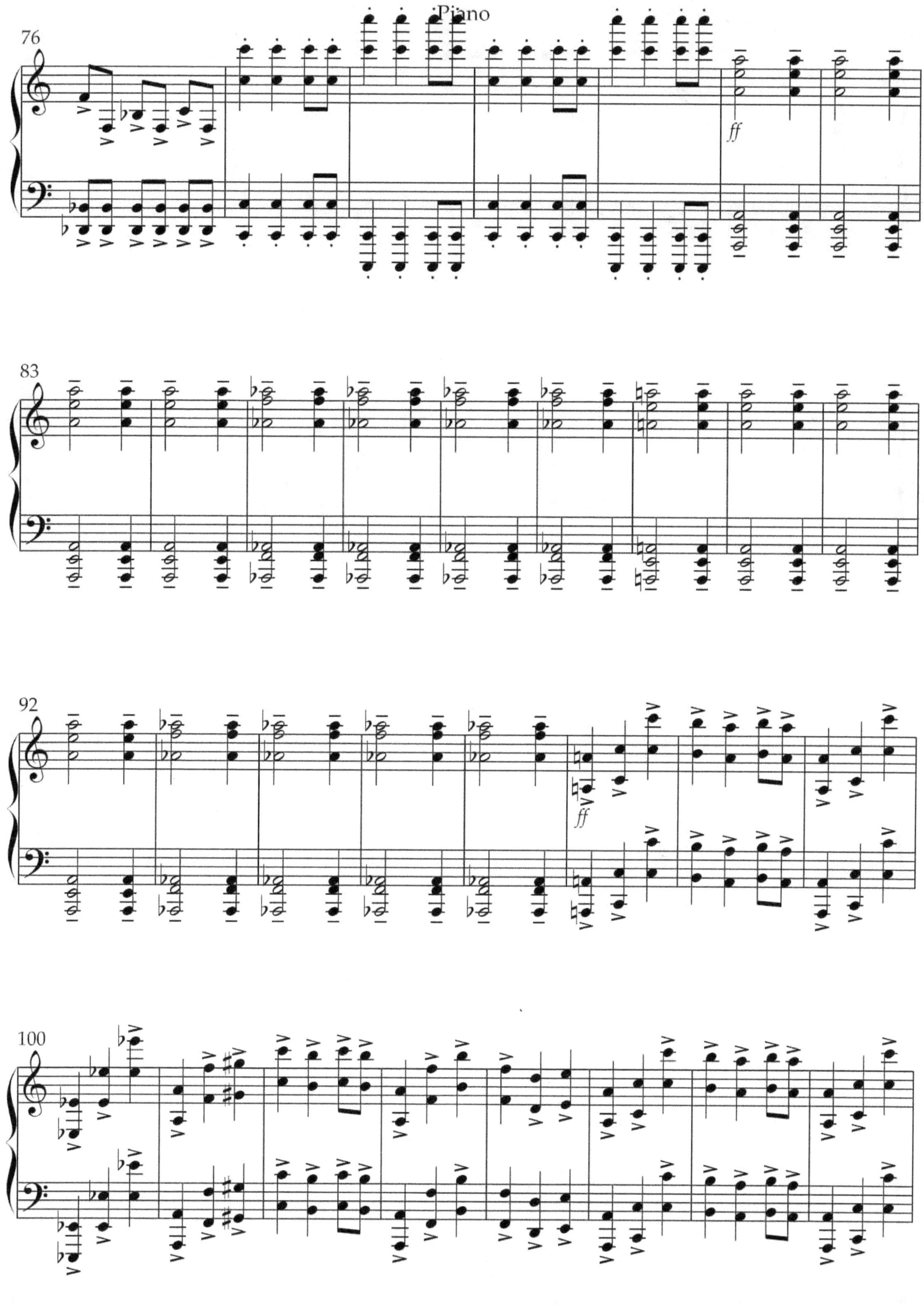
Piano
76
ff
83
92
ff
100

Piano

Piano

Piano

Procession in D Minor
(Score)

Tito Abeleda

Andante ♩=83

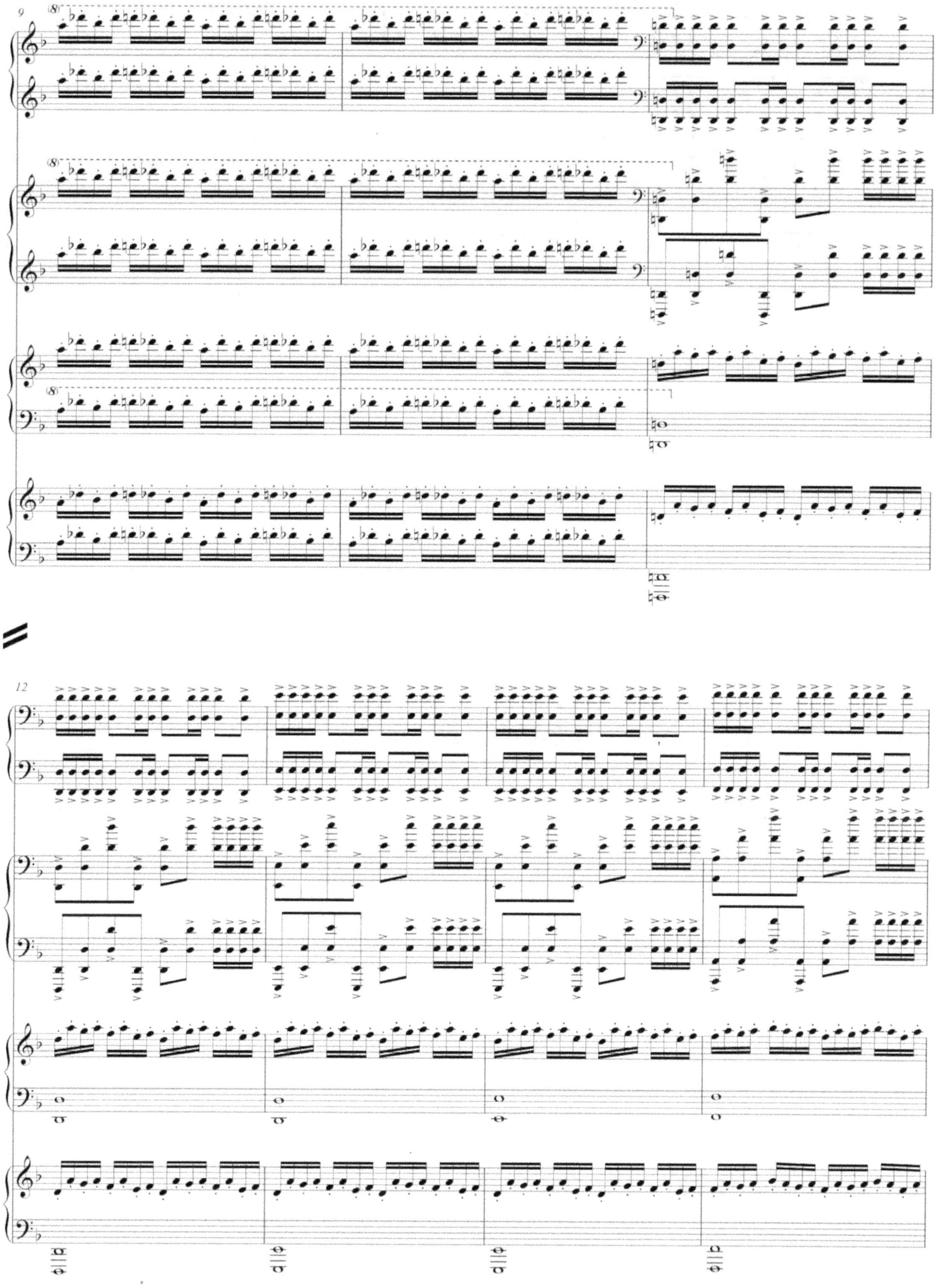
9
12

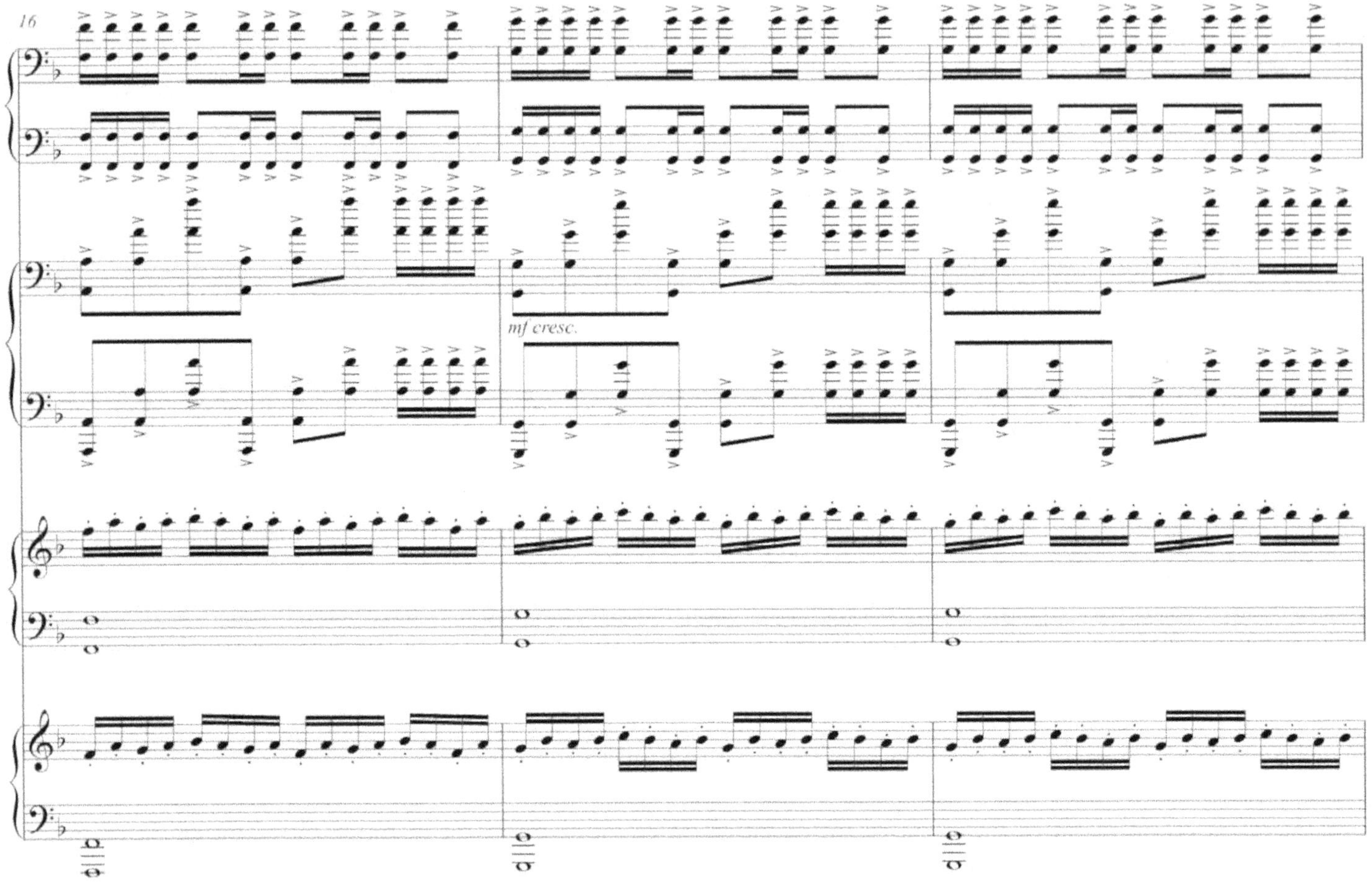
16
mf cresc.

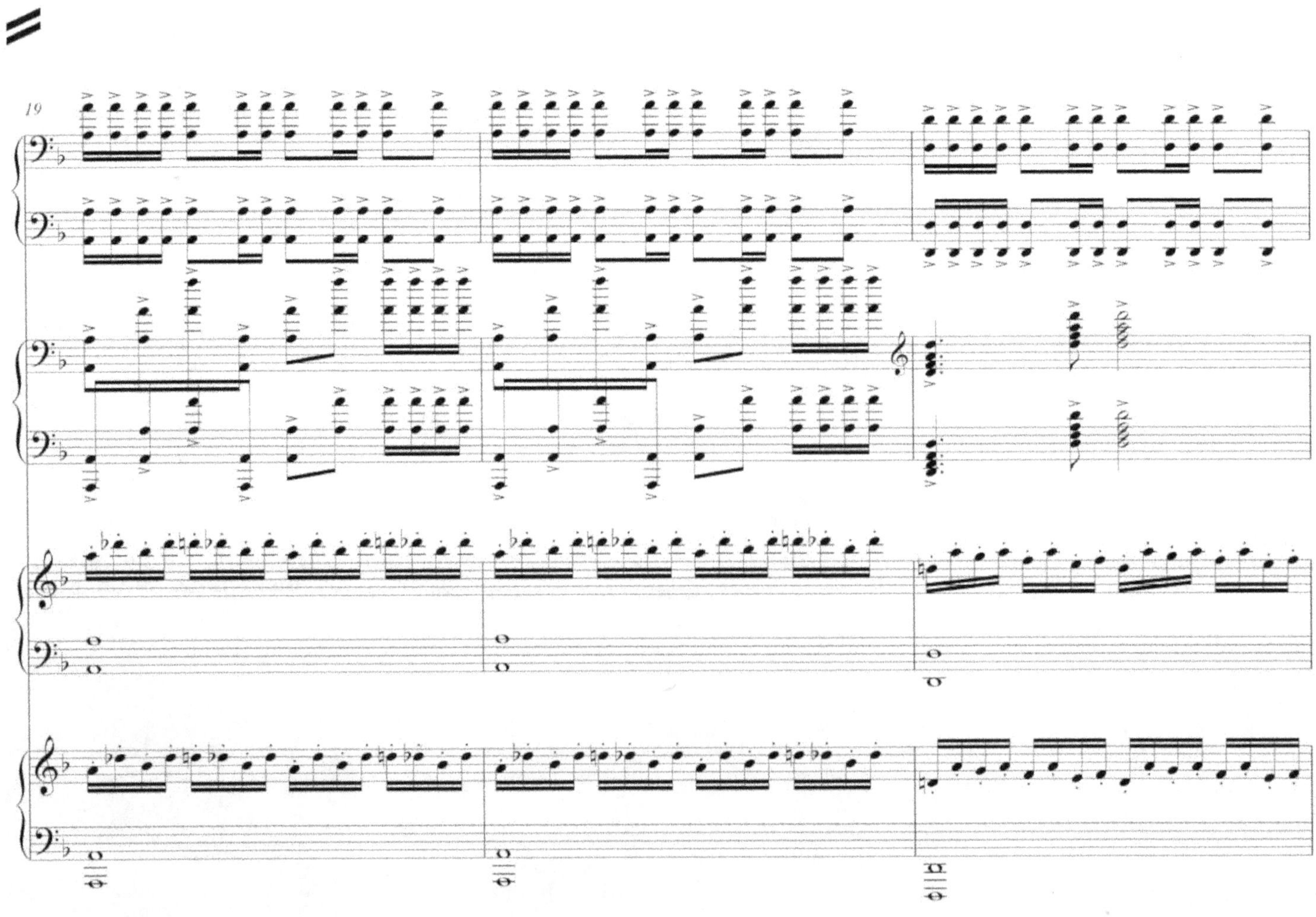
19

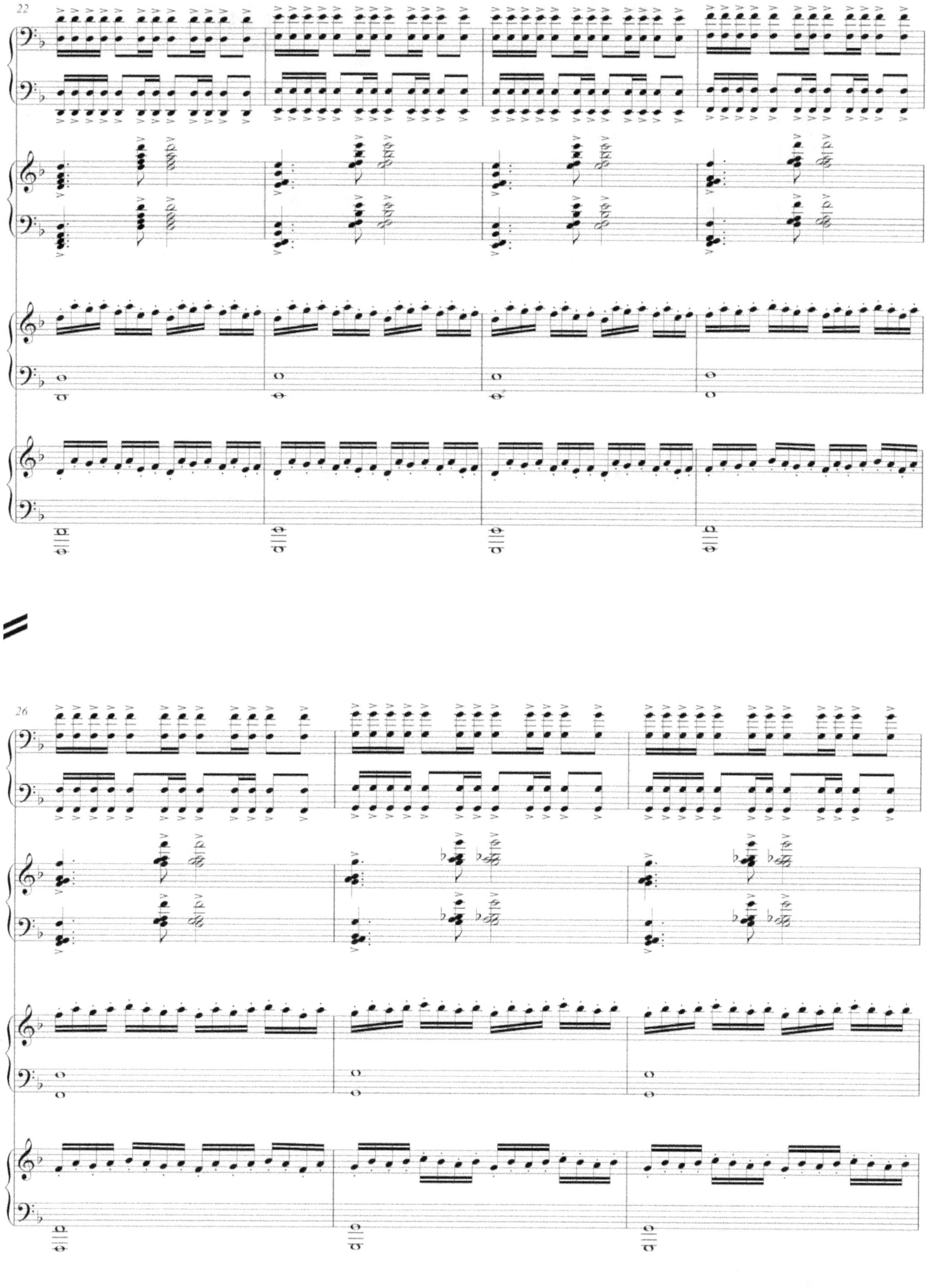
22
26

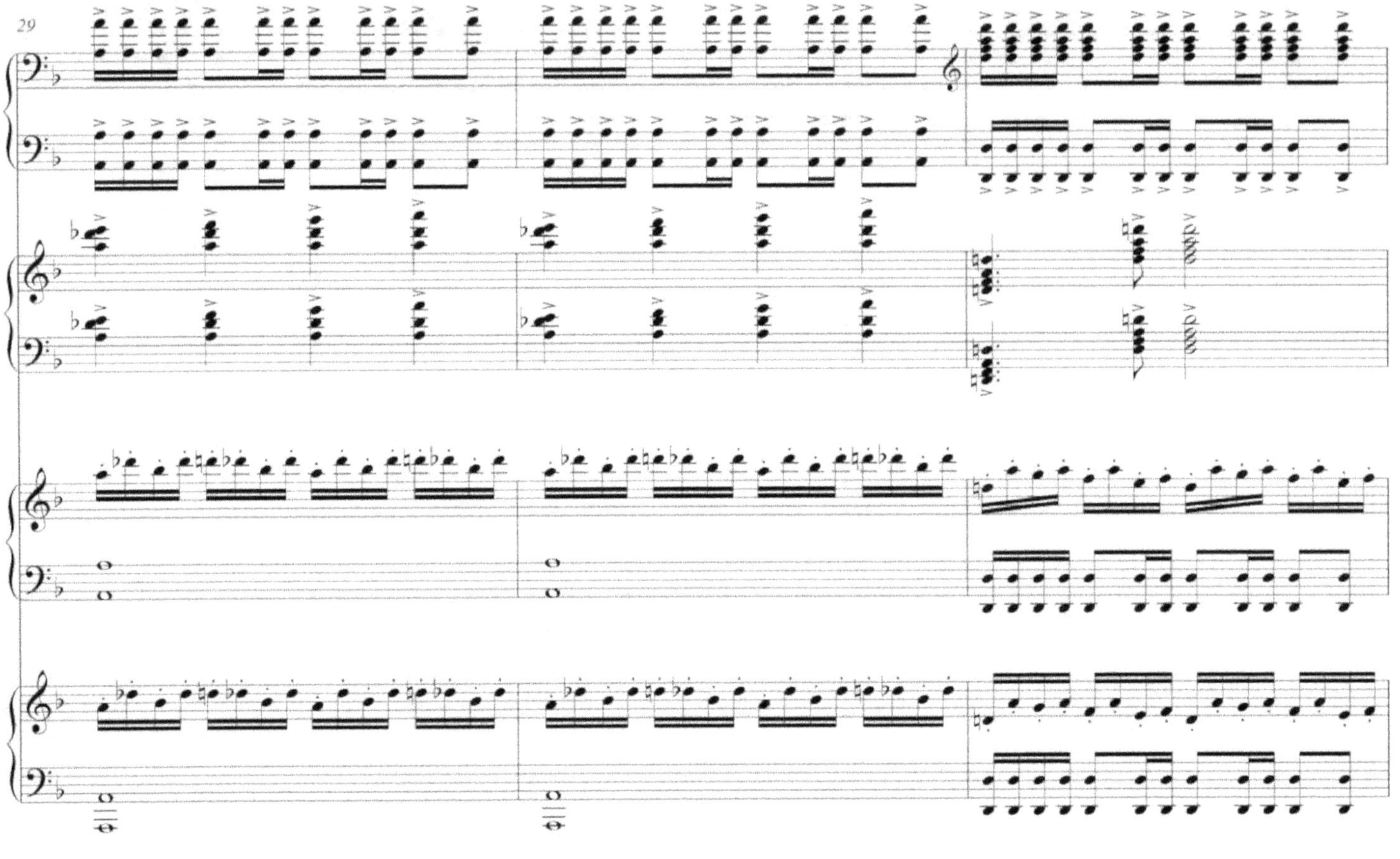
29

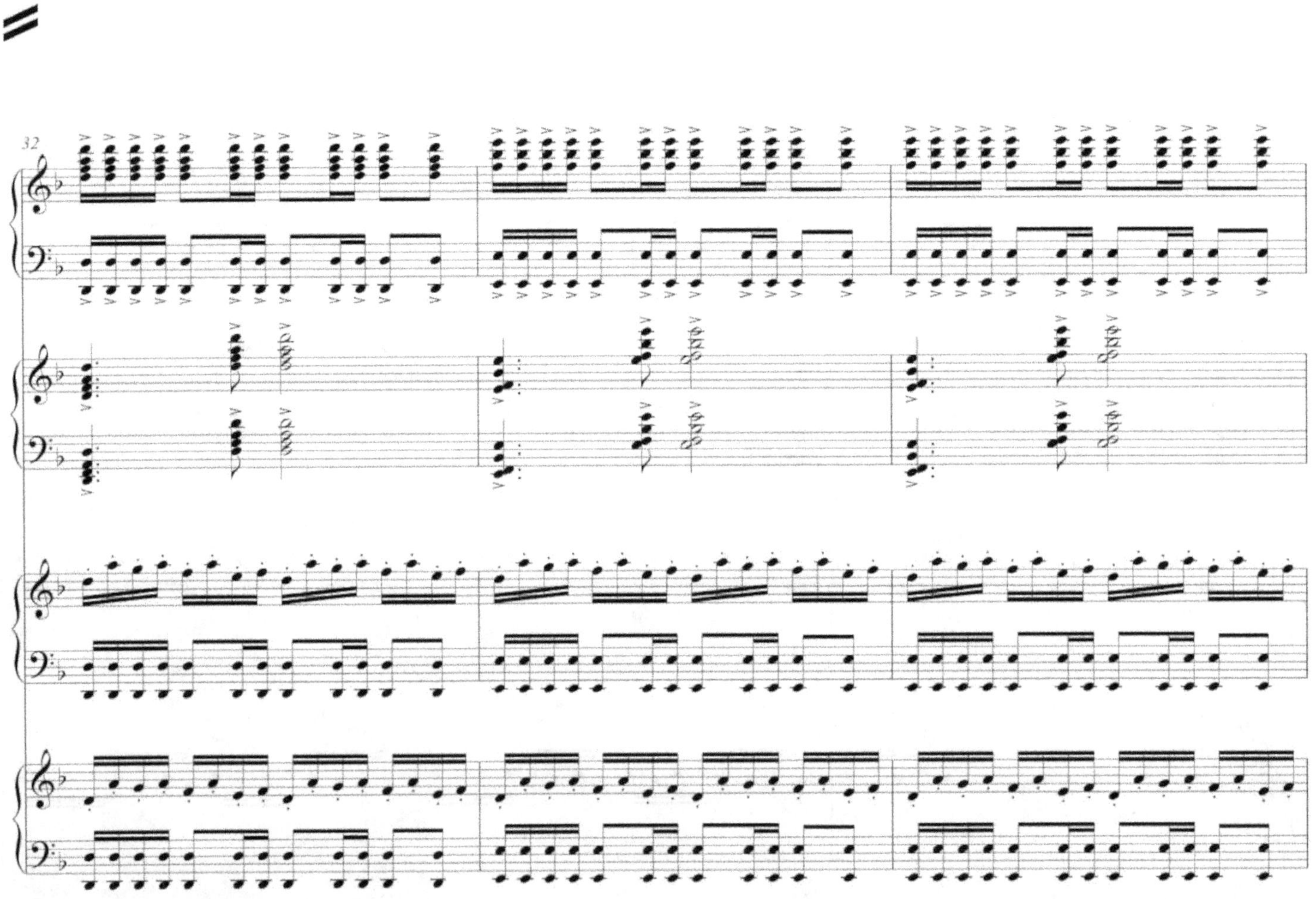
32

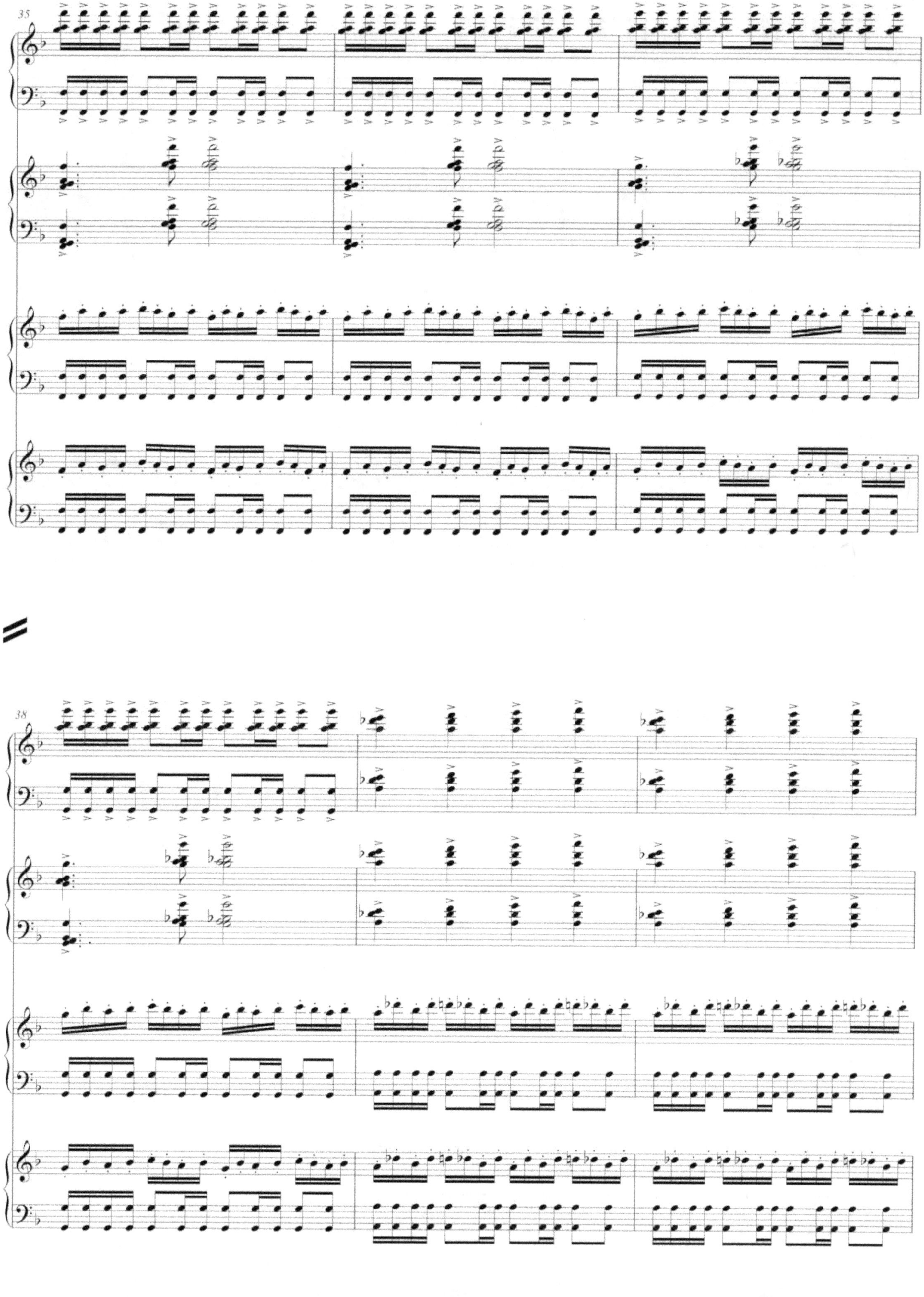

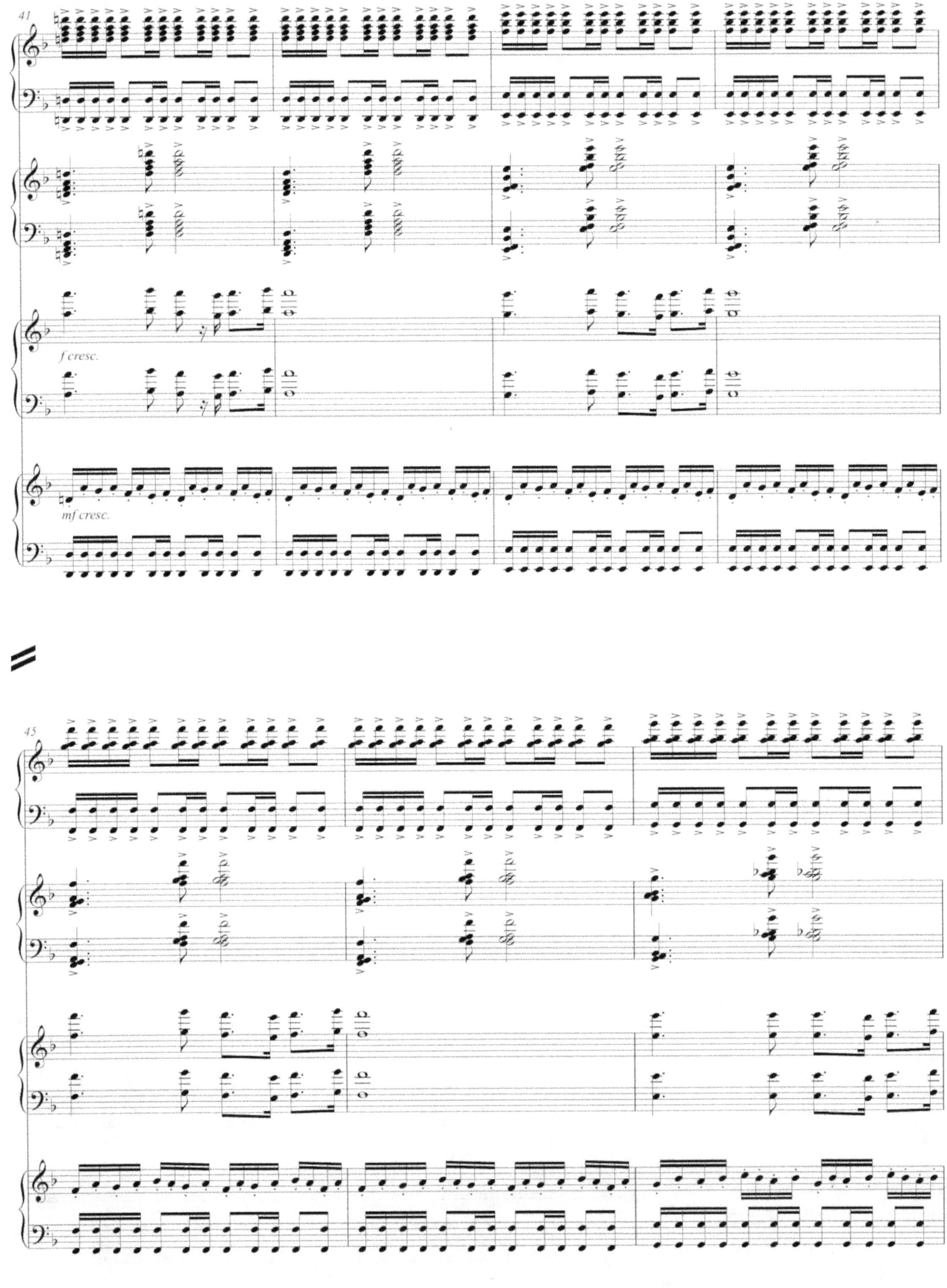
41
f cresc.
mf cresc.
45

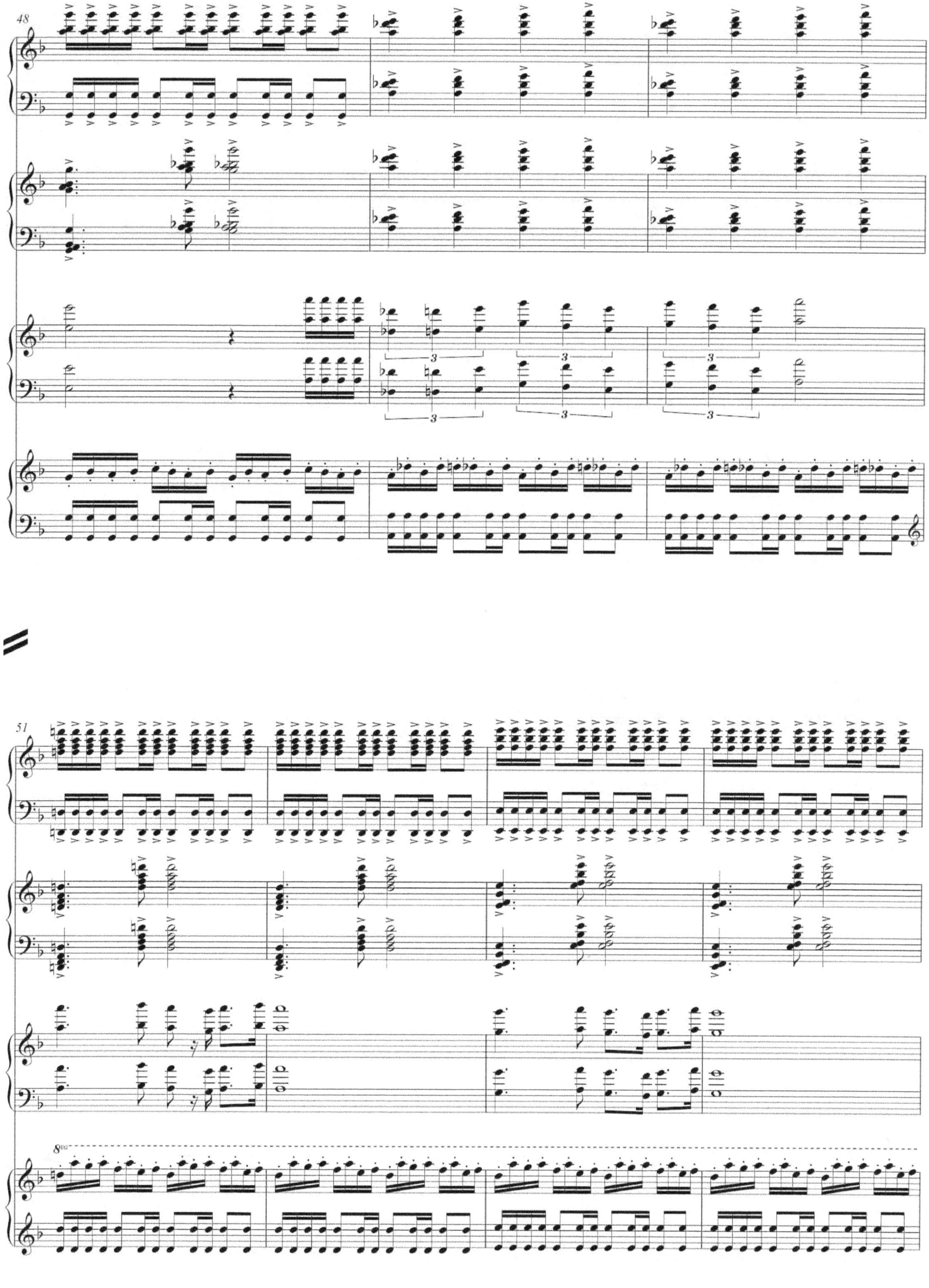
48
3
3
3
3
3
3
51
8va

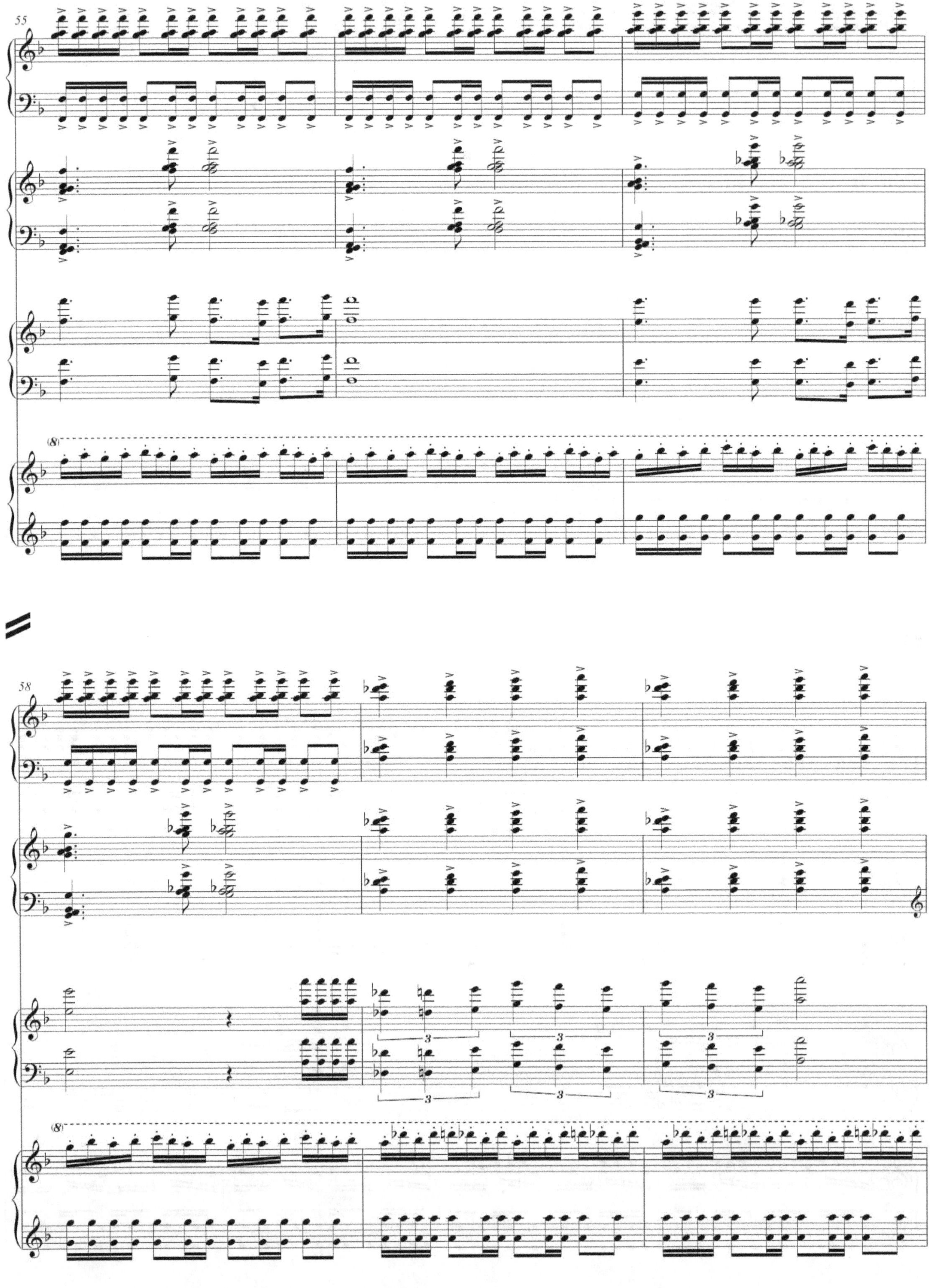

55
(8)
58
(8)

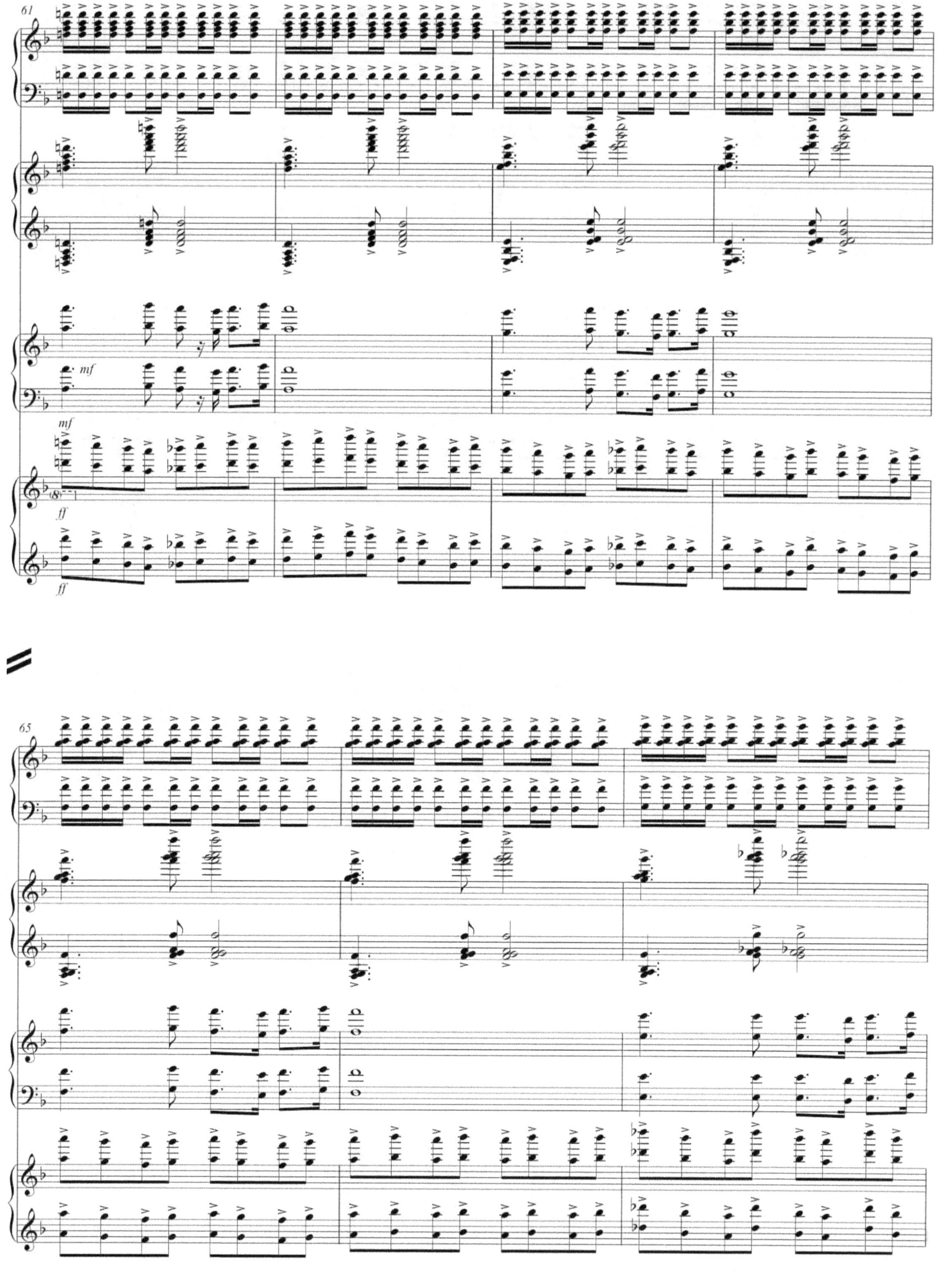
61
mf
mf
ff
ff
65

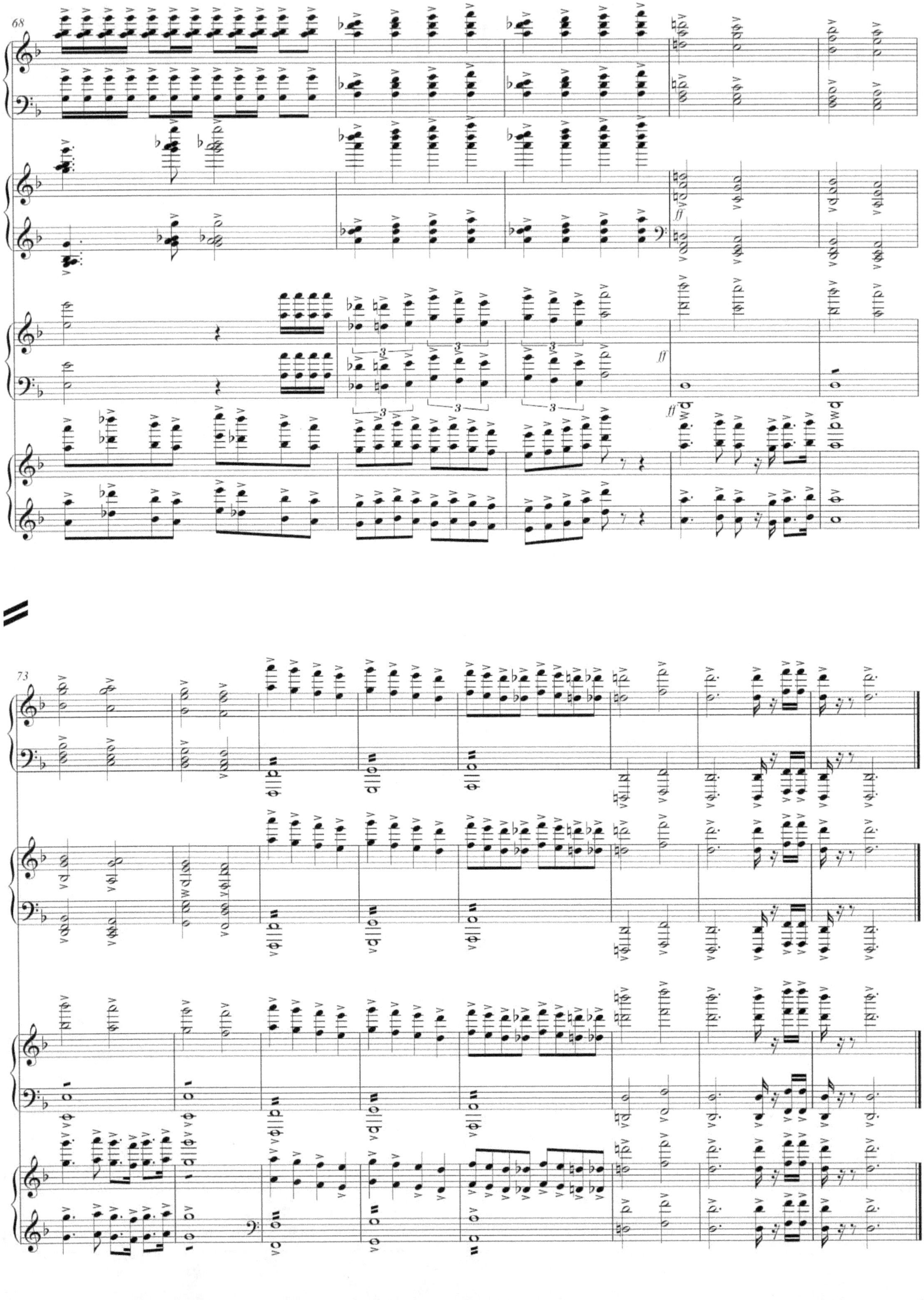
68
3
3
3
3
3
3
ff
ff
ff
73

Procession in D Minor

Piano 1

Tito Abeleda

Andante ♩=83

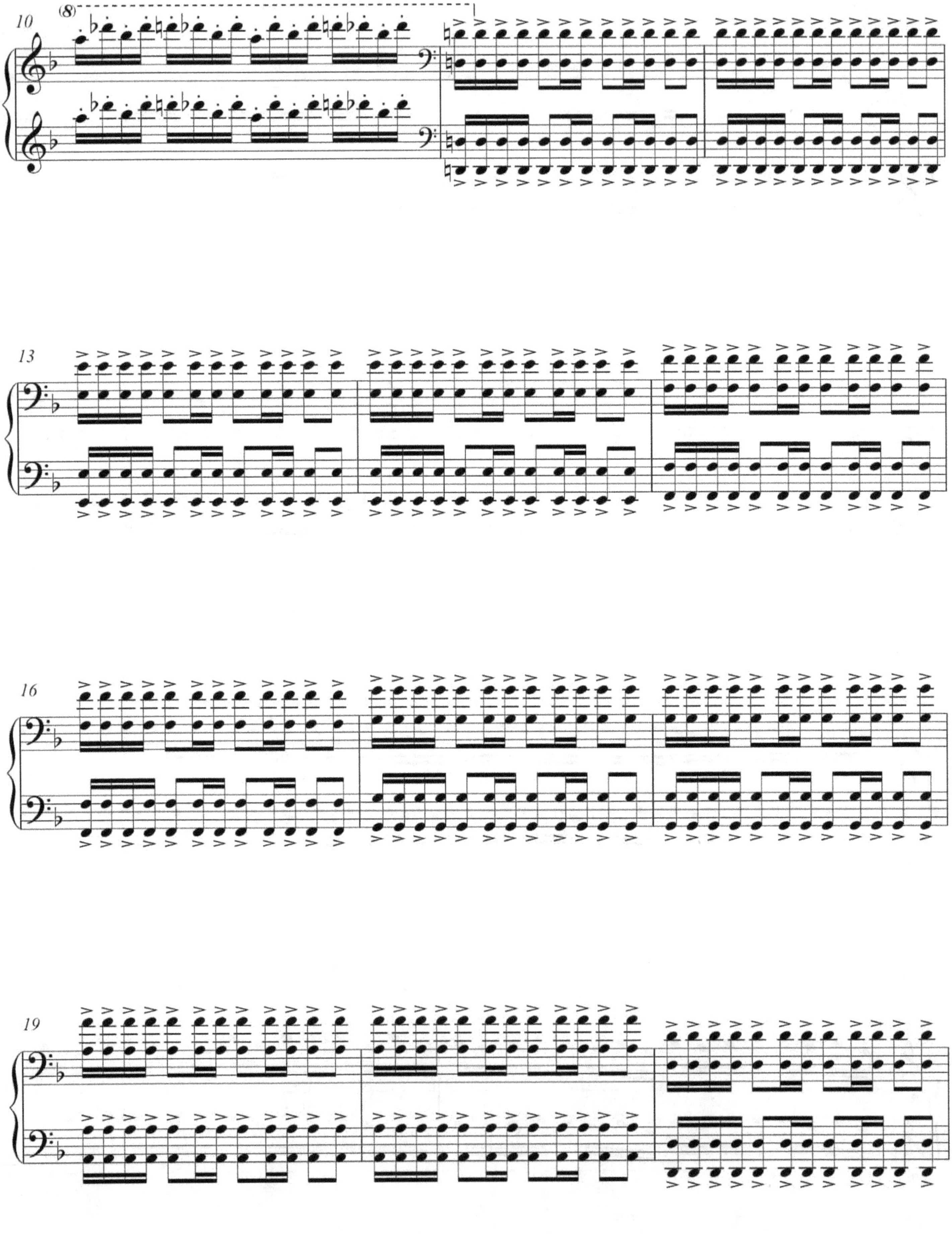
10
(8)
13
16
19

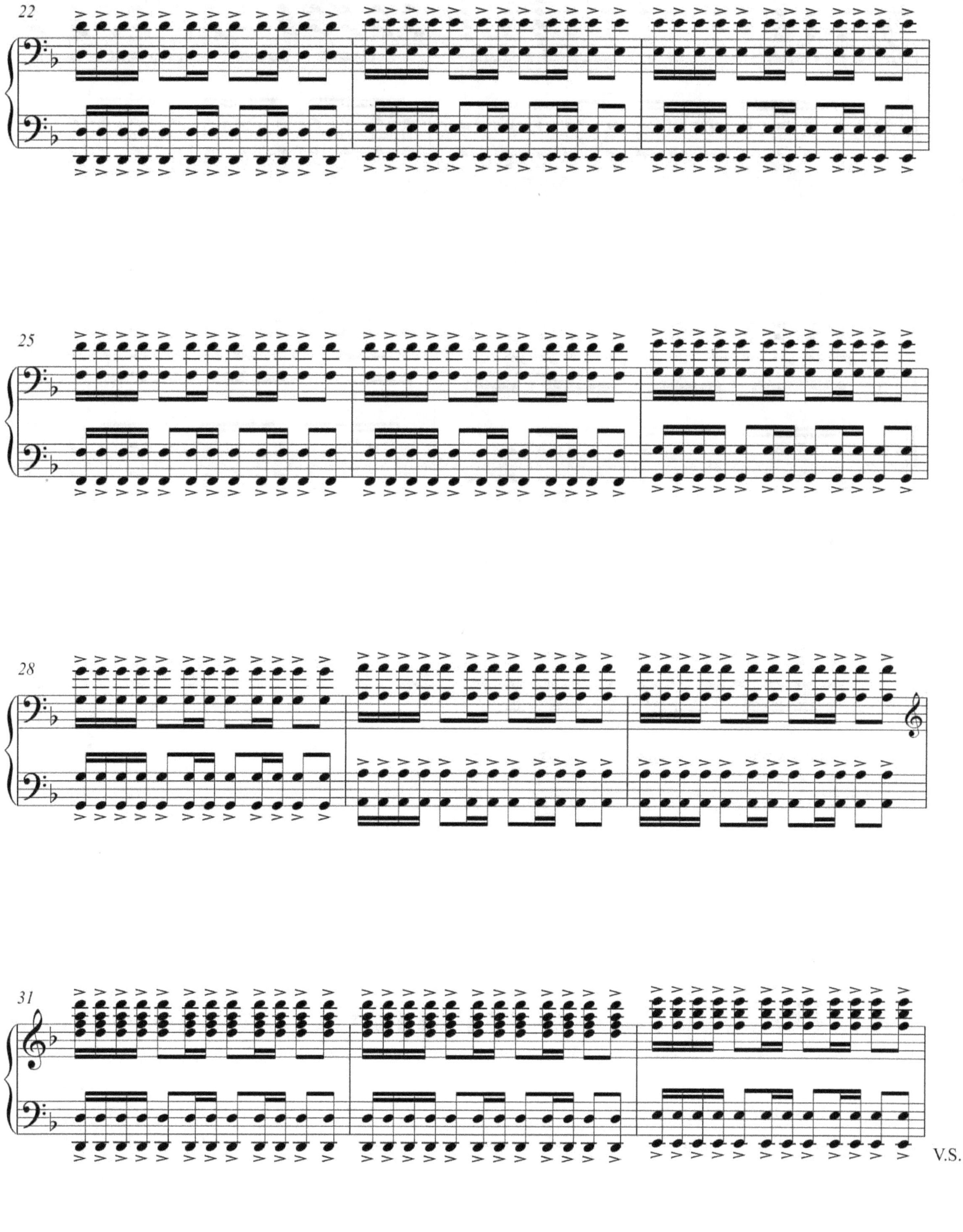
22
25
28
31
V.S.

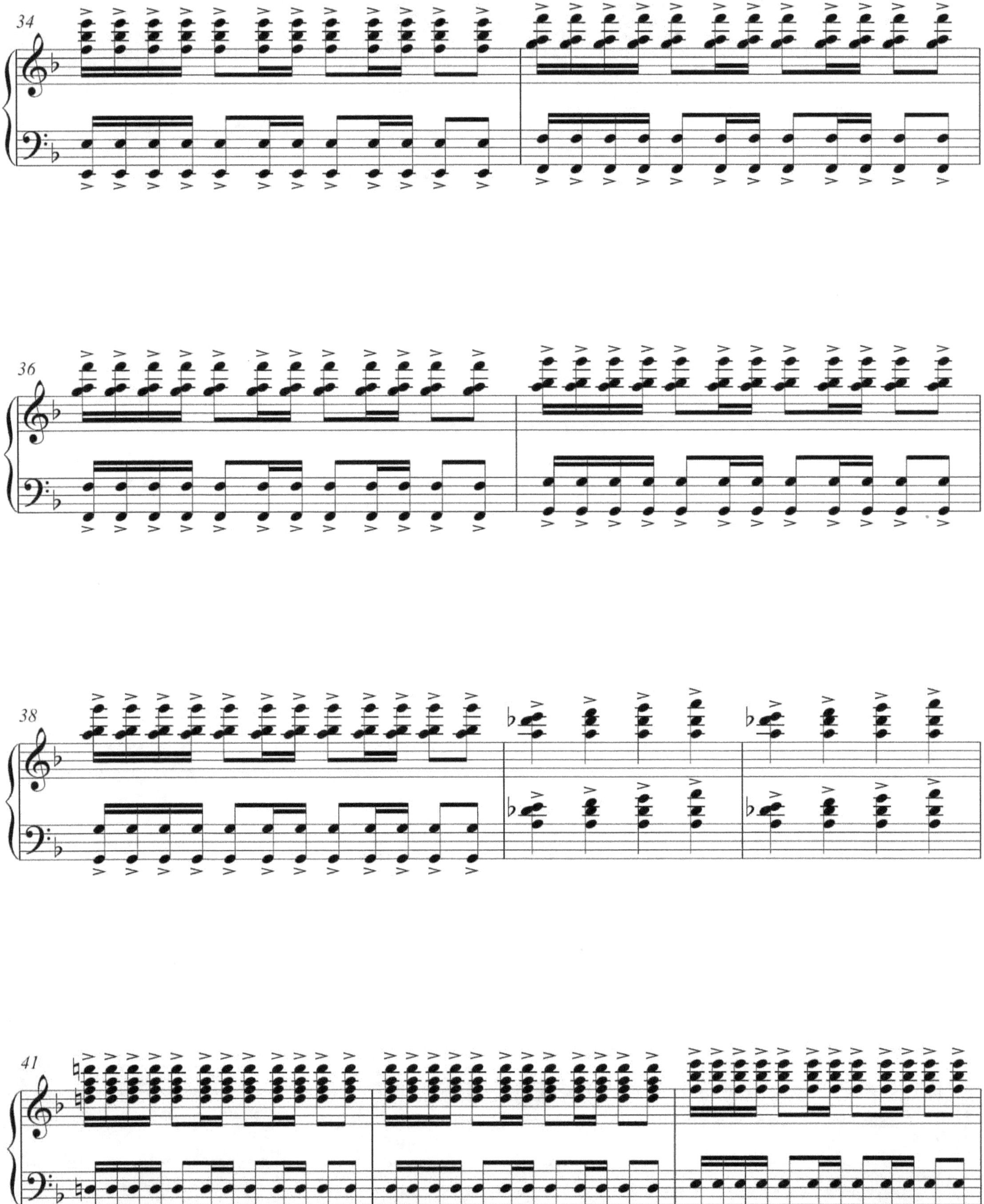
34
36
38
41

V.S.

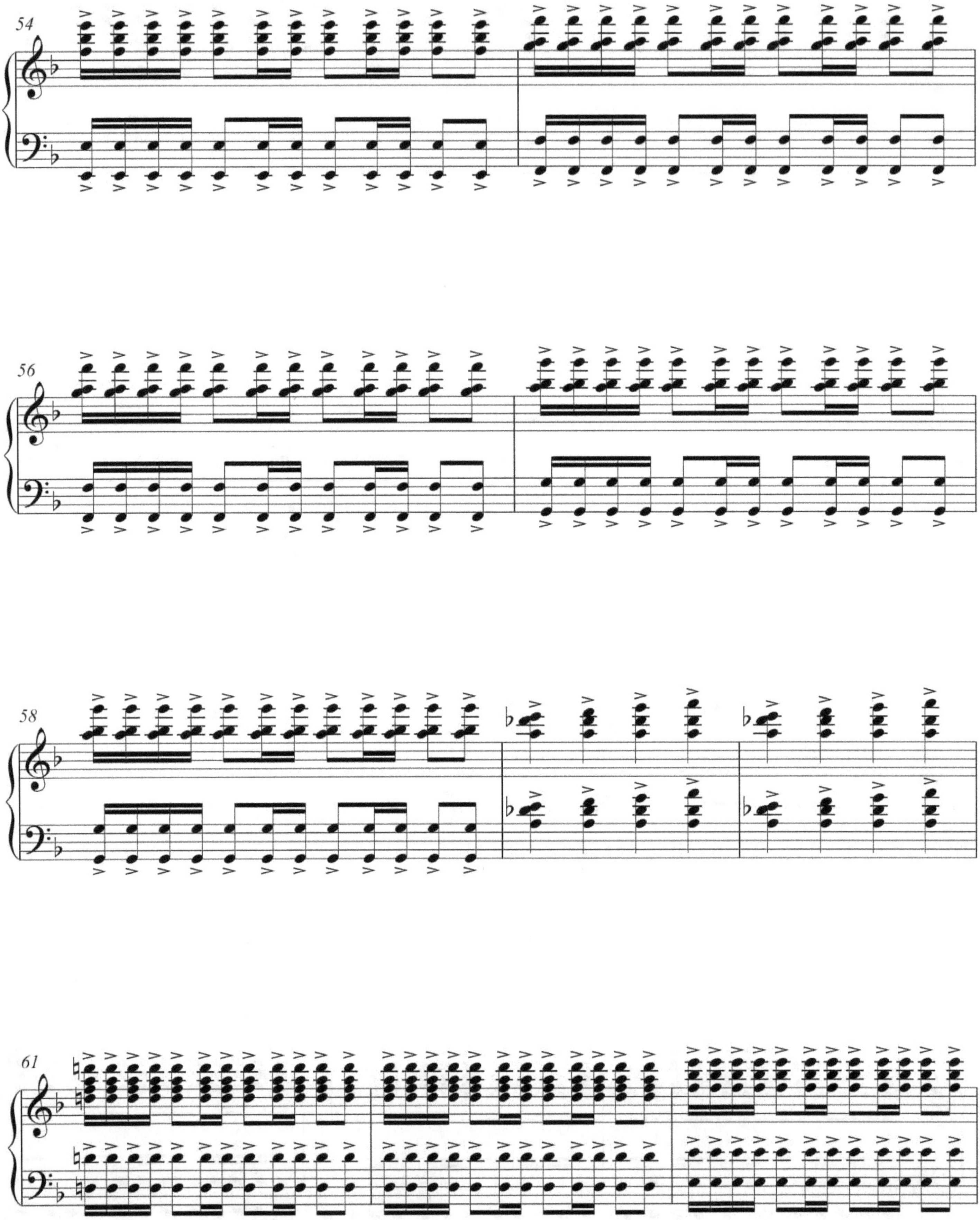
54
56
58
61

V.S.

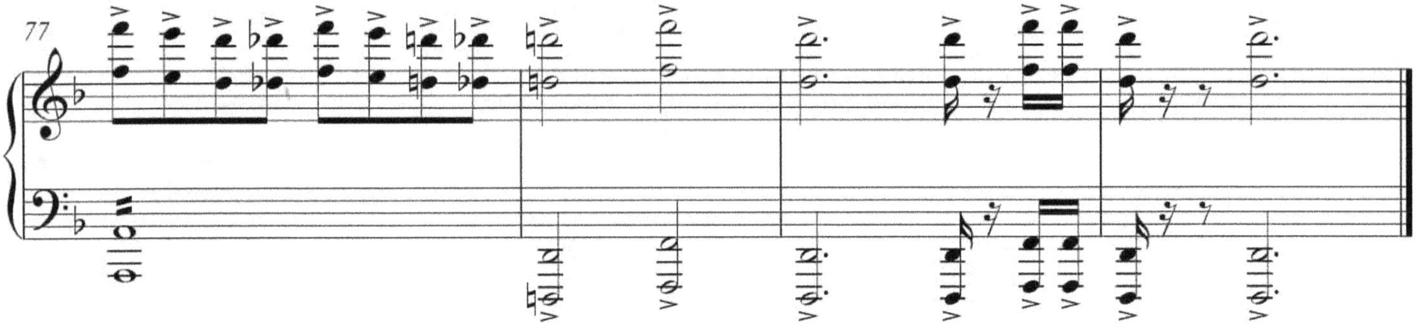
77

Procession in D Minor

Piano 2

Tito Abeleda

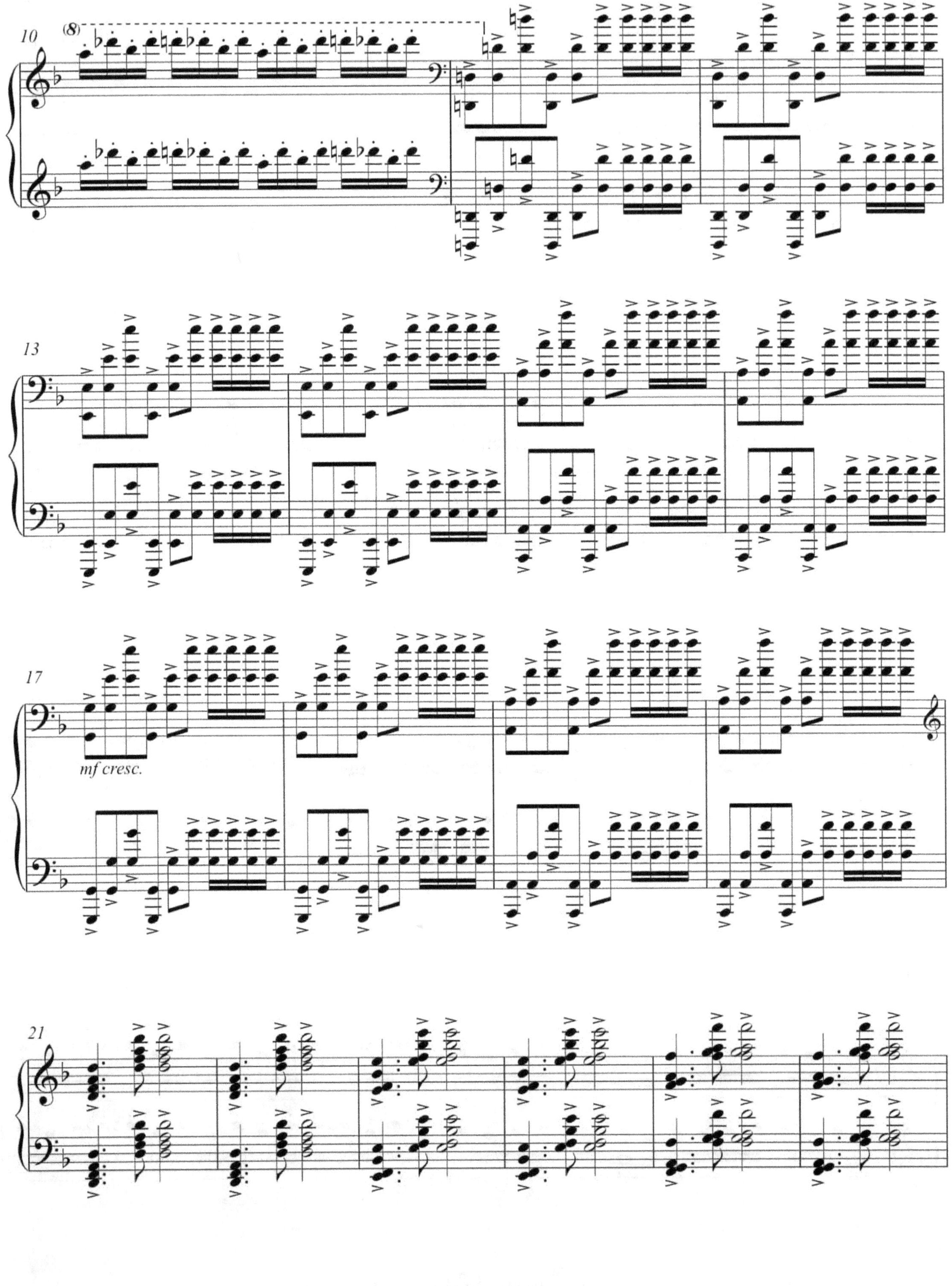
10
(8)
13
17
mf cresc.
21

V.S.

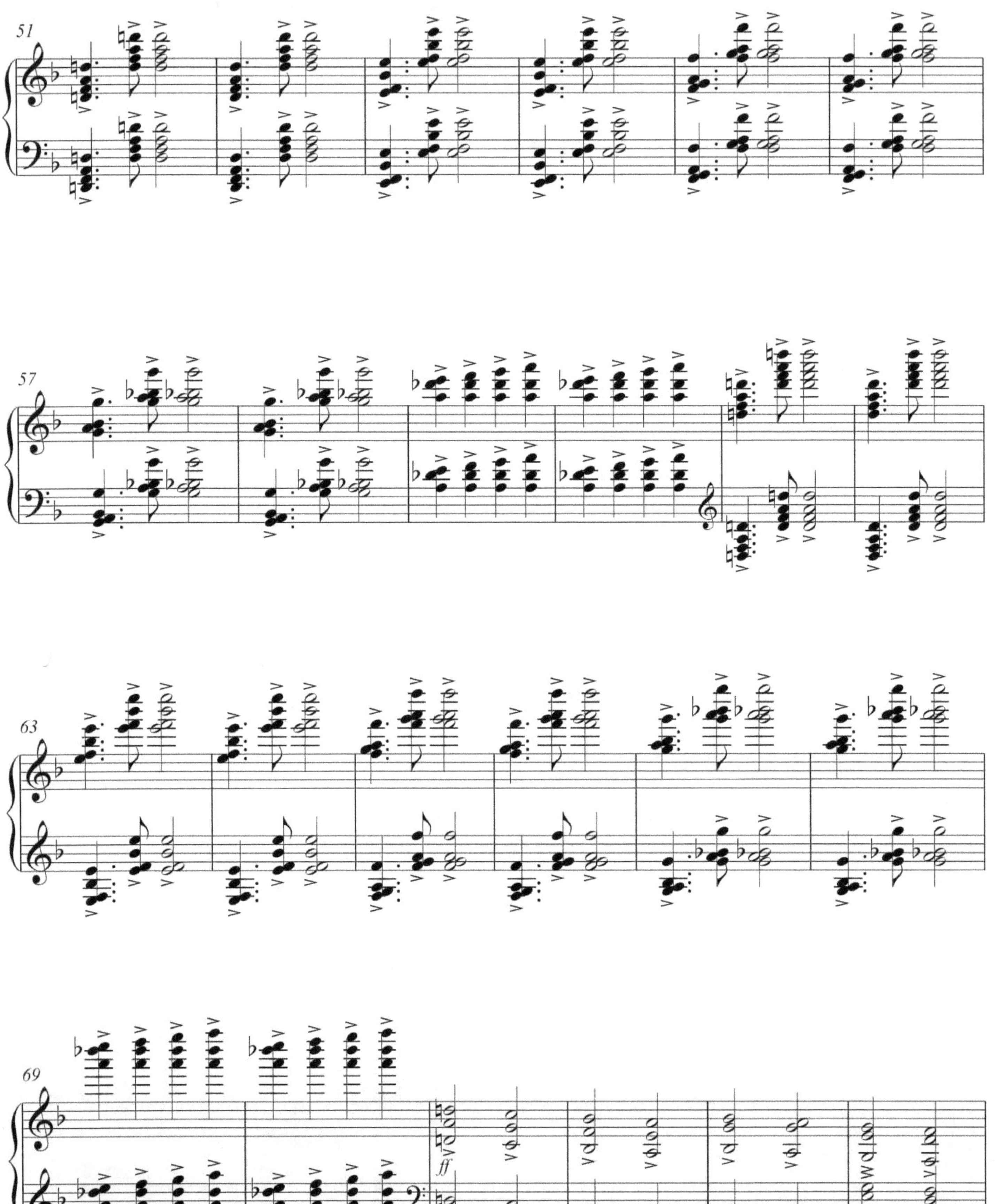
51
57
63
69
ff

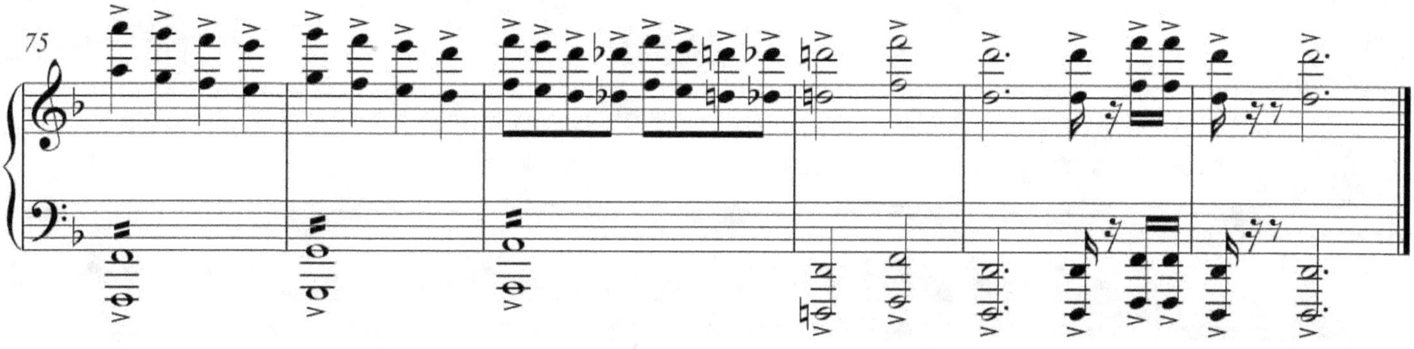
75

Procession in D Minor

Piano 3

Tito Abeleda

Andante ♩=83

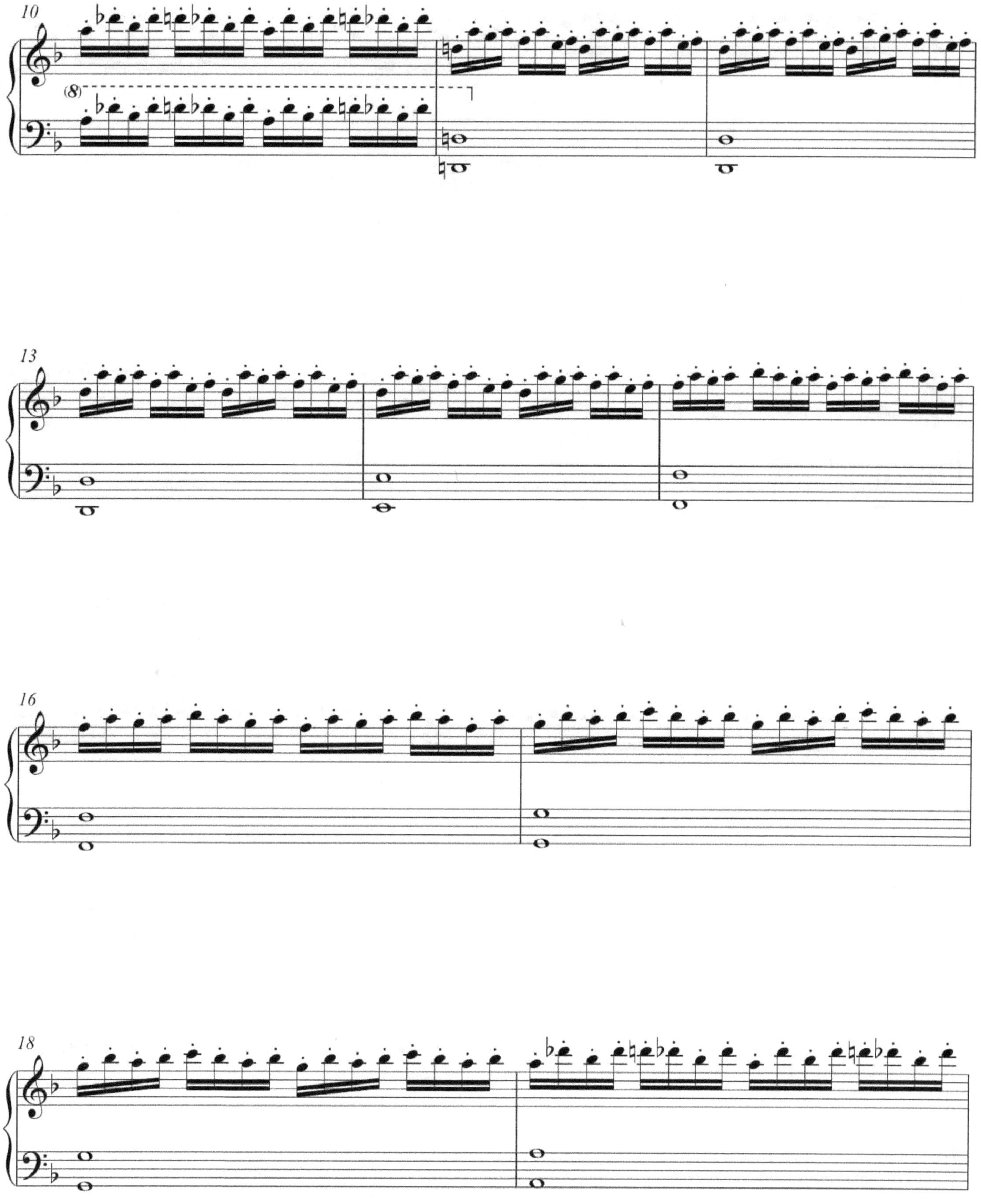
10
(8)
13
16
18

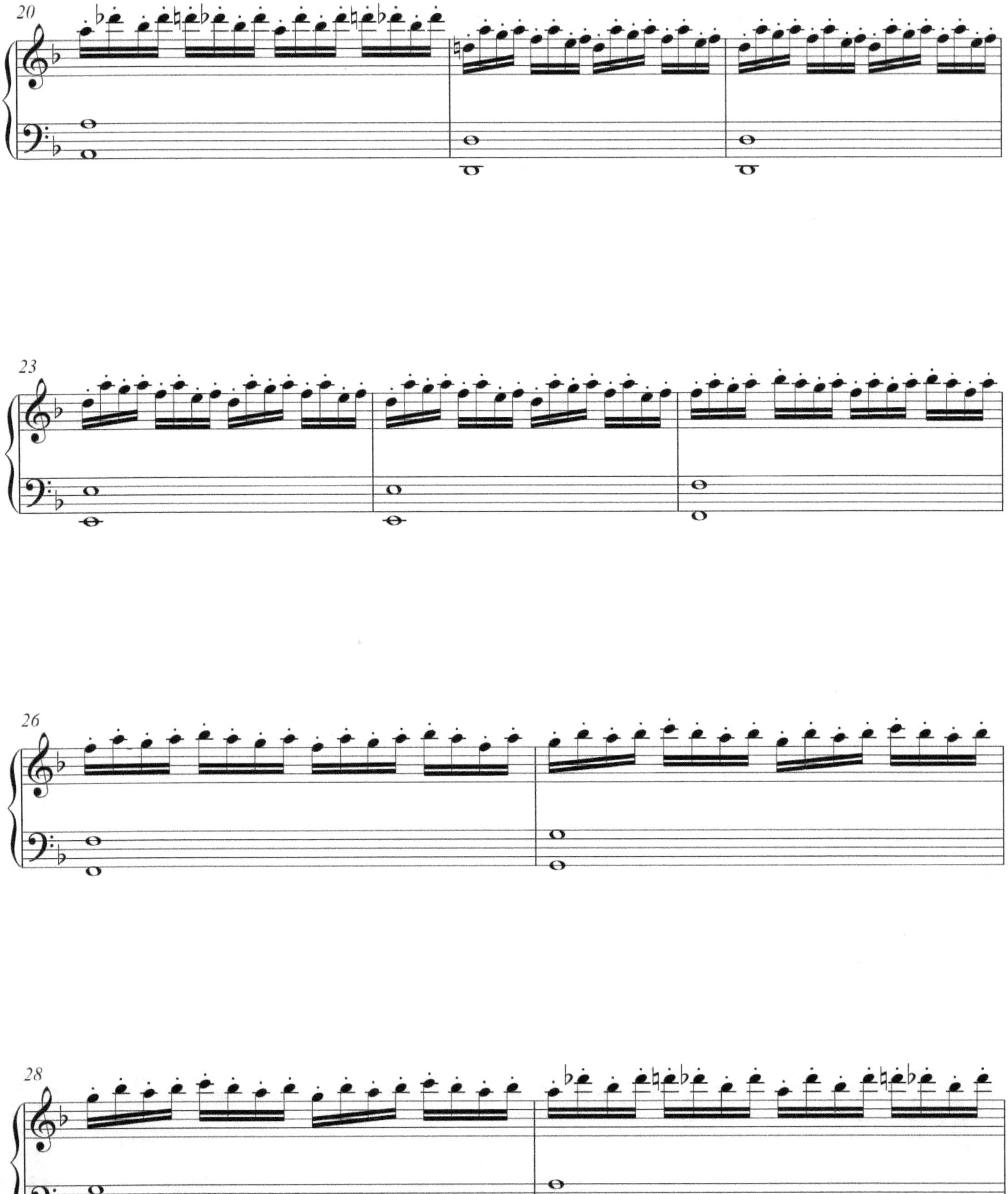
20
23
26
28

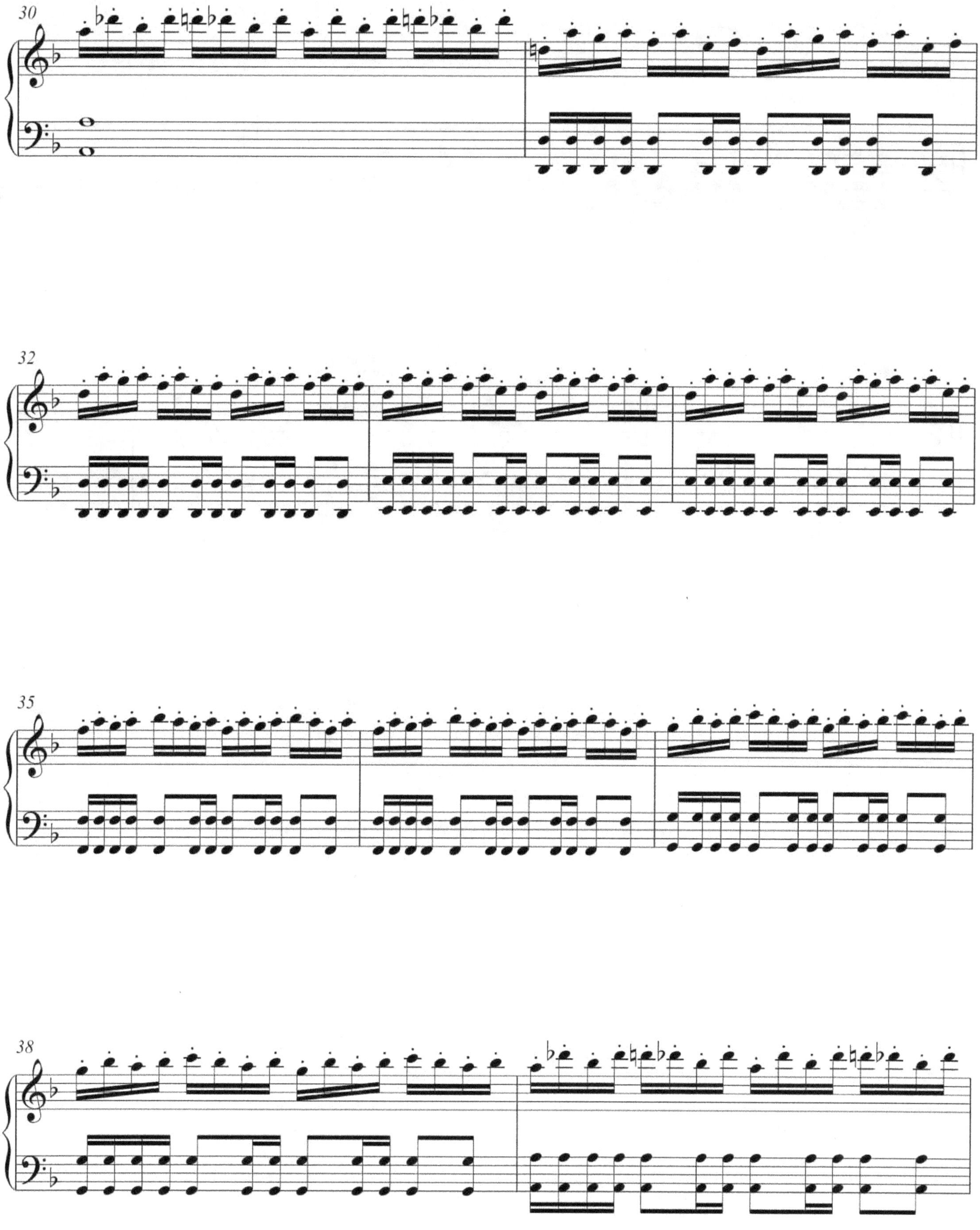
30
32
35
38

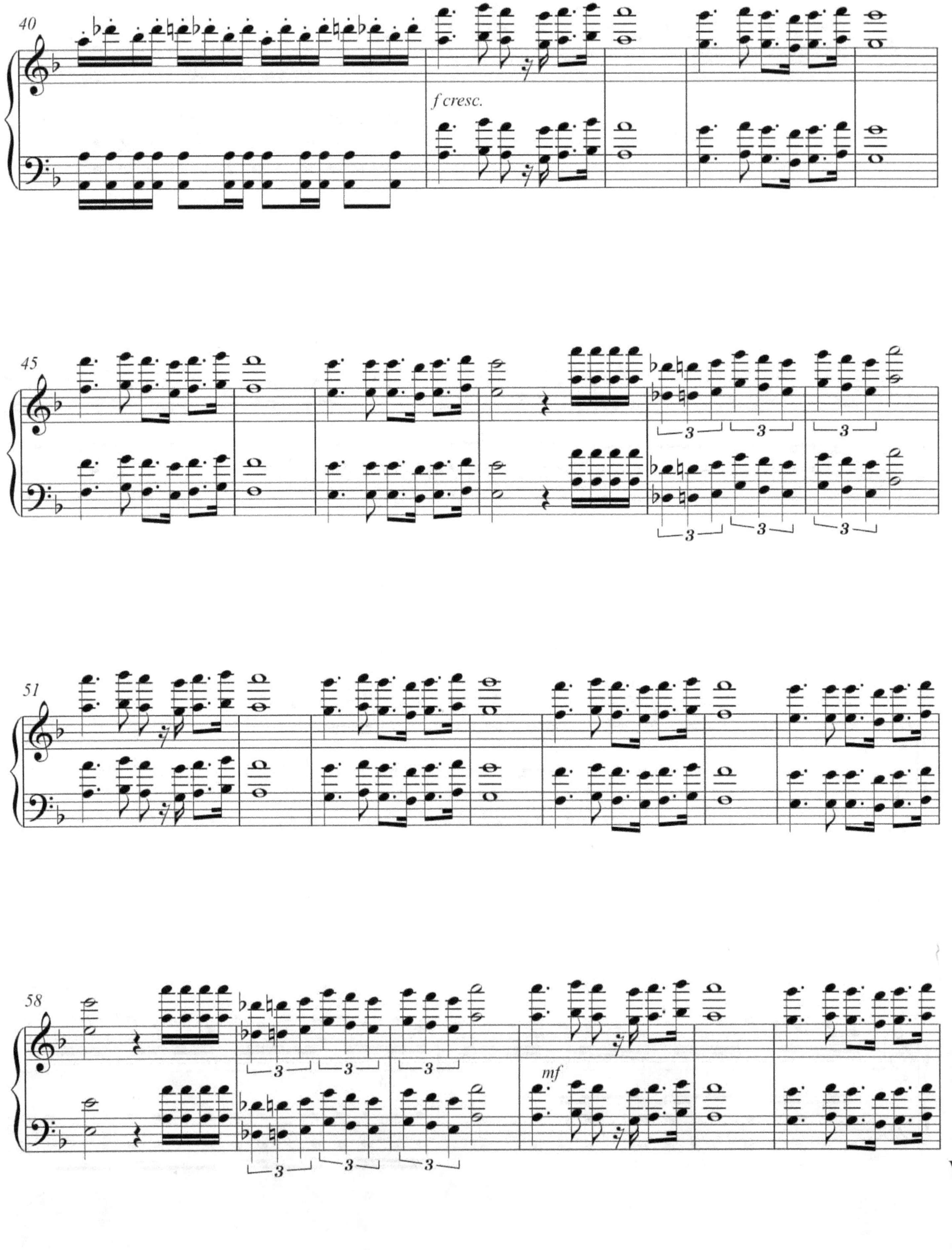
40
f cresc.
45
51
58
mf

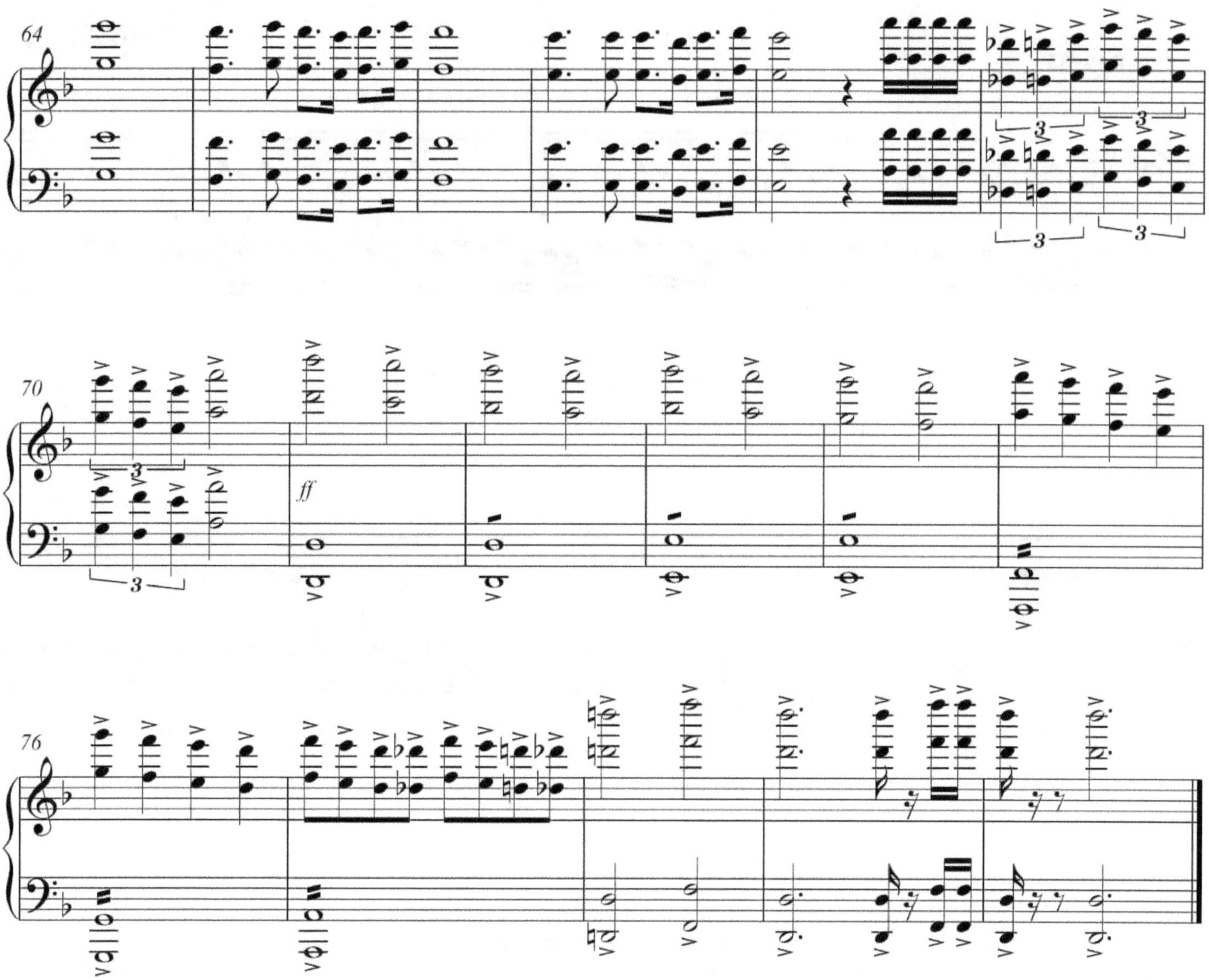
64
70
ff
76

Procession in D Minor

Piano 4

Tito Abeleda

Andante ♩=83

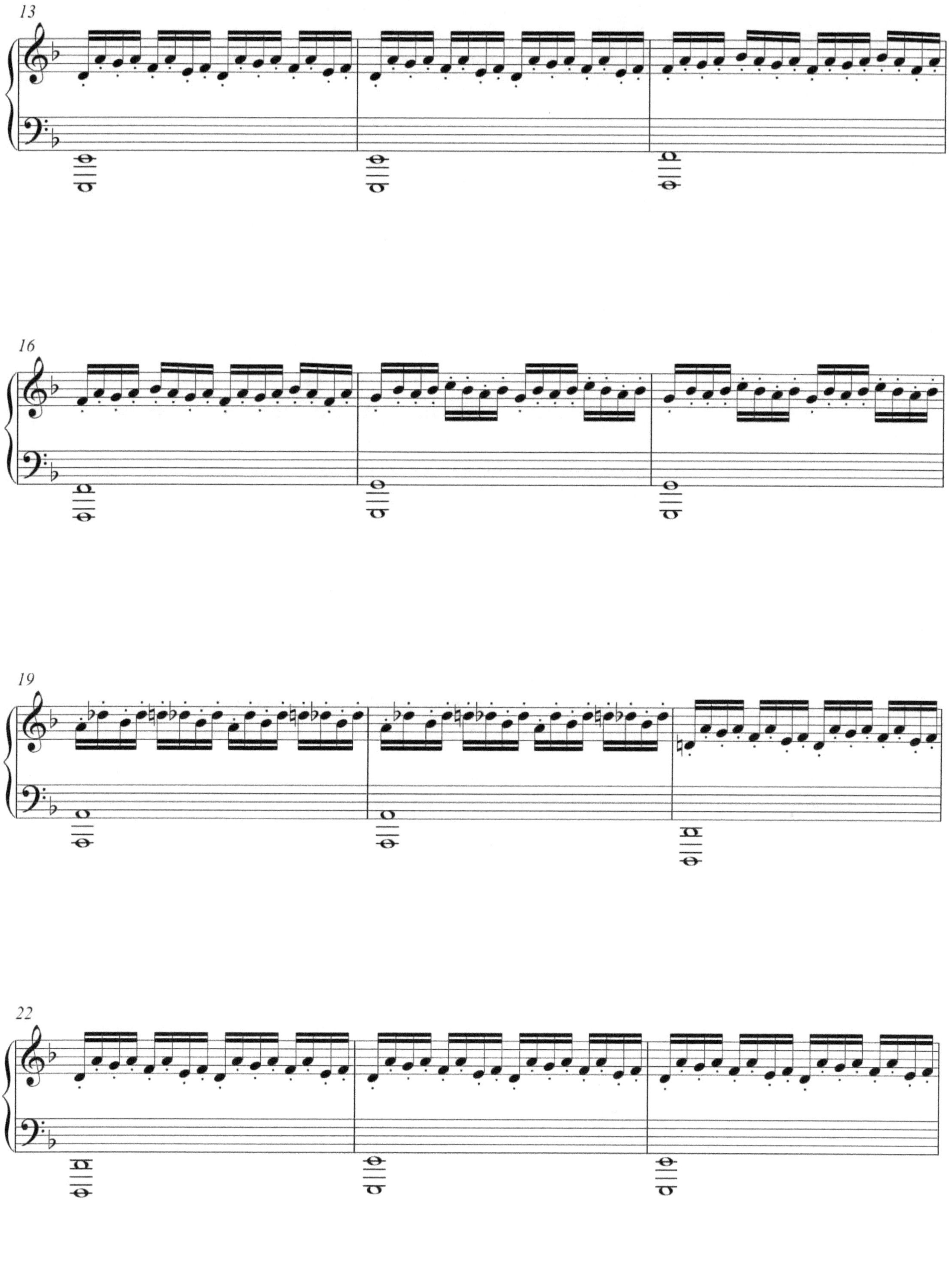
13
16
19
22

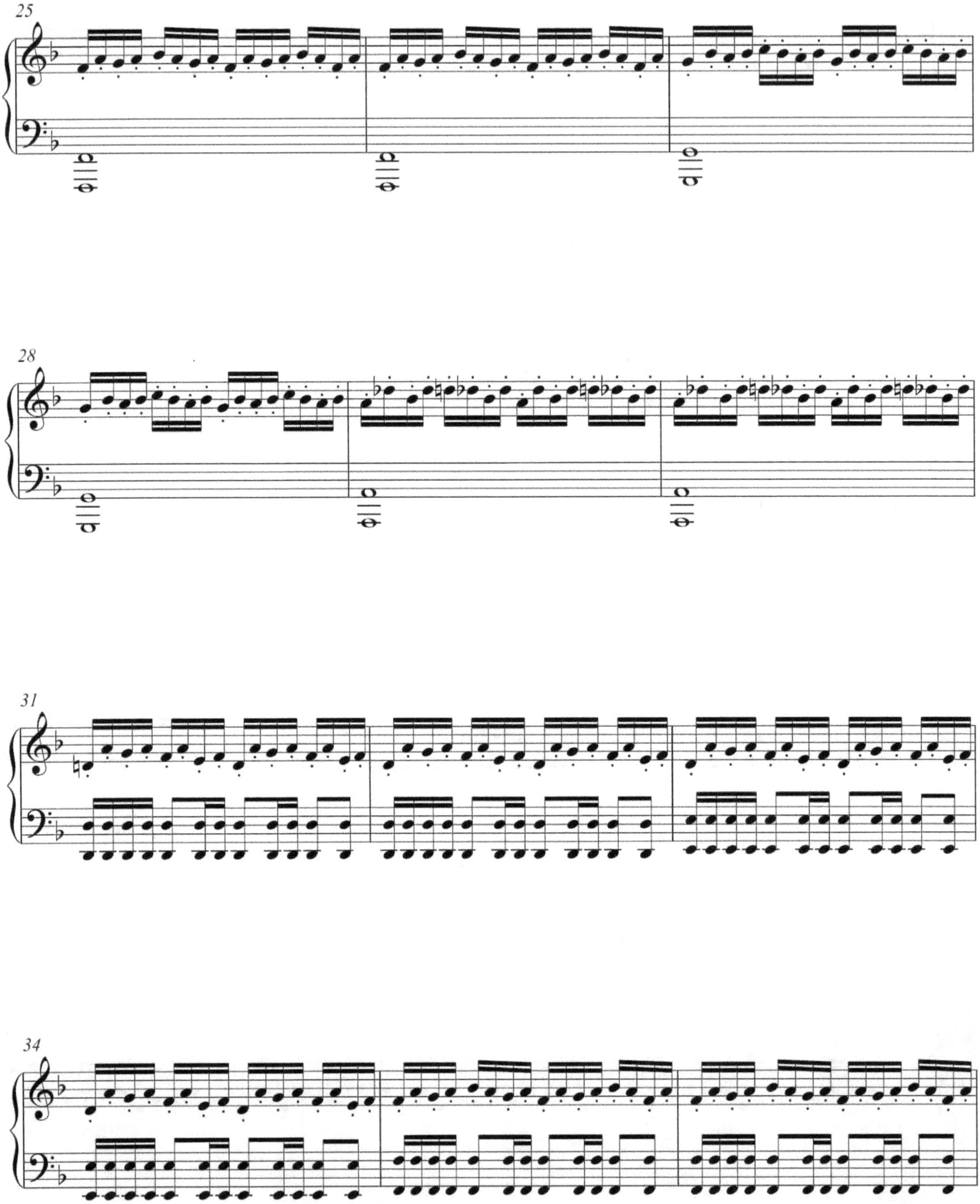
25
28
31
34

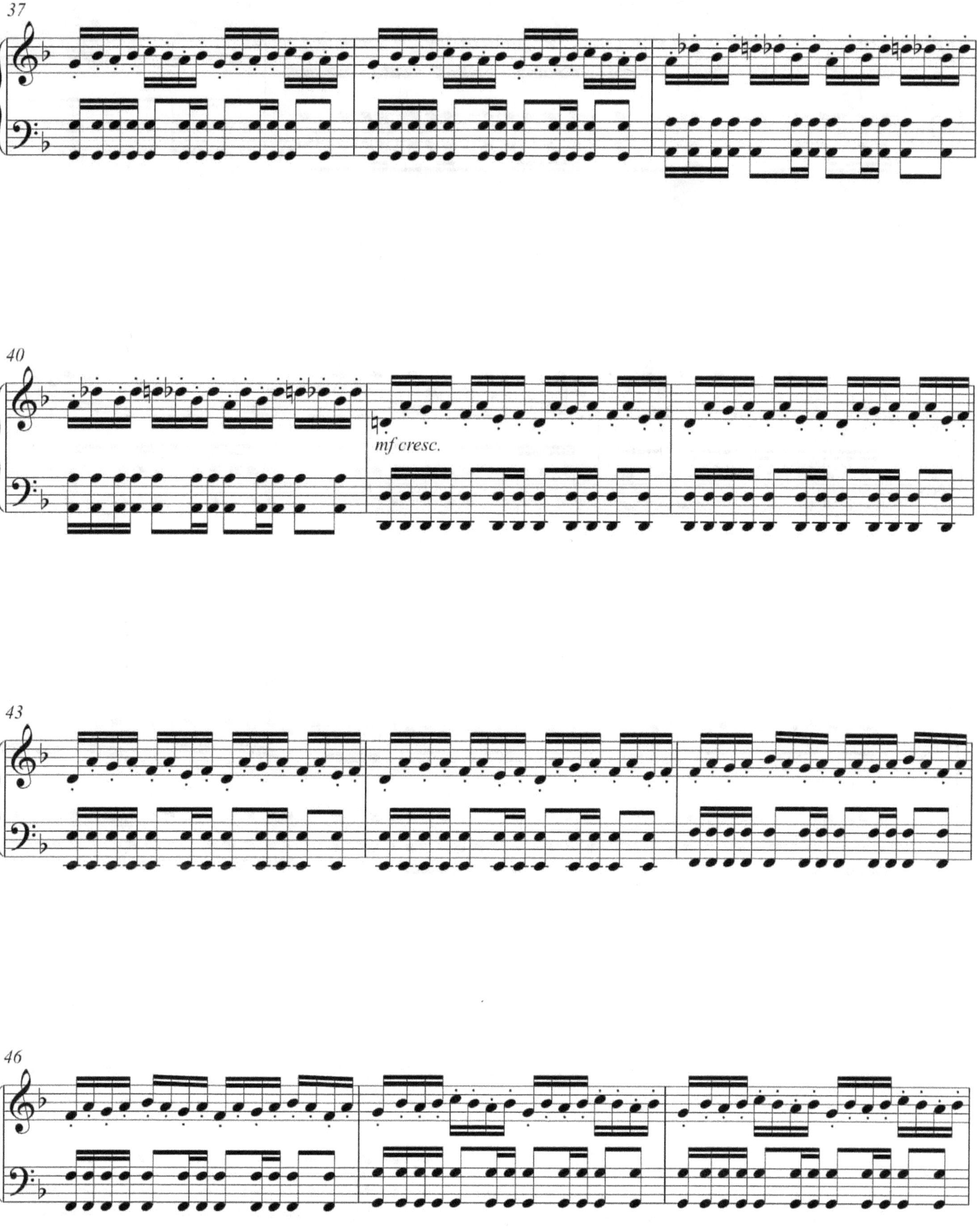
37
40
mf cresc.
43
46

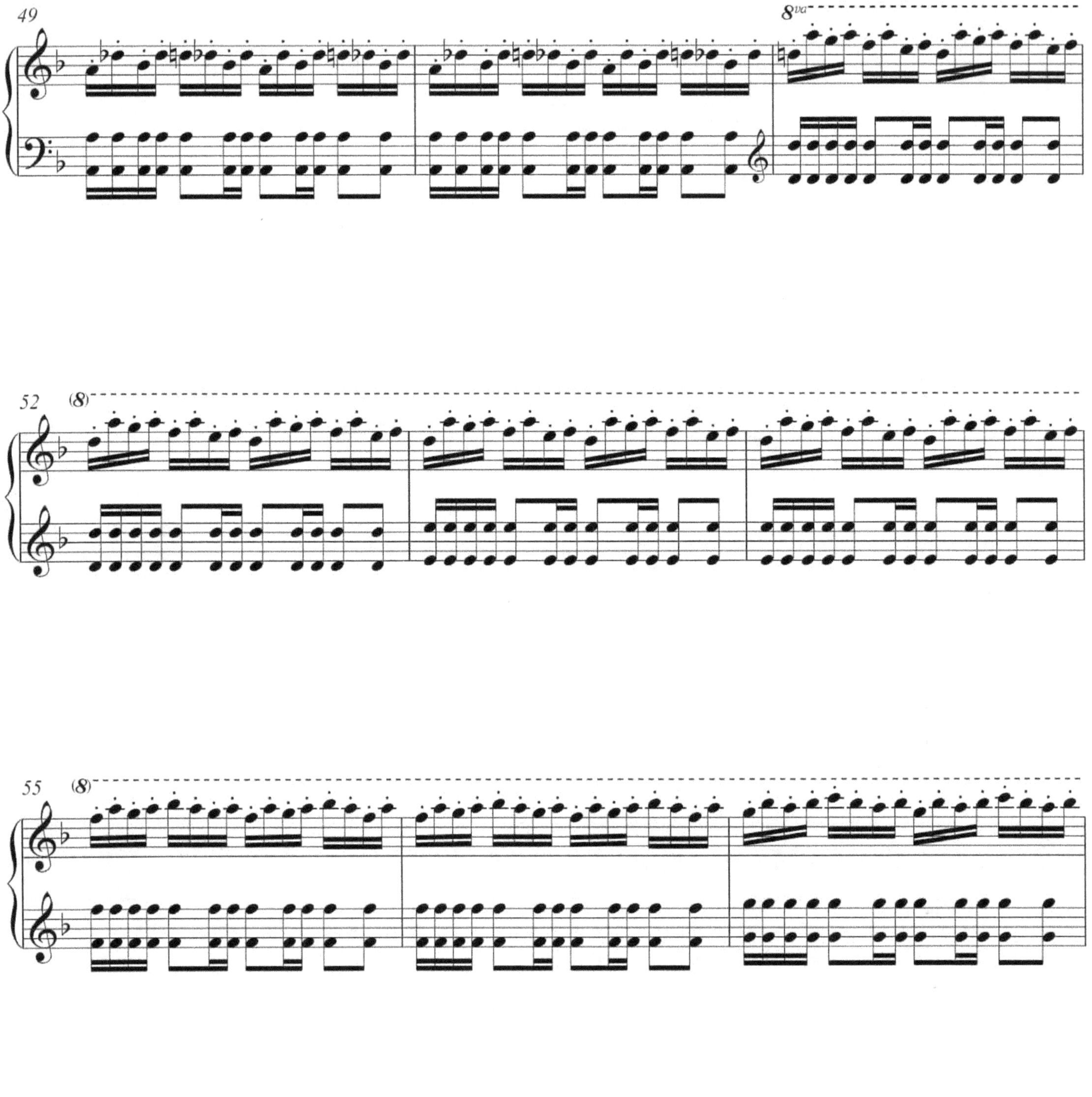
49
8va
52
(8)
55
(8)
58
(8)

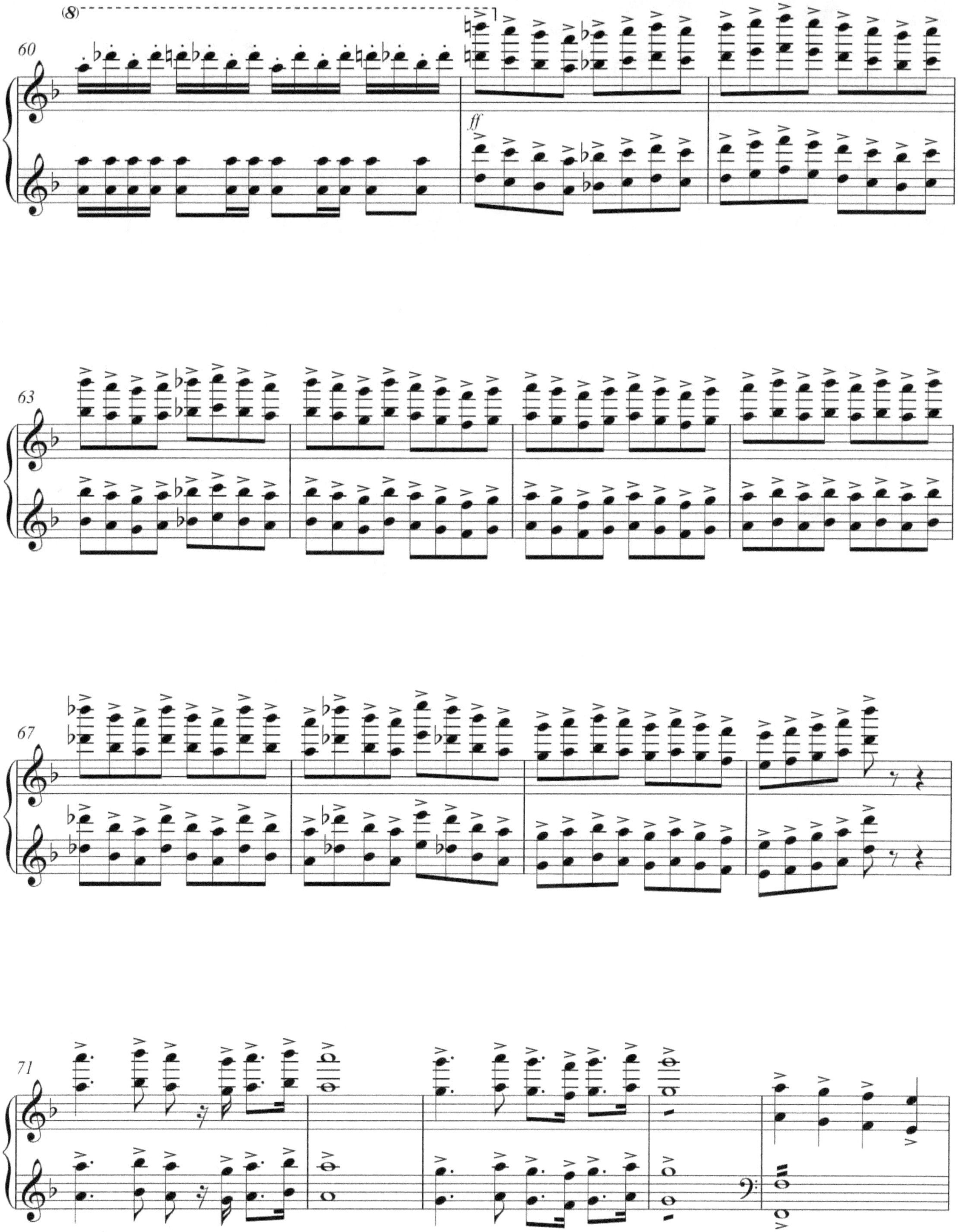
(8)
60
ff
63
67
71

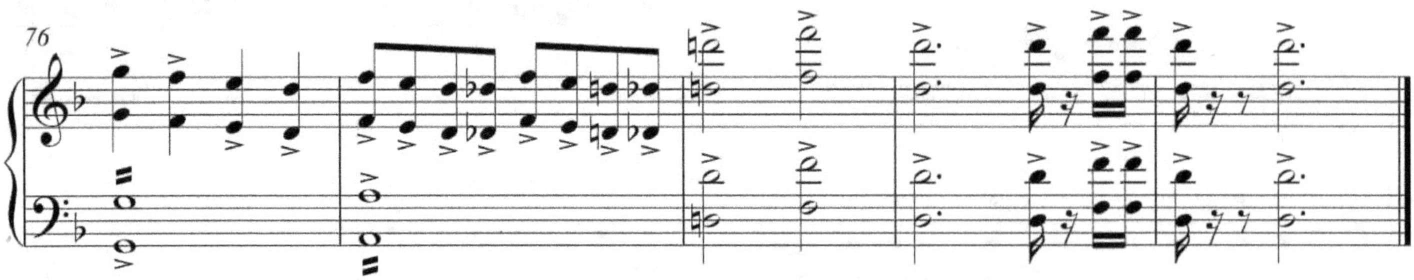
76

Tito is the founder of Visionary Quest Records composing and producing a wide range of music from modern classical to cinematic music, with a growing following of over 20,000 followers on Spotify.

He graduated cum laude and with high honors from Butler University's Jordan College of Fine Arts with a B.A. in Performing Arts majoring in Music (piano, voice), Dance, and Theatre. With more than 30 years of experience in the entertainment industry, Tito has worked as a composer, music director, director/choreographer, and producer. Tito also performed on Broadway for 10 years making his Broadway debut in James Clavell's **Shogun: the Musical**, then to **Miss Saigon** starring Jonathan Pryce and Lea Salonga, and later performing in the revival of **The King and I** as King Simon of Legree starring Lou Diamond Phillips and Donna Murphy. In 2017 Tito founded Visionary Quest Records to embody his music. Notably, Visionary Quest Records music is all instrumental. Its mission statement is to bring the creative visions of creators to life with music. Tito's music conveys a wide range of emotions from powerfully epic, suspenseful, and action-oriented to tranquil, dreamy, loving, and sorrowful.

Tito's music can also be found on Sheet Music Plus, Sheet Music Marketplace, Parts and Score, and Score Exchange.

Contact Tito for original compositions: http://bit.ly/TitoAbeleda_SoundBetter
Email: tito@visionaryquestrecords.com
Visionary Quest Records
https://www.visionaryquestrecords.com
PRO: BMI.com

Follow Tito on Social Media:

- Facebook: https://www.facebook.com/titoabeleda
- Twitter: https://twitter.com/titoabeleda
- Instagram: https://www.instagram.com/tabeleda
- YouTube: https://www.youtube.com/c/titoabeleda
- Spotify: http://bit.ly/TitoAbeleda-on-Spotify
- iTunes/Apple Music: http://bit.ly/TitoAbeleda_iTunes